TOWARD A THEORY OF RADICAL ORIGIN

TOWARD A THEORY
OF RADICAL ORIGIN

J·o·h·n P·i·z·e·r

ESSAYS ON MODERN
GERMAN THOUGHT

UNIVERSITY

OF NEBRASKA PRESS

LINCOLN & LONDON

1 · 9 · 9 · 5

Acknowledgments for
the use of previously published
material appear on page ix.
Copyright © 1995 by the University
of Nebraska Press. All rights reserved
Manufactured in the United States
of America
The paper in this book meets the
minimum requirements of American
National Standard for Information
Sciences – Permanence of Paper for
Printed Library Materials,
ANSI Z39.48-1984.

Library of Congress
Cataloging in Publication Data
Pizer, John David.
Toward a theory of radical origin :
essays on modern German thought /
John Pizer. p. cm. – (Modern German culture and literature)
Includes bibliographical references
and index.
ISBN 0-8032-3711-1 (alk. paper)
1. Origin (Philosophy)
2. Philosophy, German – 20th
century. I. Title. II. Series.
B3192.5.P58 1995 110—dc20
94-45932 CIP

Publication of this book
was assisted by a grant from
The Andrew W. Mellon
Foundation.

Tant que les épaules des collines
rentrent sous le geste commençant
de ce pur espace qui les rend
à l'étonnement des origines.

RAINER MARIA RILKE

'Quatrains Valaisans'
(1926)

CONTENTS

ACKNOWLEDGMENTS

The first two chapters of this book were previously published as individual articles, although they have been substantially revised. Chapter 1 was also entitled 'The Use and Abuse of "Ursprung": On Foucault's Reception of Nietzsche' when it was published in *Nietzsche-Studien* 19 (1990): 462–78. Chapter 2 first appeared as 'History, Genre and "Ursprung" in Benjamin's Early Aesthetics,' *German Quarterly* 60 (1987): 68–87. I would like to thank Ernst Behler, editor of *Nietzsche-Studien,* and Reinhold Grimm, former editor of the *German Quarterly,* for their permission to reuse this material.

This book has come into existence after years of research, writing, and rewriting, and a number of people provided helpful advice along the way. Professor Behler and my friend and former confrere at Louisiana State University, Adrian Del Caro, made many useful suggestions during the early stages. Numerous other colleagues at LSU also assisted me. I would also like to thank the LSU Council on Research, which provided a Summer Faculty Research Stipend in 1988. I am also beholden to the library staffs at LSU, Tulane University, and the University of Washington for their help in leading me to materials I needed.

I would like to acknowledge three early readers of the manuscript who influenced its ultimate trajectory: Alan Udoff, Anthony J. Cascardi, and John H. Smith. An equally fruitful later reading was provided by Richard Wolin. Two other readers who provided useful advice remain unknown to me, but I would like to express my thanks to them nevertheless. Much credit is also due to Peter Hohendahl, the general editor of the Modern German Culture and Literature series, for his patience, time, and advice.

Finally, I would like to express my thanks to friends and family who encouraged me to continue when I had grave doubts about this project. They include my friend and former fellow graduate student at the University of Washington, Azade Seyhan; my parents, Roselle and Marvin Pizer; my sister Liz and her family; and my wife, Patricia, to whom I dedicate this book.

A NOTE ON TRANSLATIONS

Unless otherwise indicated, all translations from the German are my own. When discussing works that have appeared in previously published translations known to me, I refer to the works by their English titles after the initial citation. Otherwise, I use the German titles after the first reference. In quoted passages where lexical nuances are particularly subtle or especially central to my argumentation, I provide the German original along with the English. Although competent English-language versions of many of the primary works discussed in this book exist, much of my reasoning revolves around minute but critical lexical distinctions. Because these distinctions have often been either ignored or interpreted in ways I have found inadequate, I felt that providing my own translations was essential to my presentation.

TOWARD A THEORY OF RADICAL ORIGIN

Origin. *Origine. Ursprung.* No term, in any of its linguistic guises, can be counted on to arouse greater aversion among the vast majority of contemporary poststructuralist thinkers than this one. Although an otherwise extraordinarily diverse group, virtually all thinkers who are identified with poststructuralism and its offshoots – deconstructionism, destructionism, Foucauldian genealogy, Barthian semiotics, and so forth – share the view that the notion of origin is opposed to everything they sanction, to all the principles favored in their writing – from dissemination to Nietzschean genealogy, from alterity to *différance* to textual (and indeed sexual) pleasure (*jouissance*).

These and other poststructuralist concepts have faced, particularly of late, powerful challenges from both the right and the left. Conservative critics have tended to regard this movement as nihilistic, arbitrary, and lacking an ethical foundation. Those on the left accuse poststructuralism of being essentially apolitical and relativistic. Although the issues raised in this debate will inevitably emerge in the arguments advanced in these pages, the main purpose of this book is to address a problem all but ignored in the to-and-fro between poststructuralism's advocates and detractors: Is the condemnation of origin valid? More precisely, given the virtually universal and unchallenged criticism of origin as a philosophical concept in the last thirty or so years, can anyone still treat origin as a fruitful concept, as a valuable heuristic principle? Is there a productive place for what the Germans call *Ursprungsphilosophie* – the philosophy of origin – in contemporary critical thinking?

I believe that the answer to these questions is 'yes' and that the problematic of origin is worthy of a renewed and sustained focus. This book will attempt to demonstrate why origin is once again worthy of critical attention, why *Ursprungsphilosophie* should no longer be dismissed or ignored by almost all philosophical circles. The grounds for this dismissal are quite easy to summarize: the pursuit of origin is regarded as nostalgic, as a search for authoritarian 'first principles,' as univocal, and as an attempt to attain philosophical closure and thereby foreclose debate entirely. In order to demonstrate origin's continued validity and potential vitality, I will show why these accusations are not inevitably correct and what positive contributions a radical theory of origin has to offer in their place.

Perhaps the best place to begin is by summarizing this project's own origins. In a doctoral dissertation on the development of a historical perspective in German genre theory in the eighteenth and early nineteenth centuries, I briefly addressed modern theories on the interrelationship between literary genre and history. I then decided to explore in greater depth the most interesting modern work to treat this problematic theme, namely, Walter Benjamin's *Ursprung des deutschen Trauerspiels* (1925; *The Origin of German Tragic Drama*).[1] As I studied his definition of 'origin' in the 'Epistemocritical Prologue' to this work, I observed that this term seemed to serve as the ultimate 'straw man' in many seminal poststructuralist works. While *Ursprung* was a tremendously vital principle in Benjamin's work, which sought to grasp phenomena as constituted by the dialectic of Becoming and disappearance, his many admirers in the deconstructionist camp either ignored it or, as in the case of J. Hillis Miller, severely distorted it to suit their own critical priorities. Subsequent readings and rereadings of other modern German thinkers led me to realize that certain German philosophies of origin contained rich nuances and complexities ignored or simply papered over by contemporary theorists. This neglect or misconstrual occurred even though certain tendencies in these philosophies, and in less tendentious uses of *Ursprung* as a heuristic lexical signifier, anticipated the methodologies explicated by these very theorists. 'Poststructuralism' tended to ignore or run over *Ursprungsphilosophie*, despite its roots in the thought of such philosophers of origin as Benjamin, Friedrich Nietzsche, and Martin Heidegger.

I then began to see the need to articulate a differentiated theory of origin in order to point out these contiguities and to show that the one-sided dismissal of this concept was unwarranted. The reason 'origin' is worth focusing on at length, however, goes beyond such demonstrations, although they constitute a major portion of this book. A sustained reflection on origin can provide a corrective to the central principle of 'difference' that is key to most poststructuralist discussions. 'Difference,' 'pluralism,' 'alterity' (or otherness), 'the unlimited play of signifiers,' the demonstration of 'unlimited semiosis' in literary and extraliterary 'texts,' the 'death of the author' as the site of discrete aesthetic production: these terms and formulas are all variations on poststructuralism's central theme – that nothing in life and art can be reduced to single intentions, constructs, or units of knowledge ('epistemes').

Given this all-encompassing presumption, the pursuit of origin is inevitably seen as invalid because it is associated with the attempt to demonstrate a singular, foundational locus. If such a locus cannot exist, the attempt to establish one is at best innocuous and at worst guided by malicious intentions, that is, the attempt to achieve political or philosophical 'mastery' by demonstrating 'autochthony' or 'first principles.'

What if *Ursprungsphilosophie*, however, is not inevitably equated with such reductive ends? What if sites of origin can be seen as 'always already' (to borrow Louis Althusser's seminal term) multiple and plurivalent? If this is possible – and I believe the oeuvres of the five thinkers treated in this book show that it is – then etiology, the theoretical pursuit of origins, can be established as a valid epistemological enterprise even in a critical environment highly suspicious of establishing anything as temporally and ontologically primary. One would be then able to relegitimate the search for historical foundations – of political institutions, of physical and social phenomena, of literary texts – without thereby being accused of attempting to bring about the 'end of play' (Jacques Derrida), that is, the ultimate suspension of debate.

Clearly, traditional attempts to establish national, religious, linguistic, and textual origin can be legitimately accused of harboring authoritarian tendencies. The effort to ground what comes first in any domain's historical flux is almost invariably linked to the desire to exercise a particular dominion, be it political, scientific, or aesthetic. No one demonstrated this more forcefully than Theodor Adorno in his many denunciations of *Ursprungsphilosophie* (particularly in Heidegger), although I will call upon Adorno in chapter 3 as an ally in my attempt to legitimate a theory of radical origin. What I want to show is that the goal of etiology may be diametrically opposed to this traditional telos of mastery. If it can be demonstrated that all individual domains are inherently intertwined at their origin – that no construct is pristine, singular, or temporally privileged but always already linked to other peoples, other languages, other texts *in* its site or sites of origin – then the supremacism associated with philosophies of origin will be turned on its head. The aimlessness and drift associated with poststructuralism – its sanctioning of alterity and undecidability in the service of a vaguely defined ethos of difference – could then be refocused into a pursuit that *grounds* diversity *at its origin.* This would lend poststructuralism's heretofore rather feeble and abstruse confrontations with racism, ethnocentrism, and nationalism, on the one hand, and dogmatism in literary and philosophical investigations, on the other, not only a firmer historical foundation but a clearer sense of direction without sacrificing its goals.

Needless to say, such a reinvigoration cannot be accomplished by simply declaring that origin presupposes an inherent multiplicity, that 'origin' always signifies 'origins.' Without a firm philosophical ground, it would be all too easy simply to assert that the phenomena constituting social and aesthetic domains are always mixed and entangled at the locus of origin. Actually legitimizing such assertions is this book's complex and challenging task. I will attempt to show that such a legitimation can be derived from an examination of origin's treatment as a heuristic concept in the oeuvres of Nietzsche, Benjamin, Adorno, Franz Rosenzweig, and Heidegger. The following question naturally emerges: Why focus exclusively on German-language writers? The reason the theory of origin is so compelling in German thought can be educed by examining the German word for 'origin.'

Ursprung literally means primal (*Ur*) leap (*Sprung*). Discussing Benjamin's book on the German *Trauerspiel,* George Steiner characterized *Ursprung* as the 'leap (*Sprung*) into being which at once reveals and determines the unfolding structure.'[2] Steiner's definition reveals the dynamic character of the term by breaking it into its constituent parts. Nevertheless, he implicitly associates *Ursprung* with an ultimate first cause and a normative volition. The use of *Ursprung* as a heuristic principle through which one determines the root cause of a phenomenon – and is thereby able to discern a teleological regularity in its subsequent development – is certainly predominant in some German writing prior to the twentieth century. Johann Gottfried Herder, for example, whom Steiner argues is the seminal philosopher of *Ursprung*, traces the origin of human language back to man's ability to engage in reflection (*Besonnenheit*).[3] As this reflective capacity is developed, the various ages (*Lebensalter*) of human language unfold in a predictable historical continuum.[4]

This conservative use of *Ursprung* as the basis of a stable epistemological foundation, while not unusual in German thought, is not inevitable. The 'primal leap' of *Ursprung* is not inherently informed by a revelation or a determination, that is, the movement of Being toward an ontologically privileged (i.e., controlling and delimiting) inception. *Ursprung* as 'originary' (*Ur*) is outside of history. As such, *Ursprung* as an epistemological principle can be – and has been – used to project a sense of metaphysical plenitude, whereby a phenomenon's beginning is seen to contain its subsequent development right up to its end. This plenitude, however, begins to allow the representation of phenomena and epiphenomena outside the continuum of history, a representation that is particularly evident in Benjamin's writings. *Ursprung* as a 'leap' (*Sprung*) is nonlinear, is not governed, that is, by a fixed diachronic progression. The 'Sprung' of *Ursprung* ruptures the historical continuum: one can no longer use a linear procedure to determine origin and must therefore give up the attempt to trace it back to a discrete site. Alternatives – such as a genealogy of intersections or 'interstices' – suggest themselves, and I explore these in my chapter on Nietzsche.

The expression 'radical origin' is not 'original' with me; one encounters it, for example, in an essay on Freud by Paul Ricoeur, who borrows it in turn from Leibniz.[5] The term 'radical' itself, derived from the Latin *radix* (root, foundation), has in its dialectical double significance an affinity to *Ursprung* as I attempt to define it here.

Particularly in modern usage, 'radical' implies a break with the normative, a departure from concepts, traditions, and institutions as they are usually defined and maintained. Most poststructuralist critics tie the concept of origin to such traditions, and their varied attempts to employ it as the catchall signifier for the hoary practices they are attempting to subvert will be explored later in this introduction. *Ursprung* in the works of the five writers treated in this book resonates with both meanings of 'radical'; it is inscribed by foundation-oriented principles but, at the same time, seeks to undermine historical norms and authoritarian usages. In these writings, the principle of origin is used to *undermine* those elements of philosophic, historiographic, and aesthetic discourse most contemporary poststructuralists *associate* with origin. I will show how originary thinking is used to challenge a linear, historicist view of temporality (Nietzsche and Benjamin), to attack an aesthetics that privileges the univocality of the symbol (Benjamin), to call into question dialectical teleology (Adorno), to confront the subjective authoritarianism of German idealism (Rosenzweig and Adorno), and to distance the *archē* from causality (Heidegger).

Most of these thinkers are employed as authorizing voices in poststructuralist discourse. Nietzsche and Heidegger provided and continue to provide the main inspiration for the attempt to demonstrate self-deconstructive impulses allegedly embedded in language, literature, and philosophy. Benjamin's complex allegorical theorems are (often wrongly) seen to validate current views on the problematic character of the literary symbolic and on the fragmentary status of literary texts. Adorno's aesthetics are frequently cited in postmodern aesthetic theories. Rosenzweig's confrontation with German idealism and his unusual intertwining of theology, origin, and existential facticity (concrete, material Being) have received increased attention in recent years. In short, these writers' use of origin as a dynamic heuristic principle challenges poststructuralist attempts to treat it as the universal straw man.

Although the various movements signified by the umbrella term 'poststructuralism' generally are regarded as antifoundational, their treatments of origin as a purely oppositional category ironically constitute a virtual foundational characteristic for poststructuralism. Origin is the negative pole in the binomial polarities most poststructuralists claim they avoid; it is the antithesis of alterity, undecidability, *jouissance*, and *clôtural* reading. Such harsh critiques are so common they seem to have become almost a reflex action, but their inception within the poststructuralist enterprise is quite easy to fix chronologically. The famous conclusion to Derrida's seminal 1966 lecture 'Structure, Sign, and Play in the Discourse of the Human Sciences' has served to inspire many deconstructionists:

> There are thus two interpretations of interpretation, of structure, of sign, of play. The one seeks to decipher, dreams of deciphering a truth or an origin which escapes play and the order of the sign, and which lives the necessity of interpretation as an exile. The other, which is no longer turned toward the origin, affirms play and tries to pass beyond man and humanism, the name of man being the name of that being who, throughout the history of metaphysics or of ontotheology – in other words, throughout his entire history – has dreamed of full presence, the reassuring foundation, the origin and the end of play.[6]

The dichotomies Derrida articulates could not be more clear; the pursuit of origin encompasses a movement toward closure and full metaphysical plenitude. Origin is antithetical to the infinite openness of play and semiosis. Those who turn toward the origin seek to overcome deferral and escape alterity. Derrida deconstructs the turn toward origin as plenitude throughout the course of his writing and in connection with figures as varied as Plato, Rousseau, Lévi-Strauss (the focus of the essay just cited), Hegel, Edmond Jabès, and Heidegger. The metaphysics of presence Derrida discerns within Heidegger's notion of origin is an especially persistent theme in his writing, and I will address it in chapter 5. It is worth noting here, however, that Derrida's recent book-length work on Heidegger tends to be less radically antipathetic toward the notion of origin than his previous efforts.[7]

Roland Barthes's 1968 essay 'The Death of the Author' is another early example of the poststructuralist equation of origin and univocality. The essay is celebrated for its early elucidation of intertextuality, the view that a text should not be seen as the product of a single author but as the construct of the reader and the infinite semiotic web to which he or she performatively links it. Writing properly understood as unrestricted dissemination subverts any favoring of a discrete historical locus, of the authorial site of textual production. This is what Barthes means when he claims that 'writing is the destruction of every voice, of every point of origin.'[8] The destruction of origin for Barthes is the destruction of the author as a unique point of reference for guiding the direction of critical inquiry. The homogeneity of a book's author is replaced by the performative heterogeneity of its readers, and Barthes sees this replacement as a displacement of origin. He thus equates origin with the domination of criticism by single governing subjects, by the authoritarianism of the author. This domination leads to univocal readings of texts, whereas true interpretation for Barthes must evoke the text's plurality. To speak of a text's author is to find an origin, which reduces the text to a singularity. To speak of an 'I' who reads the text is to invoke the plurality of the intertext and to cause the origin to vanish. As Barthes puts it in *S/Z* (1970), 'This "I" which approaches the text is already itself a plurality of other texts, of codes which are infinite or, more precisely, lost (whose origin is lost).'[9] To find intertextuality is to lose origin. To write is to obliterate origin. Like Derrida, Barthes finds it necessary to banish origin in order to introduce the unclosable play of semiosis.

Barthes's and Derrida's attempts to evoke the infinite openness of the literary text have been extended and redirected in the United States by the 'destructive' poetics of Paul Bové and William Spanos. As Vincent Leitch has shown, the destructionists resist critical closure by creating a poetics that emphasizes the ontological and temporal dimensions of literary texts. Largely ignoring the temporal elements in deconstructionism, such as the moment of deferral in *différance*, they find the allegedly spatial orientation of deconstructionist readings insufficient to the task of demonstrating 'the inexhaustibility of literary texts.'[10] However, 'destruction' shares the aversion directed by 'deconstruction' toward the notion of origin. Like Barthes, Bové equates origin as a convention in literary criticism with a privileged authorial presence, although, consistent with destructionism, he emphasizes the atemporality he regards as inherent in such criticism.[11] His former teacher, Spanos, also redirects deconstructionism by emphasizing the temporal and ontological dimensions of literary activity, but his work tends to mirror the Derridean view that origin seeks to escape discontinuity, difference, and openness.[12]

The opposition of American deconstructionists to the notion of origin is, of course, as strong as that of Bové and Spanos. Among them is Leitch, who asserts that 'the idea of a discontinuous and differential unity or origin is unthinkable.'[13] In supporting his view, Leitch cites passages from the best-known American deconstructionist, J. Hillis Miller, who displaces origin by emphasizing the metaphorical status of words and by executing an allegorical mode of reading. At the outset of his collection of essays *The Linguistic Moment* (1985), Miller equates 'the interpretative power of origins' with the attempt to simplify literary history; he claims origin-based criticism would explain 'complex' contemporary literary developments by going back in time to their roots in 'earlier' and 'simpler' periods.[14] He tries to debunk this explanatory model by demonstrating the plurality of meanings inherent in literary texts and by invoking Walter Pater's prescient embrace of intertextuality.[15] Miller's rejection of the notion of origin because of its link to a search for simple, univocal first causes and its concomitant lack of interpretative power is paradigmatic of virtually all American deconstructionists. They privilege allegorical modes of reading because allegory supposedly subverts the reductionism they also associate with the search for origins.[16]

Feminist thinkers often tie the question of origin to Freudian notions of origin. Julia Kristeva, for example, believes Freud suppresses the unique character of feminine *jouissance* and the sense of alterity opened to the mother in the mother-child relationship. Freudian analysis is imbued by an all-determining generative force centered in the father, which joins 'origin and becoming.'[17] Origin for Kristeva is antithetical to otherness, to the open space of the nondetermined, and to the dissemination inherent in feminine *jouissance*. Luce Irigaray, another well-known French feminist, is

even more radical in her linkage of origin to the Freudian phal-
locentric universe. She implies that rape fantasies stem from the
male's desire to 'appropriate' – that is, overcome the mysterious alterity of – the source of his 'origin.'[18] For Irigaray, only in connection with woman are there 'origins' rather than a single 'origin' –
for example, she condemns Freud's 'nonelaboration of [woman's]
relation to her own origins.' She also links the concept of origin to
the mystification and mythifications of the philosophico-phallo-
centric tradition.[19] For Kristeva, Irigaray, and many feminists, the
origin monopolized is a Freudian origin and is concomitant with
the exclusion of the feminine. Writing concerned with the question
of origin and origins is thus authoritarian, paternalistic, and phal-
locentric. Although in other ways they differ considerably from
their poststructuralist male contemporaries, writers like Kristeva
and Irigaray sometimes use a similar strategy, and manifest a similar attitude, in dealing with questions of origin.

There is much talk today of the 'death' of poststructuralism
in general and of deconstructionism in particular. They are supposedly being replaced by a 'New Historicism' more willing to return to the past in order to establish the interaction between texts
and their cultural and socioeconomic contexts. Although its practi-
tioners constitute a group as diverse, in terms of methodology and
purport, as the poststructuralists, they generally share poststructuralism's aversion to the notions of direct causality and human
agency in generating history and textual production. Inspired by
Michel Foucault's antihumanist stance – and his concomitant view
of power as produced by nonindividuated networks and constellations perceptible as a trace in literary and other cultural artifacts –
New Historians tend to reject the principle of origin as a methodological tool.[20] Stephen Greenblatt, for example, perhaps this
movement's most celebrated advocate, argues against the existence
of any 'originary moment' in the literary text, a moment he associates with the discrete agency of a 'master hand.'[21]

Even talk of deconstructionism's demise, however, shows a continuing bias against any tendency toward originary thinking. In a
recent article, Jeffrey Nealon summarizes the proclamations of deconstruction's death and proceeds to show its waning influence in

America can be partly attributed to distorted adaptations of Derridean ideas by his American adherents. He equates '"origin-al" concepts' in Derrida's scheme of things with 'those that wish to rule the chain, ensure its decidability.'[22] In a response to this article, Jeffrey Williams accuses Nealon of attempting 'to recuperate deconstruction by projecting Derrida as origin, as founder, as ur-text to which all others must refer,' an approach a more authentic reading of Derrida would never allow.[23] Such vigorous debates lead one to suspect that claims concerning deconstruction's demise are exaggerated. However, even if we accept the assertion as valid, its proponents can be seen continuing to invoke 'origin' as the ultimate authoritarian dictator in the realm of epistemological constructs as they argue over deconstruction's apparently prostrate body.

Many other examples of individual thinkers attacking the notion of origin could be cited. For example, the views of Foucault, one of origin's most relentless foes, will be examined in the first chapter in connection with his reception of Nietzsche. Poststructuralist discourses – deconstructionist, destructionist, feminist, and so forth – are united in linking origin to authoritarianism, univocalism, and the suppression of alterity. The remainder of this book will attempt to show how five German-language writers point the way toward a new approach to origin by using *Ursprung* as a heuristic principle that would avoid these and other forms of closure.

Of course, a new approach to origin must do more than simply elude closure if it is to possess any heuristic value. I explore some positive applications of a reinvigorated theory of origin in this book's postscript. The concept of *Ursprung*, for example, may help invest current critical priorities such as alterity (or difference), interdisciplinarity, undecidability, and otherness with a clearer methodological focus and a greater sense of direction in any number of domains. 'Difference,' after all, is often invoked by extreme nationalists and turf-jealous academicians; they highlight their alterity vis-à-vis other countries, other ethnic groups, and other researchers. After the worldwide collapse of socialism, left-wing politics seems to have lost its ability to touch the masses with appeals to universal brotherhood and equality. The embrace of ethnic identity seems to be the only gesture left to fill the void. Bereft of ideology aside from the often cold comforts of international capitalism, most groups and ethnic factions are trying to touch base with what they dimly perceive as an autochthonous identity. Poststructuralist appeals to diversity have helped to spawn a multiculturalist movement in American academia, but this intellectual course is sometimes marked by the same quest for a foundationally established franchise – for origins putatively demonstrating historically grounded superiority and privilege (for example, the recent 'ice people/sun people' debate) – that is currently leading to 'balkanization' on a worldwide scale. Deconstructionists may seek to circumvent this trend by delineating a *clôtural* form of reading and knowledge, situated between origins and seeking to preserve undecidability and infinitely extend hesitation, but this will never prove satisfactory to most readers, scholars, and others who pursue truth.[24] Virtually all historical research is driven by etiology, the striving toward origins. New Historicists may eschew the attempt to identify an 'originary moment' in literary texts because they associate such moments with a bogus first cause, but their interest in historical, social, or cultural milieus as generators of literature betrays a clear etiological impulse. The search for 'roots,' for genealogical (in the traditional, non-Nietzschean sense) identity is so ancient as to seem an integral part of the human psyche. One might debate the universality of humanity's genealogical tendencies, but the fact that this quest – currently too often tinged by fascism – has rushed in to fill the void left by socialism's demise is simply beyond question.

How can a theory of radical origin help to counteract the negative consequences of this trend? There is no reason to pretend a complex epistemological concept will lead to any panacea. What it *can* do for thinking people involved in this and other kinds of foundational quests, however, is to take the twin ideals of alterity and diversity so eloquently expounded by poststructuralism and show how they are inherent *in* – indeed fundamental *to* – the origin of discourses, of branches of knowledge, and, indeed, of all the world's individual ethnic, racial, and religious groups. Authentic origins are inherently plural and divergent, and an extended meditation upon them both reinvigorates attention to history and subverts the supremacist claims of particular groups by showing that their ethnicity, religion, or discipline is 'always already' – from the origin – entangled with others.

This is perhaps the most all-encompassing and profound lesson offered by the *Ursprungsphilosophie* developed by the five thinkers I examine in the following chapters. The goal of teaching people to cherish pluralism, tolerance of difference, and the nonclosed character of art and knowledge will be better served by showing how such qualities inhere *within* origin than by vainly trying to discredit it. In the process, we may perhaps discover the multivalent richness that will enable us to feel once more what Rilke called 'the astonishment of origins,' an astonishment that can rekindle our openness to the Other.[25]

CHAPTER 1

The Use and Abuse of *Ursprung:*
On Foucault's Reception
of Nietzsche

One of the most tenacious warriors in the battle against origin was Michel Foucault, who not infrequently called Nietzsche into his service. In the introduction to *The Archaeology of Knowledge,* Foucault attacks the search for an 'original foundation' capable of generating a 'total history' that attempts to overcome the disruption and difference of genuine history through the synchronic embrace of a closed and immobile system. Such an approach is opposed to the 'decentring operated by the Nietzschean genealogy.' Even worse, it attempts to coopt Nietzsche by viewing him according to the precepts of transcendental philosophy and by regarding his genealogy merely as 'a search for origins.'[1] In *The Order of Things,* Foucault discerns in philosophy's attempt to locate an original foundation (referred to here as the 'real and fundamental ground') a deliberate avoidance of the terrain of language, an avoidance based on the fear that the chimera of the unity of Being would vanish forever when confronted with language's irreducible complexity and multiplicity. He credits Nietzsche with being the first to face the abyss, 'to connect the philosophical task with a radical reflection upon language.'[2]

In *The Order of Things,* Foucault does not speak as disparagingly of origin as he did later in *The Archaeology of Knowledge.* In the earlier work, he rejects origin as the site of transcendent, synchronic plenitude but locates in the experience of Nietzsche (along with Hölderlin and Heidegger) the negation of origin as plenitude. Their works make an approach toward the restoration of the 'void' of the origin, the 'void created both by its recession and by its approach.' Foucault sees modern thinkers such as Nietzsche encountering origin as a recession, as a continuous movement backward, toward a region (really a void) 'where the Gods have turned away.' This backward hunt creates a 'ceaseless rending open which frees the origin in exactly that degree to which it recedes; the extreme is therefore what is nearest.'[3]

Foucault addresses Nietzsche's concept of origin (*Ursprung*) most cogently in his seminal essay 'Nietzsche, Genealogy, History,' and this essay will be the focus of this chapter. Foucault here discerns two modalities at work in Nietzsche's attempt to articulate the opening sites, the foundational spaces, where historico-philosophical constructs may first be identified. He believes Nietzsche implicitly denigrates one of these modalities, constituted by traditional diachronic approaches to history. What he sees as the more adventurous, volatile account of how paradigms constituting Western thought and society emerge through the conflict of oppositional epistemologies in Nietzsche's oeuvre is more in harmony with – indeed largely provided the inspiration for – Foucault's own methodology. In differentiating these two approaches between (apparently) antiquated and revolutionary styles of praxis, Foucault creates rigorous terminological distinctions. He alternates between critiques of broad-based concepts and explorations of the words designating them. Any attempt, for whatever purpose, to extensively examine Foucault's essay thus runs the risk of seeming to engage in terminological quibbling. However, I cannot avoid this risk, because I, like Foucault, believe there are two forms of originary thinking, because these forms are, for both of us, closely tied to minute lexical issues, and because I want to show how Foucault ties terminological conventions to larger, conceptual matters. As Stanley Corngold has shown, Nietzsche consistently adhered to a rigorous 'distinction about names' throughout the course of his writings, and Foucault is quite in keeping with the spirit of Nietzsche's philosophy when he pays close attention to Nietzsche's choice of words.[4] Despite this care, however, Foucault almost completely inverts Nietzsche's priorities. In his eagerness to create an image of Nietzsche's work as an anticipation of contemporary efforts to denigrate the concept of origin as inherently metaphysical and authoritarian, he often overlooks Nietzsche's appreciation for the dynamic and polyvalent nuances of the term that designates it in Nietzsche's native German.

Foucault's disparagement of the metaphysics of origin is at its

most extreme in 'Nietzsche, Genealogy, History,' and, in rejecting *Ursprung* as a historiographic principle in this essay, Foucault
sought to align his approach to history with Nietzsche's. Foucault
was, after all, the foremost proponent of the modern antilinear
view of history. Thus, Foucauldian history does not unfold as a
chronological pattern of events emanating from a mystified but
all-determining point of departure. This apotheosized and metahistorical point, the object of the search of traditional philosophers
looking for the foundations of Being, is termed the 'origin' by Foucault and his followers, particularly Edward Said. In opposition to
this tradition, Foucault seeks to evoke and magnify the field of
disruptions, differences, and displacements he sees operating un-
derneath the apparently seamless evolution of diachronic history.
This documentary approach – Foucault's own – is labeled a 'genealogy' in his essay on Nietzsche. The antithesis of genealogy is seen
here as the metaphysics of *Ursprung,* and Foucault discovers Nietzsche to be the anti-*Ursprung* genealogist par excellence.

Foucault seeks to establish his image of Nietzsche as a genealogist opposed to the metaphysics of origin by examining his use of
the term *Ursprung* in a variety of works, especially *Zur Genealogie
der Moral* (1887; *Toward a Genealogy of Morals*) and *Die fröhliche
Wissenschaft* (1882; *The Gay Science*). Particularly in his reading
of the *Genealogy,* Foucault locates a dichotomy in Nietzsche's use
of the terms *Ursprung* and *Entstehung.* Foucault asserts that Nietzsche indiscriminately interchanges the words *Ursprung, Entstehung*
('emergence' or 'genesis'), and *Herkunft* ('ancestry' or 'provenance')
in *The Gay Science* when discussing the origins of knowledge and
logic. According to Foucault, in *Genealogy Entstehung* and *Ursprung*
are also used interchangeably to demarcate the origin of duty and
guilty conscience. This is, however, only one of two uses of *Ursprung* in Nietzsche's vocabulary – its 'unstressed' or indeterminate use. In its 'stressed' use, *Ursprung* becomes the metaphysical
antithesis of other terms commonly translated as origin (NGH
140–41).

Foucault's postulation of an 'unstressed' use of *Ursprung* is certainly valid. Nietzsche and the other writers treated in this book
employ the term frequently without displaying a conscious aware-

ness of its special resonances. To speak of the origin or *Ursprung* of a phenomenon or idea does not inevitably imply an acceptance or rejection of origin as a specific philosophical and critical principle. However, the passages selected by Foucault to illustrate Nietzsche's 'unstressed' use of origin tend to undercut his argument. For example, Foucault refers to passages from *The Gay Science* that denote the 'origin' of logic and knowledge (NGH 140). One of the three fragments to which Foucault refers is entitled *Herkunft des Logischen* (*Ancestry of the Logical*). Nietzsche asks here where origin was 'emergent' ('entstanden') and answers, 'Certainly from illogic.'5 In *Menschliches, Allzumenschliches* (1878; *Human, All-Too-Human*), Nietzsche asks how it is possible for something to emerge ('entstehen') from its opposite and uses the emergence of logic from illogic as an example (2:23). The posing of such a dilemma signifies a causal ontology, a 'progression' corresponding to a 'process' (3:472) that is generally foreign to Nietzsche's elucidation of origins as leaping into being in the nonplace or interstice between or among polarities. A causal and diachronic chain is even more in evidence in another passage from *The Gay Science* singled out by Foucault as evidence of Nietzsche's unstressed denotation of epistemological origin. Nietzsche speaks here of 'preludes' to science and asserts that the promises and delusions of magicians, alchemists, astrologers, and witches create the hunger for hidden and forbidden powers, which leads to the emergence of the sciences (3:538–39).

The first of the three fragments cited by Foucault as examples of the unstressed signification of knowledge's origin is entitled *Ursprung der Erkenntniss* (*Origin of Knowledge*). As with the 'ancestry of logic,' the 'origin of knowledge' comes into being here as the unmediated negation of its opposite, in this case those primal errors of perception that nevertheless sustained and furthered human existence. However, such a negation is only the weakest form of knowledge. Knowledge as 'truth' itself becomes a life-sustaining drive, and the origin of knowledge can no longer be distinguished as a clearly definable site. Instead, it is caught up in a 'coil' of clashing drives and wills. The modern origin of knowledge in 'the thinker' is disseminated in the irreconcilable internal conflict be-

tween the 'drive for truth' and those *primal*, life-sustaining epistemological errors still latent in the individual consciousness
(3:469–71). Such an *Ursprung* is unfixed and multivalent, an indeterminate 'interstice,' to borrow Foucault's term again (NGH 150).

Most of Foucault's article is devoted to exploring the uniquely
consistent nuances in the various German signifiers of 'origin'
when Nietzsche uses them in their 'stressed' form. Foucault notes
that '*Entstehung* and *Herkunft* are more exact than *Ursprung* in re-
cording the true objective of genealogy; and, while they are or-
dinarily translated as "origin," we must attempt to reestablish their
proper use' (NGH 145). He believes *Entstehung* denotes 'emergence,'
which is not a point of origin giving rise to an uninterrupted continuity but the locus of the interstices where the historical forces of
domination and subjection can be illuminated as they meet, clash,
and struggle. Foucault suggests that there is a sporadic quality to
the moment of *Entstehung*. *Entstehung* opposes itself to the meta-
physician's search for an *Ursprung* that can only be located at the
base of a chain of events locked in an uninterrupted continuity
(NGH 148–49).

Foucault's view that *Entstehung* is a site – actually a '"nonplace,"
a pure distance' (NGH 150) – of struggle and disruption is somewhat belied by Nietzsche's use of the predicate form of this noun in
the preface to the *Genealogy*. Nietzsche seeks to sanction his search
for the provenance (*Herkunft*) of moral prejudices through the use
of an organic metaphor. He is confident of the validity of his
thoughts precisely because they have *not* emerged sporadically
('nicht sporadisch entstanden'): 'Even today I still hold fast to
them, they hold ever faster to each other, and have indeed grown
into, coalesced into each other. This strengthens my cheerful as-
surance that they did not emerge in me individually, arbitrarily,
sporadically, but from a common root, from a *fundamental* will to
knowledge that speaks with ever greater resolution, demands ever
greater resolution, enjoins the plumbing of ever greater depths'
(5:248; Nietzsche's emphasis). Nietzsche's metaphor of a common
root ('Wurzel'), signifying continuity, evolution, and a firm foundation that has as its origin the fundamental will to knowledge
forces us to question Foucault's view that Nietzsche's genealogy

opposes itself to metaphysical approaches stressing evolution and 'unbroken continuity' from a point of origin (NGH 146). Paul de Man comes closer to the mark when he speaks of Nietzsche as a writer of 'organic or, in his terminology, *monumental* history.'[6] Nietzsche clearly wants his readers to view the *Genealogy* as an organically developing history. As a tree emerges from its roots, so Nietzsche's work will emerge from his will to knowledge. It does not emerge sporadically, as an 'eruption' or 'leap,' but steadily and progressively (NGH 149–50). Nevertheless, the methodological ideals expressed here by Nietzsche are undercut precisely by his concept of *Ursprung*.

Foucault speaks of Nietzsche's concept of *Entstehung* as signifying the eruption of clashing forces emerging in the pure distance of the interstice by citing Nietzsche's use of the term 'Entstehungs-herd' (sic) ('threshold of emergence') early in the *Genealogy*. According to Foucault, 'What Nietzsche calls the *Entstehungsherd* of the concept of goodness is not specifically the energy of the strong or the reaction of the weak, but precisely this scene where they are displayed superimposed or face-to-face. It is nothing but the space that divides them, the void through which they exchange their threatening gestures and speeches' (NGH 150). Although Nietzsche indeed superimposes the plebeian and noble valuations of goodness in the fragment cited by Foucault, he uses the term *Entsteh-ungsheerd* exactly the way Foucault claims he does *not* use it. Nietzsche claims the *Entstehungsheerd* of the concept of goodness is sought in the wrong place. It does not first emerge as a value of the weak but of the strong. It is *precisely* 'the energy of the strong' that Nietzsche situates as the *Entstehungsheerd* of the concept of goodness (5:259). The locus of the eruption of the clash of contrasting moralities, the site where Nietzsche superimposes the antitheses of good and evil, is not a site of *Entstehung* but of *Ursprung*: 'The pathos of distinction and distance, as we said, the enduring and dominating, total and fundamental feeling of a higher, reigning species in relationship to a lower species, to a "below" – *that* is the origin of the opposition "good" and "bad"' (5:259; Nietzsche's emphasis).

Foucault appears to be on more solid ground in citing the sixth section of the second essay of the *Genealogy* to build on his notion that the 'Entstehungsherd' is, for Nietzsche, the space where violently competing systems of domination emerge and reveal their disguises, displacements, and reversals (NGH 151). Nietzsche describes the threshold of emergence of the moral conceptual world as blood-spattered, consistent with the beginning ('Anfang') of everything great in the world. From this threshold arise concepts such as guilt, conscience, and duty (5:300). Where there is blood, there has been a clash. The struggle, however, must have already taken place because the combatants are nowhere mentioned in the drama of this fragment. Where do they appear head-to-head, their contraposed profiles given highest resolution because separated by the 'space' of single conjunctions or prepositions? Not until they reappear in section 8, where a résumé of their combat is given in the course of describing the *Ursprung* of guilt: 'Picking up the thread of our investigation once more, we note that the feeling of guilt, of personal obligation, had its origin in the oldest and most originary [ursprünglichsten] relationship of individuals, in the relationship between buyer and seller, creditor and debtor. Here for the first time individual went up against individual, here for the first time individual *measured himself* against individual' (5:305–6; Nietzsche's emphasis). Foucault cites this passage, but only as an example of Nietzsche's 'unstressed' use of the term *Ursprung*.[7] In point of fact, *Ursprung* rather than *Entstehung* most truly signifies the locus of the interstice where competing moral forces emerge, struggle, disappear, and dominate. *Ursprung* provides the foundation for a genealogy of morals.

The issue here is more than a minor question of semantics: Foucault's denigration of the notion of origin has resonated far beyond his own work. The most significant effect of this influence has been in the work of Edward Said. In the preface to his book *Beginnings: Intention and Method,* Said notes that his work is largely premised on the idea that 'beginning is basically an activity which ultimately implies return and repetition rather than simple linear accomplishment, that beginning and beginning-again are historical whereas origins are divine.'[8] Said formulates even stronger disjunctions between beginning and origin in the preface to the second edition to his book, where he defines origin as 'divine, mythical and privileged,' while beginning is 'secular, humanly produced and cease-lessly re-examined.'[9] Said consistently uses both Nietzsche and Foucault as authorizing voices. For example, he cites 'Nietzsche's distinctions between *origin* and *purpose*' in a passage from the *Genealogy* to ground his own distinction between the (divinely tinged) notion of an *'author* (origin)' and the (secular, ceaselessly reex-amined) concept of a *'beginning intention* (purpose and interpreta-tion).'[10] This passage, in which Said uses Walter Kaufmann's trans-lation of Nietzsche, suggests that there is indeed a distinction to be made between the 'Ursprung und Zweck einer Strafe' [origin and purpose of a punishment]. However, the terms that receive a nega-tive resonance in this passage because they are connected to the failed efforts of previous moral genealogists are *Anfang, Entstehung,* and *Entstehungsgeschichte* ('beginning,' 'emergence,' and 'history of emergence'). The earlier genealogists confused these latter con-cepts with the 'purpose' of punishment. Nietzsche only uses the word *Ursprung* as the generic, *foundational* term in this section, that is, as the *basic* issue with which 'purpose' is confused (5:313). This is not accidental. Nietzsche clearly suggests that, in their fumblings with and conflations of 'purpose' on the one hand and 'beginning' or 'emergence of a thing' on the other, the earlier moral genealo-gists never approach what truly lies at the heart of the genealogy of punishment as a moral institution – namely, its 'origin.' Moreover, in *Genealogy, Ursprung* is not divinely but dialectically grounded.

In the course of *Beginnings* Said frequently cites Foucault as a legitimizing authority for his concept of origin, a practice that oc-curs in Said's later works as well.[11] Said, in turn, has influenced the terminological conventions of other critics. For example, writing on William Carlos Williams's *Kora in Hell,* Stephen Fredman cites Said in making the following distinction: 'First and foremost a beginning, an improvisation begins from the middle, not from a point of origin.'[12] Fredman's distinction demonstrates Said's suc-cess (and, by extension, Foucault's) in making origin seem an in-evitable corollary of metaphysical thought. Metaphysics subverts spontaneity and improvisation by engendering a teleological cau-sality that emanates from a divine (or at least privileged) point of origin. Origin as the 'site of truth' that 'makes possible a field of

24

knowledge whose function is to recover it' (NGH 143) pursues the goal of a 'timeless and essential secret' (NGH 142). This ultimate plenitude collapses history into a continuum, into the ever-the-same. Spontaneity and improvisation can only emerge through the evasion of the timeless and essential. For writers such as Said and Fredman, this means a critical praxis informed by the 'meta-physics' of origin must be abandoned in favor of a genealogy that evokes secular, disruptive, and volatile beginnings.

Foucault himself contrasts the 'lofty origin' – divine, prelap-sarian, and prior to temporality – with 'historical beginnings.' Such beginnings are 'lowly: not in the sense of modest or discreet like the steps of a dove, but derisive and ironic, capable of undoing every infatuation' (NGH 143). For Said and Foucault, the infatua-tion of origin is the infatuation with a divine, timeless, and regula-tive truth. This priority of *Ursprung* is subverted, in the vocabulary of Foucault's Nietzsche, by *Entstehung,* with its sporadic and unsta-ble dynamism. Despite his qualifications concerning the stressed and unstressed uses of *Entstehung* and *Ursprung,* it thus seems odd that Foucault cites the following passage from *Human, All-Too-Human* by way of defining the 'lofty origin' (NGH 143):

> '*Am Anfang war.*' – Die Entstehung verherrlichen – das ist der metaphysische Nachtrieb, welcher bei der Betrachtung der Historie wieder ausschlägt und durchaus meinen macht, am Anfang aller Dinge stehe das Werthvollste und Wesentlichste.

> ['*In the beginning.*' – To glorify the genesis – that is the meta-physical aftershoot that sprouts when one contemplates his-tory and that leads us to believe that the most valuable and essential stands at the beginning of all things.]

Entstehung is used here to demarcate a metaphysically privileged site of emergence or genesis, solemnified as the firm and regula-tive foundation for subsequent history. This passage is one more example of Nietzsche's employment of the term to evoke the *anti*-genealogical bent inherent in traditional approaches to historiogra-phy. The site of *Entstehung* is unitary, a solitary point of temporal reference that sets a normative standard for judging value and es-sentiality. The univocal transcendence of *Entstehung* can only be overcome through the (genealogical) pursuit of origin, origin *as multiple.* Nietzsche's celebration of the pursuit of multiple origins is especially evident in *Also sprach Zarathustra* (1883–85; *Thus Spake Zarathustra*): 'Whoever has become wise concerning old origins [Ursprünge], behold, he will at last seek after new sources of the future and after new origins' (4:265). Nietzsche here implies that the multiplicity of origins is boundless because the search for origins is tied to the search for the 'sources of the future,' a future not governed by the divine cosmogony or regulative metaphysics of the priestly and philosophical castes and thus open, unfixed, endlessly heterogeneous. The very fact that there are *new* origins to be pursued counteracts Foucault's argument that origin is inevitably prelapsarian, that it 'always precedes the Fall' and 'comes before the body, before the world and time' (NGH 143). This description can be more accurately applied to *Entstehung,* a focus for adulation because it stands 'at the beginning of all things' (2:540). By contrast, the *origin* of all *good* things is manifold and recurrent: 'Aller guten Dinge Ursprung ist tausendfältig, – alle guten muthwilligen Dinge springen vor Lust in's Dasein: wie sollten sie das immer nur – Ein Mal thun!' (4:219) [The origin of all good things is thousandfold – all good mischievous things leap for joy into being: how should they always do that – but once!].

Few passages are more suggestive of the latent volatile and disseminatory quality of *Ursprung* than this proclamation from *Zarathustra*. The 'leap into being' (Steiner) of *Ursprung* is declared by Nietzsche to be ceaselessly reenacted, capricious, and joyful.

The delineation of multiple origins is not, however, confined to evoking phenomena in their unfettered and carefree heterogeneity. Origin is also the multiplied locus where individual will, strength, and renunciation come into conflict with the creature comforts and slavish mentality of the herd. This locus is the manifold *Ursprung* of genuine virtue (4:99). Foucault believes the genuine genealogical project must define the site of the emergence of ideas as an interstice, as the space between clashing ideologies. Foucault is quite correct in attributing a similar point of view to Nietzsche. However, contrary to Foucault's interpretation, this interstice is governed not by *Entstehung* but by *Ursprung*.

Ursprung and *Entstehung* are also operative terms in *Die Geburt der Tragödie* (1872; *The Birth of Tragedy*). For Nietzsche, the *Ursprung* of Greek tragedy is a labyrinth: 'We must call upon all of the previously discussed principles of art for aid, in order to find our way in the labyrinth, the term with which we much characterize the *origin of Greek tragedy*' (1:52; Nietzsche's emphasis). Nietzsche rejects as bizarre the theory, widely accepted in the nineteenth century, of 'the emergence [Entstehung] of the tragedy from the chorus' (1:55). *Entstehung* connotes here a continuous, natural progression, an evolution from one genre to another. This affiliation of *Entstehung* with unbroken continuity again points out Foucault's error in associating such linearity with *Ursprung* while seeing in *Entstehung* 'the scene where forces are risked in the chance of confrontations' (NGH 159). Even the full title of Nietzsche's work, *Die Geburt der Tragödie aus dem Geiste der Musik* (*The Birth of Tragedy from the Spirit of Music*), implies a certain continuity from the one artistic sphere to the other, whereas *Ursprung* suggests dialectical tension and confrontation. The true *Ursprung* of Greek tragedy lies in the interstice between the Apollonian and the Dionysian.[13] At the very outset of *The Birth of Tragedy*, Nietzsche speaks of 'an enormous contrast, as regards origin and objectives, between the Apollonian art of the sculptor and the Dionysian, nonpictorial art of music' (1:25). The discussion following this passage, which contraposes the two spheres (1:25–52), suggests that the 'enormous contrast' between them itself forms the 'labyrinth' of the Greek tragedy's *Ursprung*.

Nietzsche also uses the terms *Ursprung* and *Entstehung* toward the close of *The Birth of Tragedy* when talking about the beginnings of the opera where the two terms even appear in the same sentence. Nietzsche speaks of the *Ursprünge* of the opera but only to indicate where its origins *do not* lie: 'What sort of influence on art can one expect from an artistic form whose origins [Ursprünge] lie entirely outside the aesthetic domain, a form that, indeed, trespassed into the region of art from a semimoral sphere, and that is able only occasionally to deceive one concerning this hybrid genesis [hybride Entstehung]?' (1:125–26). The question Nietzsche leaves hanging in the middle of posing his question is: What are the origins of opera? The answer might very well be that it has none. Reviewing Nietzsche's discussion of the emergence of the opera in the context of his discussion of the birth of tragedy brings to mind Marx's well-known dictum in *The Eighteenth Brumaire of Louis Bonaparte* that world history's greatest events and characters occur twice: once as tragedy, then as farce. In Nietzsche's *Birth of Tragedy,* the hybrid *Entstehung* of the opera farcically repeats the origin of Greek tragedy. Tragedy's *Ursprung* finds its ground in the convulsive merging of two antithetical spheres: the Apollonian dream world and the orgiastic sensuality of the Dionysian realm. Opera's *Entstehung* is also based on the union of dissonant sensibilities, the Renaissance idyllic and the ancient tragic worldviews. However, the 'tremendous contrast' that constitutes Greek tragedy's 'origin' has been devalued to the 'hybrid genesis' of the opera. Hybridization is the farcical modern equivalent of the convulsive union of antithetical modes of Being, and this farce reflects the substitution of a modern *Entstehung* for an ancient *Ursprung* as the ontological foundation of form.

Like Nietzsche, Heidegger appears to privilege origin as a temporal modality. In one of his controversial lectures on Nietzsche, he speaks of Nietzsche's rejection of the Darwinian concept of self-preservation in favor of his own concept of self-assertion. Of course, the doctrine of self-preservation belongs to evolution, and thus lacks the genealogical qualities Foucault associates with Nietzsche – eruption, discontinuity, and the dialectics of the interstice.[14] According to Heidegger, self-preservation is so preoccupied with what is at hand that it becomes blind to its own essence. Self-assertion, on the other hand, is connected to change at its primal level: 'Selbstbehauptung, d.h. im Haupt, d.h. oben bleiben wollen, ist ständig ein Zurückgehen in das Wesen, in den Ursprung: *Selbstbehauptung ist ursprüngliche Wesensverwandlung*'[15] [Self-assertion, that is, at the top, that is, to wish to remain above, is consistently a return to the essence, to the origin: *self-assertion is originary transformation of the essence*]. This passage reminds us of the continuous search backward associated by Foucault with Hölderlin, Nietzsche, and Heidegger.[16] What is the nature of the primal, fundamental transformation engendered by self-assertion – transformation as

Ursprung? Heidegger believes Nietzsche's concept of self-assertion is rooted in the will to power, which Heidegger believes is at the same time self-destructive and self-creative, dictatorial and annihilating.[17] Thus, Heidegger's Nietzsche shares with Foucault's an opposition to the metaphysics of evolution and continuity as well as the view that the drive to domination engendering history is located in the interstice between destruction and creation. Heidegger, however, more accurately situates the dynamics of this dialectical change in the *Ursprung*.

Although Nietzsche rejected Darwin's self-preservation postulate and directed a fair amount of invective at evolution's most significant theorist in aphorisms such as 'Against Darwinism' and 'Anti-Darwin' (1887–88), Darwin exercised a major influence on Nietzsche's thought. Nietzsche rejected the metaphysical teleology implicit in evolution but embraced the principle of natural selection. As R. J. Hollingdale has noted, 'Natural selection was for Nietzsche essentially evolution freed from every metaphysical implication: before Darwin's simple but fundamental discovery it had been difficult to deny that the world seemed to be following some course laid down by a directing agency; after it, the necessity for such a directing agency disappeared, and what seemed to be order could be explained as random change.'[18] To be sure, Darwin did not directly attribute random change to natural selection; he saw a clearly defined purpose behind all of nature's modifications and the directing agency of the Creator God behind all evolving life-forms. His *Origin of Species* (1859), however, emphasizes that 'there will be a constant tendency in natural selection to preserve the most divergent offspring of any one species.'[19] Although he surmises that all living things can be traced to a mutual origin, his book militates against the idea that this origin can be established historically. Indeed, he subverts the significance of linear continuity in evolution by suggesting that the demonstration of direct linkages between species lacks primary significance in questions of biological origin.

Darwin's theory, then, bears some resemblance to the notion I am articulating here. Darwin tends to undercut the principle that origins can be situated in a univocal, clearly discernible locus. Although he may surmise a common origin for all life-forms, this origin becomes so occluded by his famous, enthusiastically proclaimed 'tangled bank' metaphor that it emerges as unfixed, destabilized, and polyvalent.[20] Werner Stegmaier has shown how Darwin's conceptualization of the enormous variability and differentiation among the divergent biological genres was particularly attractive to Nietzsche; the 'random change' that such variability suggested to him undoubtedly helped to sustain his formulation of volatile and multiple *Ursprünge*.[21]

Heidegger's emphasis on the refutation by Nietzsche of Darwin's self-preservation concept as being concomitant with the development of a thesis of aggressive self-assertion is consistent with Heidegger's own overemphasis on certain strains in Nietzsche's work. His obsession with the Nietzschean concepts of the will to power and the eternal recurrence of everything represents, as Ernst Behler has suggested, a one-sided misappropriation of Nietzsche's philosophy.[22] The dialectics of their notions of origin, however, reveal similarities, which are more evident in Heidegger's essay 'Der Ursprung des Kunstwerkes' (1935–36, 'The Origin of the Work of Art') than in his work on Nietzsche. As Fredric Jameson has noted, Heidegger's essay 'is organized around the idea that the work of art emerges within the gap between Earth and World.'[23] For Heidegger, the unconcealedness of Earth and the concealedness of World exist in a dialectical tension and in the 'nonplace' or 'interstice' ('non-lieu,' 'l'interstice') between them, to again use Foucault's terminology in his discussion of Nietzsche's *Genealogy* (Heidegger uses the term *Riß* – 'fissure'), the work of art is situated.[24] To be more precise, art (*Kunst*) is itself the *Ursprung* of the work of art.[25] *Ursprung,* however, provides the ground of the artwork's 'primal leap into being' (Steiner), its emergence into the *Riß:* 'Etwas erspringen, im stiftenden Sprung aus der Wesensherkunft ins Sein bringen, das meint das Wort Ursprung'[26] [To bring something into creation through a leap, to bring something out of its essential provenance and into being through a founding leap; this is the meaning of the word origin].

Heidegger's use of the term *Wesensherkunft* – 'essential provenance' – to describe the preontological (i.e., prior to Being) condition of phenomena reminds us that Foucault finds not only *Entstehung* but also *Herkunft* a more precise term than *Ursprung* in designating genealogy's genuine purpose. Foucault also gives *Herkunft* a preontological status when he asserts, 'the traits it attempts to identify are not the exclusive generic characteristics of an individual, a sentiment, or an idea, which permit us to qualify them as "Greek" or "English"; rather, it seeks the subtle, singular, and subindividual marks that might possibly intersect in them to form a network that is difficult to unravel' (NGH 145). As existent phenomena are characterized by individuation, their subindividual marks are traces pointing back to the nonspace prior to their coming into temporal and spatial being. Their intersections form the individual phenomena or ideas. In sustaining this interpretation, Foucault has recourse to Nietzsche's discussion of the '*Herkunft der Gelehrten* [*Ancestry of the Scholars*] in *The Gay Science* (NGH 147). Nietzsche's descent into the prehistory of the modern scholar attempts to locate the subindividual social traits (derived, for example, from the classificatory obsessions of the bureaucrat and the naive confidence of the Protestant minister) that intersect to form the modern scholar's identity. This confirms, in part, Foucault's sense of the resonance of *Herkunft*. Nietzsche, however, uses an organic metaphor to sanction his search for the *Herkunft* of moral prejudices in the introduction to *Genealogy*. He uses a similar metaphor – indicative of steady growth and continuity – in describing the scholar's *Herkunft*: 'The scholar in Europe grows from all kinds of social and class conditions, as a plant that doesn't need a specific kind of soil' (3:583). This clearly runs counter to what Foucault links to Nietzschean *Herkunft* – namely, the identification of 'complete reversals' or even 'minute deviations' (NGH 146).

Just a few sections after discussing the 'ancestry of the scholars,' Nietzsche adopts a different tone in exploring the '*Ursprung der Religionen* [*Origin of the Religions*]. Religious origin finds its ground in disruption, conflict, and reversal. The most significant aspect of the founding of a religion lies in its founder's ability to lend to the character of a specific sort of everyday propriety a moral patina that makes it appear worth fighting and dying for. Jesus, for example, lends this gloss to the virtuous but oppressed life of Rome-dominated Judaea: 'He analyzed it, he invested it with the highest meaning and value, and thus supplied it with the courage to despise every other way of life, the quiescent Herrenhut fanaticism, the secret, subterranean self-confidence, which grows and grows and is finally prepared "to overcome the world" (that is, Rome and the more elevated classes throughout the entire empire)' (3:589). This is the *Ursprung* of Christianity. As with *Entstehung*, then, Foucault's interpretation of Nietzsche's use of *Herkunft* as a corrective to *Ursprung* is contrary to Nietzsche's actual procedure. It is *Ursprung*, not *Herkunft*, that identifies the site where competing systems of domination give rise to human institutions.[27]

What, then, are we to make of the opening section of *Human, All-Too-Human*, in which, as Foucault correctly states, 'the miraculous origin (*Wunderursprung*) sought by metaphysics is set against the analyses of historical philosophy, which poses questions *über Herkunft und Anfang*' (NGH 140)? At the opening of this aphorism, Nietzsche notes that the fundamental issue subsuming questions of modern philosophy is basically the same as it was two thousand years ago, namely, how can something emerge (*entstehen*) from its opposite? Metaphysics had previously resolved this dilemma by denying its possibility and presupposing a 'miraculous origin' for objects of highest value, which stem directly from the 'thing in itself.' Nietzsche, however, is no more kindly disposed toward historical philosophy, which simply dismisses as exaggerated the notion that oppositions such as those between logic and unlogic and reason and unreason exist by claiming that apparent ethical antitheses are merely sublimations (2:23). As an alternative, Nietzsche proposes 'a *chemistry* of the moral, religious, and aesthetic representations and sensations' that would attempt to win 'the most magnificent colors from lowly, indeed despised materials.' Such a chemistry would be concerned with 'Herkunft und Anfänge' [ancestry and beginnings] (2:24; Nietzsche's emphasis). Nietzsche goes on to advocate genuine historical philosophizing, but this activity must be based on a historicist sensibility absent in all philosophers, presumably even those he would include under the rubric of 'historical philosophy' (2:23–25).

As Foucault suggests, Nietzsche rejects the notion of a *Wunder-*

ursprung. The miraculous origin posited by the metaphysicians is the exact reverse of origin as we have seen it employed in Nietzsche's works previously. The metaphysical notion of the complete unity, the undifferentiated and holistic nature of objects belonging to the higher spheres, is contrary to Nietzsche's view of *Ursprung* as the site of a primal division between competing ideologies or phenomena. He finds that contemporary philosophy strives for the same systematic totality in the form of its postulations as that sought by questions posed two thousand years ago (2:23). This was the period of the birth of Christianity, which also marked the birth of Christian morality. The origin of this morality – like that of the *Wunderursprung* sought by contemporary metaphysics – would place it in a sublime realm of inviolable certitude. As Nietzsche puts it in *Götzen-Dämmerung* (1889; *Twilight of the Idols*), 'Christian morality is a command; its origin is transcendental; it is beyond all criticism and all right to criticism' (6:114). To speak of religious and philosophical discourses as inscribed by such a transcendent origin is to presume that they are directed toward a search for metaphysical plenitude, for absolute closure. To speak of such a transcendent origin is to speak of a miraculous origin. In principle, however, *Wunderursprung* is the antithesis of *Ursprung* in Nietzsche's vocabulary. The latter is a term resonant with division, alterity, multiplicity, and dissemination when Nietzsche employs it in most nontranscendent contexts. For example, *Twilight of the Idols* refers to the earthly orgiastic origin of the Hellenic worldview. This origin gave rise to an alienating and differentiated wealth of rites, symbols, and myths that spread over the entire world of antiquity (6:158).

Nietzsche also refers in the *Twilight of the Idols* and elsewhere to *false* origins, such as the one he connects with the fundamental principle of psychology. This principle holds that the origin of every action is grounded in consciousness, and the error of this postulation is engendered by the priestly caste's desire to procure for itself the right to inflict punishment (6:95). Modern metaphysicians, however, do not even pose the question of origin. The dilemma evoked by the question 'how can something emerge [entstehen] from its opposite?' signifies a causal rather than a dialectical ontology. A chain leading from something to its opposite is implied here, whereas *Ursprung* implies the coming-to-being of concepts and sentiments through the convergence of primally irreconcilable spheres. Metaphysics itself comes to being in the interstice between two such spheres, the worlds of dreaming and waking: 'In the age of crude, primal culture, man believed he was becoming acquainted with a *second real world* through the dream; here is the origin of all metaphysics. Without the dream, one would never have found an occasion to divide the world into two' (2:27; Nietzsche's emphasis). This primal division of one world into two antithetical worlds constitutes the ancestry ('Herkunft') of the belief in spirits. Although Foucault is correct in asserting that Nietzsche contrasts the 'miraculous origin' of metaphysics with the search for the 'ancestry and beginnings' of historical philosophy, the same relation does not pertain to *Ursprung* and *Herkunft* themselves. Although it does not easily yield itself to the efforts of historians, *Herkunft* can ultimately be discerned in the course of the 'patiently documentary' search through 'entangled and confused parchments' that lies at the heart of the genealogical endeavor posited by Foucault's Nietzsche (NGH 139). *Ursprung* subsumes *Herkunft* and cannot be located in the examination of a causal network. Only through the contraposing of ideological and phenomenological extremities can *Ursprung* be approximated.

Nietzsche's use of *Herkunft* in the framework of a causal rather than dialectical epistemology becomes even more obvious in the fourteenth section of the first volume of *Human, All-Too-Human*. Here Nietzsche considers the concept of resonances: 'All *stronger* moods bring along a sympathetic resonance of related feelings and moods; it is as though they churned up the memory. They cause us to remember something within ourselves, and we become aware of similar states and their provenance [Herkunft]' (2:35; Nietzsche's emphasis). *Herkunft* is the telos of a chain of interlocking, diachronically descending signifiers. Nietzsche goes on to dispute the authenticity of the perception of cohesiveness that results from the resonances of strong dispositions. Moral and religious feelings are not genuine unities but 'rivers' with many 'sources and tributaries' (2:35). The *Herkunft* of religious and moral feelings is perceived as lying at the intersection of these sources and tributaries, and, as Foucault notes, these intersections form 'a network that is difficult to unravel' (NGH 145). However, the very notion of unraveling a network in order to locate the intersection of the powerful dispositions that combine to create ideologies and theologies still implies a search backward. The exploration of *Herkunft* involves both simple diachronic and complex intersecting causal chains.

The exploration of the *Ursprung* of morals is dialectical. In a passage from *Morgenröte* (1881; *The Dawn*) cited by Foucault to illustrate Nietzsche's 'ironic' approach to '*Ursprung*' (NGH 140–41), Nietzsche grounds the '*Ursprung aller Moral*' [origin of all morality] in the interstice of the antithetical poles 'good – bad' and 'the hostile – the friendly.' Whether we perceive someone as good or evil or friendly or hostile depends entirely on whether we perceive their actions to be harmful or beneficial to our own interests. It is true, as Foucault stresses, that Nietzsche judges this origin of morals to be shameful, a '*pudenda origo*' (NGH 141 and 3:90). This is a good example of what Jeffrey Minson refers to when characterizing Nietzsche's pioneering genealogy as 'the attempt to debunk cherished values by demonstrating their contingency and ignoble origins,' an attempt which, as Minson shows, lays the groundwork for Foucault's own genealogical enterprise.[28] It is one thing, however, to argue that origins are ignoble and shameful and quite another to see an epistemological error in the notion of 'origin.' Foucault's article leads us to believe that Nietzsche, 'at least on those occasions when he is truly a genealogist,' would 'challenge the pursuit of the origin (*Ursprung*)' (NGH 142), and this is simply not the case. It is more accurate to say that Nietzsche seeks to demystify the metaphysics of *Ursprung* by shifting its locus from the paradise of metaphysical plenitude to the interstices between antithetical, self-interested ideologies.

The use of the term 'antithetical' in connection with the dialectics of Nietzsche's *Ursprung* concept should not be taken to mean that this aspect of his genealogy follows a Hegelian model. Although such antitheses as the Apollonian and the Dionysian may come together to engender a new ideology or form – the Greek tragedy, for example – they are never actually resolved into a synthesis. This allows Foucault to use Nietzsche as his own model in developing a genealogy based on disparity, disruption, difference, and rupture, on a dialectics, that is, of the interstice. Of course, the assertion that Nietzsche's dialectics involve the conjunction of antitheses without their resolution breaks no new ground. As Peter Heller has noted, 'Nietzsche rarely recommends any mediation which would result in a toning down or neutralization of opposites. He is hostile to a balance achieved at the expense of intensity and adverse to adjustment or compromise.'[29] Nietzsche's rejection of analogical reasoning, of an epistemology based on simple cause and effect, and of the concept of succession (3:115) is related to this refusal to diminish the intensity of the oppositions he brings together. What has not been adequately demonstrated – and what Foucault's reading of Nietzsche would deny – is that Nietzsche's dialectics are largely centered around his concept of *Ursprung*. I have tried to illustrate this from a variety of aphorisms taken from several of Nietzsche's works that employ the concept of *Ursprung*, aphorisms that are often the very same ones that Foucault believes point to Nietzsche's *rejection* of the pursuit of origin.

The bulk of this chapter has been devoted to showing that Foucault has misread Nietzsche's use of the term *Ursprung*. We have now arrived at the thornier issue of what generates this misreading, an issue that leads to the historical dimension of Nietzsche's principle of origin and Foucault's interpretation of it. It is impossible to resolve this issue with any degree of certainty, but Minson's treatment of the dilemma lying at the heart of both Nietzsche's and Foucault's genealogies suggests a plausible cause. For Minson, this dilemma is grounded in their inability to face up to the inevitable connection between origin and outcome. Origins may be multiple, and this multiplicity may counteract Western metaphysical tendencies to manufacture a teleological *Wunderursprung* at some mystical, prelapsarian site. However, if one denies any connection at all between origin and outcome, one effectively nullifies the purpose of the genealogical enterprise. Minson's summary of the quandary of genealogy as praxis has implications for both Nietzsche and Foucault:

On the one hand, it can remain faithful to its methodological starting point and maintain the dissociation of origins and outcome, in which case its moral-critical presumption falls down since origins are no longer constitutive of their product. On the other hand, it can insist on the constitutive and telling character of origins, but then the original grounds for distinguishing genealogy from teleological history collapse. Either genealogy remains a variant of teleological history or it is irrelevant by its own standard of relevance.[30]

Minson's commentary suggests that there is a fundamental split between the origin of an idea or phenomenon and its subsequent history – between origin and outcome – in the genealogies of Nietzsche and Foucault. It seems quite plausible that Foucault wishes to avoid this dilemma by implying that his genealogical precursor has so effectively deconstructed the principle of *Ursprung* as to make it methodologically irrelevant. No aporia can result from the conflict between origin and history if there is no origin, only historical disruptions, conflicts, and differences. In defense of Foucault (and Nietzsche), Minson's critique can be amended by noting that there can be a middle ground between finding no connection between origin and outcome and seeing the two as linked by unmediated causality. Creative misreadings and partial distortions of origins may also lead to outcomes, and the genealogies of Nietzsche and Foucault reflect this fact. They often oscillate between inventive juxtapositions and strategies designed to relentlessly expose historical distortions. The two methods are often tied together, as in Nietzsche's analysis of the origins of Christianity (3:589) and Foucault's examination of the 'birth' of the clinic. Nevertheless, Foucault seeks to subvert the notion of origin entirely. In 'Nietzsche, Genealogy, History,' he comments that 'history also teaches us how to laugh at the solemnities of the origin' (NGH 143). Much of his essay is devoted to showing the division between origin and history, a divorce he believes has been methodologically sanctioned by Nietzsche's genealogical practices. Of course, Foucault believes Nietzsche comes down on the side of history, or at least 'effective' history – a history 'without constants' (NGH 153) because without any stable origins. However, Minson's critique allows us to see that the division between origin and history ('outcome'), far from being a laughing matter, is the fundamental dilemma facing genealogical praxis.

Foucault is certainly correct in suggesting that Nietzsche believes 'history becomes "effective" to the degree that it introduces discontinuity into our very being' (NGH 154). Effective history is contraposed with the suprahistorical perspectives that use teleological principles to establish 'history' as a 'totality.' Foucault is also justified in citing the second of the *Unzeitgemäße Betrachtungen* (1873–76; *Untimely Meditations*), 'Vom Nutzen und Nachteil der Historie für das Leben,' (1873; 'On the Uses and Disadvantages of History for Life') as a premier document of Nietzsche's development of an antitotalized, antiteleological view of history (NGH 152, 161–62, 164). In his essay, however, Foucault fails to isolate what it is that propels Nietzsche's 'effective' history – and with good reason. It is precisely forgetting – *das Vergessen* – that overcomes the 'transcendental construction of a historicity' and constitutes the dynamic and vital element in Nietzschean history, as Walter Gebhard's book on Nietzsche's notion of totality has suggested.[31] In 'On the Uses and Disadvantages of History for Life,' Nietzsche equates forgetting with the ahistorical. Both the historical and the ahistorical are necessary for the well-being of individuals and cultures. Nevertheless, the ability to perceive ahistorically is the more original mode of human existence: 'On the other hand, we saw the animal, which is completely ahistorical and dwells within a horizon reduced practically to a point, but with a certain amount of happiness and, at any rate, without boredom and dissembling. Thus, we must regard the ability to perceive to a certain degree ahistorically as more important and originary, insofar as within this capacity lies the foundation enabling the growth of the just, the healthy, the strong, the truly human' (1:252). Ironically, the origin of noble, genuinely human qualities is dialectically engendered in the interstice between activity (as only in activity can noble abstractions such as justice, health and grandeur be made manifest) and forgetting.

Foucault's genealogies seek to overcome such forgetting; in exploring the historical foundations of such institutions as the clinic, the prison, and the asylum, Foucault acts to jog the memory by painstakingly documenting these institutions' marginal or 'lowly' origins for our conscious consideration. In this sense, Foucault is, of course, a far more traditional chronicler of events than Nietzsche ever was. Foucault's own 'forgetfulness' regarding Nietzsche's establishment of forgetting as a dynamic principle in human history is thus understandable because his essay seeks to establish Nietzsche as a methodological ally.

In one of the more comprehensive monographs on Foucault's oeuvre, Hubert Dreyfus and Paul Rabinow note that, particularly after the *Archaeology,* Foucault 'uses Nietzsche's genealogy as a starting point for developing a method that would allow him to thematize the relationship between truth, theory, and values and the social institutions and practices in which they emerge.'[32] Foucault's landmark studies of these social institutions and practices have proven to be of great value in stimulating fruitful new discourse and research in such fields as sociology and historiography. It might seem ironic that Foucault's pioneering insights were themselves in great measure stimulated by a certain blindness to Nietzsche's notion of *Ursprung.* But as Paul de Man has taught us all, blindness and insight are inextricably intertwined.

CHAPTER 2

Ursprung's Destructive/Redemptive
Rhythm: Walter Benjamin

In *The Origin of German Tragic Drama,* Walter Benjamin criticizes Nietzsche for essentially ignoring the historical character of the tragedy. He sees Nietzsche's view of tragic myth as informed by an aestheticism that renounces historico-philosophical knowledge. This renunciation does not allow Nietzsche an insight into the essence of the tragedy, which is grounded in historico- or religio-philosophical concepts.[1] Ferenc Feher discerns in Benjamin's critique 'a defense of the *right to existence of the specifically modern drama* against the overwhelming authority of Nietzsche.'[2] It also suggests the resolutely historico-philosophical approach Benjamin brings to bear on the question of origin. More than Nietzsche and the other thinkers discussed in this book, Benjamin sees origin as a 'historical category' (1:226). This does not mean, however, that Benjamin equates origin with a simple diachronic starting point for the emergence of phenomena and ideas. In fact, the *philosophical* component of Benjamin's *Geschichtsphilosophie* allows him to see phenomena and ideas under the sign of origin as stamped by the *totality* of their history. Moreover, Benjamin's notion of historical totality is not to be equated with the bad infinite of metaphysical absolutism; rather, he equates historical totality with the pre- and posthistory of phenomena. This pre- and posthistory is both encompassed and generated by origin and is related to concrete historical findings; it is not above or beyond phenomenal facticity (1:226). The phenomena examined by Benjamin in the guise of such a historical totality are not caught up in the stasis of homogeneous time. Instead, this configuration of phenomena inscribed by the 'rhythm' (1:226) of origin will ultimately allow Benjamin to articulate the explosion of the continuum of history.

The underpinnings of Benjamin's view of origin are theological and informed by a belief in prelapsarian semiotic plenitude. In the

1916 essay 'Über Sprache überhaupt und über die Sprache des Menschen' ('On Language as such and on the Language of Man'), Benjamin distinguishes between the limited, analytical nature of human language and the infinite, creative nature of the divine word. Human language is the language of knowledge, but knowledge is perfect prior to the Fall – that is, there is no split between signifier and signified or between subject and object. For Benjamin, the human word attains its 'hour of birth' only at the moment of the Fall, when it becomes disassociated from the language of names (2:153).

The immanent bond between man and nature forged by primordial language is thus broken. The language of names – the Adamic language – allowed man a perfect cognition of the external world. As Richard Wolin has noted, the recuperation of this language is Benjamin's telos: 'The pure language of names is the "origin" that has become the "goal," inasmuch as its affinity to the divine language of creation lends it the greatest proximity to a state of redemption.'[3] Benjamin never loses sight of this goal, and the passage from Karl Kraus to which Wolin alluded greatly inspired Benjamin toward the end of his life. Clearly, Benjamin's thesis concerning the mimetic character of language and his embrace of the ideal of a prelapsarian moment informed by divine perfection indicate a yearning for metaphysical plenitude that is at odds with the thrust of poststructuralist thought. The site of Benjaminian origin appears to lie in a domain outside of – prior to – history.[4] However, Benjamin as well as Kraus came to regard the attainment of such an origin as indefinitely deferred. Moreover, Kraus helped inspire Benjamin to equate origin with *dis*ruption, *dis*continuity, and a *destructive* critical praxis. This perspective is evident in Benjamin's discussion of Kraus's use of citations in the essay 'Karl Kraus' (1931) on the Austrian journalist: 'Language shows itself to be the mater of righteousness in the redemptive and punitive citation. The citation summons the word by its name, destructively wrests it from its context, but it thereby recalls the word to its origin' (2:363). The recuperation of the language of names as the recuperation of origin can only be generated through a fragmenting of the bond between the cited word and the context from which it was taken.

Benjamin's advocacy, in this essay on Kraus, of the annihilation of contextual harmony parallels his embrace of allegorical fragmentation and his concomitant refutation of the harmonious conjunctions of the symbol in the *Trauerspiel* book. Both instances reflect a destructive critical praxis closely related to Benjamin's notion of origin, a notion most fully articulated in the 'Epistemocritical Prologue' to the *Trauerspiel* book. An adumbration of this prologue will show the close links between Benjamin's ideal aesthetics, his favoring of fragmentary forms, his view of truth as open-ended, and his concept of *Ursprung*. While some leading deconstructionists sanction certain elements in Benjamin's poetics of mortification, especially its embrace of the allegorical and its refusal of critical closure, they, perhaps deliberately, overlook the connection between these elements and Benjamin's unique theory of origin.

Benjamin opens the prologue with a discussion of the problems of representation. Knowledge is implicated by its desire for possession. The intentionality of the subject who would cognitively possess an object makes representation of this object peripheral; its self-representationality is not an a priori condition (1:209). Truth, however, is self-representing and blocks all attempts at closure. Fragmentary forms resist closure insofar as they motivate a contemplation informed by ceaseless breath-catching, an irregular rhythm, a continuous pausing for reflection. Only such forms – Benjamin cites the mosaic and the treatise as examples – subvert the intentionality of knowledge and allow noumenal truth to emerge. Contemplative representation is coterminous with a 'prosaic soberness,' the only manner of writing proper to the representation of ideas. From the dance of these represented ideas, truth is recollected (1:209). In the *Trauerspiel* book, Benjamin brings his vision of the idea into close conjunction with his vision of truth: 'Ideas are pregiven. The winnowing of the truth from the context of knowledge thus defines the idea as Being. This is the significance of the theory of ideas for the concept of truth. As Being, truth and idea attain that highest metaphysical signification emphatically attributed to them by the Platonic system' (1:210). Although ideas are essential and preexistent rather than phenomenal, an idea is only evoked in the clustering of the extremes of phenomena around it. In bodying forth the idea, the phenomena are redeemed. Only in fragmentary form, as a configuration of extremes organized by concepts ('Begriffe'), do phenomena bring an idea to life. Only the dance ('Reigen') of these represented ideas brings forth the truth. However, as the death of an intentionality nested in a false scientific coherence, truth (to paraphrase Michael Jennings) *as* 'present in the world' *must be* 'hidden in fragmentary form.'[5] Thus, as 'present in the world,' hidden truth necessarily takes on the character of redeemed phenomena.

The circle, however, is hermeneutic. If the whole (truth) takes on the character of the parts (clustered extremes of phenomena bodying forth the ideas), the redeemed parts are invested with the character of the whole. Benjamin's theory is reminiscent – particularly with regard to the epistemological framework that guides and limits all scientific and philosophical inquiry – of the hermeneutic circle as it has been sketched by Hans-Georg Gadamer. Gadamer believes truth can never be grasped as a discrete, foundational entirety, existing apart from those who pursue it. No point of beginning is anchored either in an inquiring subject or in an objective empirical content where such truth may be said to emerge. Instead, truth and understanding are only approximated through a dynamic interchange between these two poles, an interchange conditioned by their historical contexts. As David Couzens Hoy has pointed out, Gadamer 'follows Heidegger in abandoning the foundationalist enterprise that looks for a presuppositionless starting point in the self-certainty of subjectivity, and in stressing instead the interpretive and historical character of all understanding, including philosophical self-understanding.'[6]

For Benjamin, too, philosophical and scientific truth and understanding are completely inseparable from individual experiences. These individual experiences are grounded in different phenomenal extremes, but none constitutes, in itself, the basis for a methodological starting point. When he speaks of a 'configuration of extremes,' Benjamin also posits the ideal of interdisciplinarity in the sciences, the coming together of disciplines grounded in highly differentiated sorts of individual experiences. This interdisciplinarity will facilitate the ideal 'context of knowledge' mentioned by Benjamin in the passage from the *Trauerspiel* book cited above (1:210).[7] Thus, the phenomenal extremes that make up the parts that constitute the whole of 'truth' are firmly rooted in empirical reality. However, Benjamin was more a messianic idealist than a theorist of science; he saw empirical phenomena as shards of a broken whole ('*Tikkun*'). The truth affiliated with this whole is informed by metaphysical plenitude, as are the ideas established by truth as Platonic Being.[8] This metaphysical component distinguishes Benjamin's thought from that of Gadamer, although poststructuralists such as Derrida see even in Gadamer's hermeneutic circle a 'metaphysics of presence.'[9]

Before phenomena can be redeemed and inscribed by truth, they must undergo a metamorphosis. Benjamin says of the phenomena as they come into the realm of ideas, 'They cast off their false unity in order that, thus divided, they may share in the genuine unity of truth' (1:213). The relationship between phenomenon and truth recalls the rhythm of *Ursprung* that Benjamin describes as being perceivable to a cognition that recognizes this rhythm's character as both restoration *and* something incomplete and open-ended (1:226). The phenomenon is redeemed by its participation in the genuine unity of truth. Benjamin, however, also holds truth, as 'present in the world,' to be capable of apprehension only through an immersion into factical or concrete details. Truth content can only be approached through the most precise exploration of material content (1:208).

Truth as a perceptible agency is thus revealed to be necessarily open and incomplete. If truth in its representational character were other than incomplete and resistant to closure, it could never serve as the refuge and guarantor of beauty. As the self-representing realm of ideas, truth provides this refuge precisely by opening up the moment of representationality (1:211). Truth as the Platonic 'content' of beauty is not manifested through exposure but through the destructive immolation of the work's husk. Benjamin's definition of the rhythm of origin allows this fusion of otherwise seemingly disparate, even antithetical, elements in his early aesthetics: the appropriation of the Platonic idea with its ideal of noumenal

plenitude, the embrace of a destructive critical praxis with its concomitant favoring of fragmentary aesthetic forms, and the view
that truth is open-ended. As in his discussion of the Krausian citation, Benjamin's view of *Ursprung* in his *Trauerspiel* book points
toward both the telos of redemption and the infinite deferral of
closure found in deconstructive poetics.

Benjamin's definition of *Ursprung* in the prologue to the *Trauerspiel* book occurs within the context of a discussion of genre theory. Having engaged in a detailed refutation of both inductive and
deductive genre poetics (1:219–25), Benjamin is left in the apparent position of endorsing a critical relativism that treats each
particular work as an original category in toto. Because such a view
is foreign to Benjamin's aesthetics, he distanced himself from it
through a critique of the foremost proponent of the complete formal integrity of the individual work of art, Benedetto Croce. On
the foundation of his refutation of Croce's nominalism, Benjamin
formulates his concept of origin. He expresses support for Croce's
rejection of the grouping of individual works of art into aesthetic
categories and the attempt to use genres to mediate between the
universal and the particular. However, Benjamin deviates from
Croce's rejection of the literary genres in endorsing the tragic and
the comic as useful ideas. Unlike the concepts of 'pure tragedy' and
'pure comic drama,' which are informed by the artificial inclusive-
ness of rule-based genre theories, the idea as genre is an internal
structure. As such, it is neither prescriptive nor empirically comprehensive. Rather, as monad, its totality is established by its incor-
poration of both the pre- and posthistory of phenomena, including
works of art. This temporally all-encompassing totality suggests
the fundamental link between origin and monad. A criticism based
on the immanent totality of the idea rather than the extensive categories created by traditional genre poetics seeks what is generically
exemplary in the individual work. Benjamin calls this search an
investigation ('Untersuchung'), which could imply the discursive
attempt to arrive at a knowledge of normative principles. Benjamin, however, deflects any such suspicion by asserting that a
significant work will either establish a new genre or violate (and
thereby transcend) its limits (1:225).

A significant work is a transgressive work. The paradox that 'the transgressive work will become a norm or a generic paradigm' precisely as it *does away* with norms is rooted in the principle of *Ursprung*.[10] The complexity of this term in Benjamin's vocabulary can be educed by the wide variety of interpretations it has evoked. The critical passage defining *Ursprung* in the prologue to the *Trauerspiel* book follows Benjamin's critique of Croce's inability to reconcile genetic classification with an idea-based theory of art forms with respect to the problem of origin:

> Ursprung, wiewohl durchaus historische Kategorie, hat mit Entstehung dennoch nichts gemein. Im Ursprung wird kein Werden des Entsprungenen, vielmehr dem Werden und Vergehen Entspringendes gemeint. Der Ursprung steht im Fluß des Werdens als Strudel und reißt in seine Rhythmik das Entstehungsmaterial hinein. Im nackten offenkundigen Bestand des Faktischen gibt das Ursprüngliche sich niemals zu erkennen, und einzig einer Doppeleinsicht steht seine Rhythmik offen. Sie will als Restauration, als Wiederherstellung einerseits, als eben darin Unvollendetes, Unabgeschlossenes andererseits erkannt sein. In jedem Ursprungsphänomen bestimmt sich die Gestalt, unter welcher immer wieder eine Idee mit der geschichtlichen Welt sich auseinandersetzt, bis sie in der Totalität ihrer Geschichte vollendet daliegt. Also hebt sich der Ursprung aus dem tatsächlichen Befunde nicht heraus, sondern er betrifft dessen Vor- und Nachgeschichte. (1:226)

> [Origin, although an entirely historical category, nevertheless has nothing in common with genesis. The term *origin* does not signify the process of becoming of what has issued from it. Rather, it refers to what issues from the process of becoming and dying away. Origin stands within the river of becoming as a whirlpool, and it drags the material of genesis into its rhythm. The originary never reveals itself in the naked and overt presence of the factual. Only a dual insight is open to its rhythm. It must be viewed, on the one hand, as a process of restoration and reestablishment and, on the other hand, as something thereby incomplete and lacking closure. In every

phenomenon of origin there occurs a determination of the shape in which an idea will continuously confront the historical world until it is fully revealed in the totality of its history. Thus, origin does not emerge from the study of actual results but concerns their pre- and posthistory.]

Before examining the reaction of Benjamin's interpreters to this seminal passage, Benjamin's own commentary must be addressed. He was inspired by his reading of Georg Simmel's *Goethe* (1913) to note that he took Goethe's concept of the 'Urphänomen' ('archetypal phenomenon') from the realm of nature and transposed it to the realm of history, adding, 'Ursprung – das ist der aus dem heidnischen Naturzusammenhange in die jüdischen Zusammenhänge der Geschichte eingebrachte Begriff des Urphänomens' (5:577) [Origin – that is the archetypal phenomenon, taken from the pagan context of nature and brought into the Jewish contexts of history]. Simmel infers that Goethe used the term 'Urphänomen' to describe the confluence of the idea ('Idee') and the sensual object ('Gestalt').[11] Rolf Tiedemann suggests that the notion of *Ursprung* adds history to the genre's ontological makeup. An artistic genre becomes an idea as an originary phenomenon ('Ursprungsphänomen'), but origin itself is rooted in history.[12] Influenced by Tiedemann's views, René Wellek comments that '*Ursprung* does not mean origin at all, but something like the idea of a genre. It is rather Goethe's *Urphänomen* transferred to history.'[13]

In an essay on Benjamin's conception of hope, Peter Szondi is equally laconic in addressing *Ursprung,* content to note Benjamin's concern with 'the problematic nature of the ahistorical conceptions of the literary genres usually found in discussions of poetics.'[14] In a more thoroughgoing treatment of the term, Sandor Radnoti deemphasizes the connection between *Ursprung* and genre and concentrates on establishing the synchronicity of origin's historical character. What is valuable in Radnoti's commentary is his elucidation of the methodological principles nested in Benjamin's theory.[15] Bernd Witte's exegesis diverges from that of Tiedemann and Radnoti in characterizing the *Trauerspiel* under the sign of *Ursprung* as beyond history ('übergeschichtlich'). According to Witte, Benjamin determines genres to be 'ideas that are to be collected from the extreme formulations of phenomena and arranged in the series of an "intentionless Being" of truth.'[16] Thus, Benjamin's representation of the *Trauerspiel* has as its aim not mere historical accuracy but objective and metaphysical truth.[17] Michael Rumpf sees the use of *Ursprung* as an attempt to establish the substantiality of the unitary image of the tragic drama: it sheds the contingent character associated with its historical development by being elevated to the level of 'idea-based being.'[18] This transformation constitutes the transition from *Trauerspiel* as concept to *Trauerspiel* as idea.

This overview of some of the past critical struggles with Benjaminian *Ursprung* shows a remarkable range of opinions concerning the interrelationship postulated in Benjamin's theory between history and genre. In sum, *Ursprung* establishes the historical character of the genre, transcends the historical character of the genre, overcomes the *ahistorical* character of the usual view of the genre, establishes the *pre- and posthistorical* character of the genre, and transcends the *accidental* character of the history of the genre. Other treatments of *Ursprung* have emphasized the telos motivating the relationship of history and structure within the genre or work.[19] This heterogeneity suggests that the rhythm of Benjamin's origin allows him to organize entirely disparate elements into a critical constellation. Interpretations of the relationship between *Ursprung* and genre vary according to the emphasis attached to or excluded from these individual elements. However, Benjamin's idealist theory of art forms is also inclusive enough to *encompass* all these different opinions.

Some recent interpretations of Benjamin's notion of *Ursprung* have emphasized its religious dimensions. Uwe Steiner sees the core of Benjamin's theory of origin as theological. According to his interpretation, the pre- and posthistory encompassed by *Ursprung* refers not only to the empirical, historically determined character of the *Trauerspiel* but to the before and after of history on the whole ('das Vor und Nach der Geschichte'). The rhythm of origin is thus inscribed by an eschatological vision: 'As long as history awaits redemption, the restoration in history of what is addressed by revelation necessarily lacks closure.'[20] Stéphane Mosès, like Steiner, has emphasized both the Goethian and the theological underpinnings of Benjaminian *Ursprung*. He sees Benjamin's notion of origin as informed by a 'double determination': that is, it delineates that which is absolutely first in history (such as the Adamic language of names) and what is absolutely new. Origin does not signify a return to a temporal beginning but holds out the hope for a possible 'regeneration' at every instant.[21] Both Steiner and Mosès allude to something that I've underscored earlier but that bears repeating here: despite the theological – indeed eschatological – elements in Benjaminian *Ursprung*, its rhythm suggests an open-ended view of history. *Ursprung* is informed by the plenitude of pre- and posthistory, but its antilinear character subverts the closure this possibly eschatological dimension of origin seems to suggest. Leibniz's influence in Benjamin's articulation of *Ursprung* can explain this apparent paradox.

Most interpreters of *Ursprung* have ignored the concept's Leibnizian derivation. An important exception is Wolin, who states that 'the category of "monad" serves as an additional illustration of the being and specificity of the idea. Like origin, the monad knows history not in terms of its extensive empirical being, but as something *integral* and *essential*.'[22] The Leibnizian monad is characterized by 'plenitude, continuity and harmony.'[23] The plenitude – Benjamin uses the term 'Totalität' – of form grounded in the 'Wissenschaft vom Ursprung' ('science of origin') is based on its ideal character. The idea is the configuration of the apparently contradictory extremes of phenomena, giving the idea a plenitude that redeems it from the linear character of history. The idea is made essential as its 'natural (pre- and posthistorical) history' is established (1:227). Of course, the plenitude of the monad or idea also lies in the fact that each one 'contains the image of the world' (1:228).

Nevertheless, the totality or plenitude of the idea or monad does not diminish its particular individuality. In *The Monadology* (1715) Leibniz comments that 'although each created monad represents the whole universe, it represents more distinctly the body which is particularly affected by it and of which it is the entelechy.'[24] The internal, perfected nature and form-engendering energy of Aristotle's entelechy imparts to the Leibnizian monad its self-sufficient integrity. The monads find their final cause and sufficient reason in God, establishing harmony and continuity among them. However, the *Discourse on Metaphysics* (1686), which prefigures *The Monadology* epistemologically, establishes the fundamental immanence of all ideas. They are only linked externally by God.

Benjamin adapts Leibniz's monadological principles to overcome the historical problem of form and to meet the challenge he sees posed by Croce's rejection of genetic classification. In his doctoral dissertation, *Der Begriff der Kunstkritik in der deutschen Romantik* (1919; The concept of art criticism in German romanticism), Benjamin defined 'progressive universal poetry' as extensive: the individual genres are disintegrated into an endless, universal continuum of forms. Romantic 'transcendental poetry,' on the other hand, establishes the intensive unity of form. The conflicting economies of the two concepts reflect the tension in German romantic poetics between the postulation of an infinite multiplicity of genres and the idea of one all-encompassing genre. However, there is a clear fusion of the two economies in Benjamin's letter of 9 December 1923 to Florens Christian Rang: 'Their intensive endlessness characterizes the ideas as monads.'[25] In this letter, Benjamin postulates an intensive connection between works of art; the external unity of the works of art established by an extensive history of form is of no significance. The intensive cohesion of art – timeless and yet of historical significance – is established through interpretation.[26] Benjamin's care in distinguishing an essential connection between works of art from any system of forms contaminated by the exteriority of traditional histories of art reflects a praxis of critical immanence that was established in his 1923 essay on Goethe's novel *Die Wahlverwandtschaften* (*Elective Affinities*) and in *Der Begriff der Kunstkritik*. In Benjamin's letter to Rang, the dual nature of the Leibnizian monads – governed by both a self-sufficient interiority and timeless interconnectedness – also exercises an obvious influence on Benjamin's discourse. In his *Trauerspiel* book, the concept of *Ursprung* makes possible the intensive, timeless continuity of works of art precisely by evoking the historical totality of original phenomena. An immanent interpretation of exemplary works, grounded in *Ursprung*, brings about the contiguity of the extremes of a given genre (such as the *Trauer-spiel*) and thus allows it to emerge as an idea. The clustering of marginal traits culled from the individual works foregrounds their intensive, timeless interconnection. The linear historical continuity of traditional art histories is thereby overcome. These art histories seek what is average in works of art in order to establish genres characterized by historical *unity*. An idealist theory of art forms can only be reconciled to the principle of genetic classification by striving for a historical *totality*: 'The idea does not assimilate the sequence of historical formulations in order to create a unity from them and even less to extract something common to them. No analogy takes place between the relationship of the individual to the idea and its relationship to the concept. In the latter case, it falls under the sway of the concept and remains what it was – individuality. In the former case, it stands in the idea and becomes what it was not – totality' (1:227). Such totality subsumes both irreducible unity and endless multiplicity. It presupposes *all* of the relationships between genre and history outlined above. Moreover, such totality is manifested only in *Ursprung*. As with the Leibnizian monads, the historical totality of phenomena under the sign of origin both encompasses and generates their immanent connection. The monadological character of *Ursprung*, however, also allows the phenomena their individuated character so that origin is also informed by an infinite heterogeneity. Poststructuralists would be reluctant to view this radical multivalence inherent in Benjaminian *Ursprung* as a possible corollary to any notion of origin.

It is this quality, however – inscribed in Benjaminian *Ursprung* through its monadological character – that preserves the historically unique character of the *Trauerspiel* as delineated in Benjamin's book. I noted at the outset that Benjamin refuted Nietzsche's concept of tragedy because of its failure to address the historico-philosophical component of this genre, the key component for Benjamin. Benjamin's desire to foreground this element of the *Trauerspiel* caused him to alter his outlook on artistic form. Whereas *Der Begriff der Kunstkritik* equates the idea of form with a continuum of forms, Benjamin represents the idea in his *Trauerspiel* book as a unique originary essence.[27] This shift is necessary in order to establish an important thesis: the German *Trauerspiel* is not part of a continuum of the symbolic Greek tragedies, as a Nietzschean-inspired critique of this genre would suggest. Rather, the *Trauerspiel's Ursprung* is grounded in a unique historico-philosophical moment, bringing forth ideas embedded in individual works. The task of the critic is to evoke these ideas through philosophical contemplation. Benjamin devotes much of the first chapter of his treatise to distinguishing the *Trauerspiel* from Greek tragedy. He concludes the 'Epistemocritical Prologue' by establishing parallels between baroque drama and expressionist drama stemming from the decadence of both historico-philosophical epochs. However, he finds that even these parallels are limited (1:236). Only by treating the *Trauerspiel* with respect to its integrity as a discrete historical form can Benjamin illuminate *Ursprung* in the dramas themselves. The connection between *Ursprung* and the form of the individual historical object is most clearly established later in a fragment of the *Passagen-Werk* (1927–40; The Arcades Project). The term itself is not employed in this fragment. However, Benjamin's commentary in the same work defines *Ursprung* in the *Trauerspiel* book as a concatenation of history and the Goethian 'Urphänomen' (5:577). Benjamin's use of this same concatenation in defining 'dialectical image' thus allows us to sense its underlying presence: 'The dialectical image is the form of the historical object that satisfies Goethe's demands of the object of an analysis: the demonstration of a genuine synthesis. It is the archetypal phenomenon of history' (5:592).

As the title of his book indicates, Benjamin wishes to examine the *Ursprung* of the German baroque *Trauerspiel.* Only in examining this origin can the *Trauerspiel* emerge in its discrete, historico-philosophical form – as an 'archetypal phenomenon of history.' Through the technique of origin, Benjamin would inscribe the *Trauerspiel* with an alterity absent in Nietzschean and neo-Nietzschean analyses of this genre. In order to establish this alterity, Benjamin must show that its mode of representation is radically different from that of the classical Greek tragedy. The tragedy's fundamental mode of representation is the symbol. In *Der Begriff der Kunstkritik,* Benjamin had discerned a tendency among the romantics to investigate literary genres in much the same way as morphological studies, which relate essences ('Wesen') to organic life (1:115 n.307). Both the Goethian search for synthesis and this attempt by the romantics to relate form to creaturely life inform Benjamin's examination of the German baroque dramas. However, Benjamin rejects what he sees as the romantic favoring of the symbol in the search for an unconstrained knowledge of some sort of absolute (1:336). This rejection of the symbol as a privileged representational device is largely motivated by Benjamin's desire to establish that the *Trauerspiel*'s primary mode of representation – the allegory – is as legitimate as the symbol from a historico-philosophical perspective. The particular historico-philosophical constellations of the baroque age justify the use of allegory during that period. Only an ahistorical point of view could judge the symbol to be an absolutely superior mode of representation. However, Benjamin also defends allegory because it is the mode ideally suited to evoking the transient, historically mutable condition of humanity in general. Only the melancholy gaze of allegory shows the true condition of the creaturely life of man, subject to nature through his mortality. As Jürgen Habermas notes, Benjaminian allegory expresses the experience of the negative pole of life – the experience of suppression, suffering, and failure – thereby contesting symbolic art's vision of freedom, fulfillment, and positive happiness.[28] Allegory recognizes, and brings into sharp relief, the finite quality of all earthly things. At the same time, it would immortalize and thus rescue these objects from their subjection to temporality.[29] Creaturely life is inscribed by history. Allegory subverts the illusion of harmony between object and image, the temporal and the eternal, and the universal and particular fostered by the romantic symbol. Part 1 of the *Trauerspiel* book describes 'the most salient extravagances and affectations of the dramas themselves.'[30] The absolute tyranny of the Oriental despot and the silent suffering of the martyr, the splendor of the court, and the annihilated, corpse-littered landscape: such phenomenal extremities are antithetical to the totalizing conjunctions of the symbolic tragedy. They invest the baroque dramas with a unique historical content. The restoration and restitution of this historical content makes of it a philosophical truth.

This critical activity reveals the allegorical *Trauerspiel* as a ruin – that is, it establishes the *Trauerspiel*'s open, incomplete, fragmentary character. The mortification of the *Trauerspiel* is governed by the rhythm of *Ursprung*. It is reinvoked by Benjamin in the second part of his *Trauerspiel* book, implicitly informing Benjamin's view of the way philosophical criticism will help the baroque *Trauerspiel* to emerge as a ruin by foregrounding its allegorical character. This emergence is concomitant with the critical transformation of the drama's material contents into its truth content. The evocation of this truth content represents both the destruction and redemption of the work of art. The process appears to be governed by the rhythm of origin, which encompasses and generates both the evocation of the artwork's incomplete, imperfect character and the advent of its restoration (1:226). The work's formal structure must be annihilated in order for its content to be redeemed: 'This restructuring of material contents into the truth content makes the decay of the effectiveness, whereby the appeal of the earlier charms depreciates from one decade to the next, into the foundation for a rebirth, in which all ephemeral beauty completely drops away, and the work asserts itself as a ruin. In the allegorical structure of the Baroque *Trauerspiel*, such forms, reduced to rubble, of the redeemed work of art, have always stood out clearly' (1:358). The concatenation of phenomenal extremities allows the immanent ideas of the *Trauerspiel* to emerge in a formal totality, a process Benjamin defines as the 'science' of origin (1:227). The synthesis of these extremities illuminates the genre in its essential history. The fragmentary form of the *Trauerspiel* is intimately related to this redemptive recovery of *Ursprung* in the individual works. The rhythm of origin – characterized by a fragmentary, open-ended quality that also points to the redemption and restoration inherent in the work of art – can be discerned clearly in Benjamin's description of the allegorical construction of the baroque *Trauerspiel*.

The application of allegory and the articulation of allegorical modes of reading are major facets of much deconstructive criticism. Jesse Gellrich has remarked that 'allegory is used in deconstruction to reflect unresolvable properties of texts, the plurivalent or arbitrary functions of signs, and the dilemma (aporia) of choosing among them.'[31] Deconstructionists have been inspired to use allegory in this way largely through their reading of Benjamin. As Gellrich has noted, this reading tends to ignore the eschatologically redemptive element, pointing toward an ultimate referential fixity, which Benjamin sees as latent in allegorical language.[32] In the introduction, we noted that poststructuralists view origin as *antithetical* to semiotic plurivalence and the foregrounding of textual ambiguity. It is thus quite convenient for poststructuralists to ignore as well the intimate connection between *Ursprung* and allegory in the *Trauerspiel* book in their appropriation of Benjamin's views. In his essay 'The Rhetoric of Temporality,' Paul de Man includes Benjamin's privileging of the allegorical mode of representation as an example of the modern critical tendency to stress the rhetoricity of literary texts. This emphasis on rhetorical figuration is seen by de Man as part of the attempt to undermine the belief that texts have a single meaning that resides in the normative link between words and what they signify. This harmonious conjunction is inscribed in the symbol, and Benjamin is among those who call 'the supremacy of the symbol' into question.[33] In contrasting the symbol's telos of semiotic identity with the allegory's subversion of such coincidence, de Man notes that 'allegory designates primarily a distance in relation to its own origin.'[34] De Man is certainly correct to include Benjamin among those who have helped to bring about the recuperation of allegory as a metaphorical figure that foregrounds its own rhetoricity. Unlike de Man, however, Benjamin does not attempt to articulate a temporal distance between allegory and its origin. Instead, he sees allegory as inscribed by the rhythm of its origin. This inscription invests allegory with its semiotic disjunction and its attendant ability to highlight the fragmentary, pluralistic status of textual 'meaning.' However, it also provides allegory with its redemptive character, its ability to infuse the baroque drama with the resonance of an ultimate, divine 'restoration' and 'revival' (1:226). The rhythm of origin works through allegory to render the *Trauerspiel* a 'ruin' or 'fragment' (1:409) but allows allegory to 'find itself again seriously under heaven' (1:406); the rhythm of origin engenders through allegory the dialectical process of fragmentation and redemption.

Like de Man, J. Hillis Miller sees allegory as a means for invest-
ing a text with a sense of temporal disjunction and erosion. Indeed,
Miller regards these as specific attributes of Benjaminian allegory.
Miller, however, sees two forms of allegory at work in the *Trauerspiel* book. One of them appears for Miller to reflect the more
genuine dimension of Benjamin's allegorical theory, for he labels
it 'Benjaminian.' It foregrounds the self-referential, discontinuous,
fragmentary status of literary texts and the alterity of discourse.[35]
The other of Benjamin's – and Miller's – 'two allegories' points
toward dialectical resolution, an intuited grasp of textual signification, historical continuity, and 'the fulfillment of a total meaning.'
In connection with Benjamin, Miller labels this form of allegory
'Hegelian.' Miller finds that both Hegel and Benjamin 'are present
in one form or another of double person or double face, double
mask.' One form of allegory (the 'Hegelian') is 'metaphysical or
religious,' while the other (the 'Benjaminian') is 'ruinous' and 'deconstructive.'[36] However, although Miller is certainly correct to de-
tect a dual nature in Benjamin's theory of allegory, there are not in
fact two allegories in the *Trauerspiel* book. Both the 'religious' and
the 'deconstructive' elements of Benjaminian allegory – allegory as
self-consciously open and incomplete and yet pointing to the restoration of semiotic plenitude in a hoped-for messianic future – are
united by the rhythm of origin. The transcendent element in Benjaminian allegory is, at any rate, certainly not Hegelian. In the
course of his definition of origin, Benjamin emphatically rejects
what he sees as Hegel's ahistoricism and denigration of facticity
(1:226). Allegory for Benjamin is rooted in a nonlinear and non-
Hegelian historical concretion; otherwise, it could never evoke the
sense of temporal disjunction discerned by Miller. It is also resolutely factical, indeed, burdened by its facticity. Benjamin alludes
to this in noting that 'allegory corresponds to the gods of antiquity in the deadness of its palpable materiality' (1:400). Allegory's
historical and phenomenal facticity partakes of the economy of
Ursprung.

Miller's appreciation of Benjamin's ability to evoke a sense of
temporal discontinuity and rupture is not limited to his writing on
Benjaminian allegory. In his essay 'Narrative and History,' Miller

attempts to elucidate a nontraditional relationship between these two modalities. Traditional assumptions about this relationship are governed, according to Miller, by such formulas as 'unity and totality,' 'the homogeneity, linearity and continuity of time,' and (of course) 'origin and end.'[37] Miller attempts through his reading of George Eliot's *Middlemarch* to subvert such metaphysical conventions by demonstrating the dissemination, dissonance, lack of continuity, and ambiguity inherent both in the structure of this work and in its thematic treatment of history. This reading finds origin and alterity to be antithetical: '*Middlemarch* itself is an example of form arising from unlikeness and difference, a form governed by no absolute center, origin, or end' (469). Miller concludes his essay by taking note of a common ground in Benjamin's and Eliot's historiographic perspectives; both would explode the historical continuum and temporal homogeneity. In order to illustrate Benjamin's embrace of such a writing of history, Miller draws on Benjamin's 'Über den Begriff der Geschichte' (1940; 'Theses on the Philosophy of History'). As with Benjamin's two allegories, Miller sees in a passage from this work the embrace of both 'metaphysics and its deconstruction' (471). He cites Benjamin's reference to Karl Kraus's line that 'origin is the goal' and finds that this aphorism signifies 'time as the emptying out of the present by way of its eternal reiteration of a past in which the Messiah had not yet come but was coming in a now in which once more he has not yet come but is coming' (472). This remarkable run-on clause, with its double 'not yet come but was/is coming,' seems structurally designed to evoke the empty, homogeneous continuity Miller sees inherent in the very notion of origin, a notion he (and – he believes – Benjamin) would deconstruct precisely through such repetition. This stance is evident in the final sentence of Miller's article: 'This repetition disarticulates the backbone of logic and frees both history and fiction, for the moment, before the spider-web is rewoven, from the illusory continuities of origin leading to aim leading to end' (473).

Although Miller is correct to discern in Benjamin's thought an embrace of repetition as a potentially revolutionary act, Benjamin's notion of redemption makes problematic any effort to see his repetition theorem as anticipating poststructuralist techniques. He tended to see the endless repetitiveness to which the average worker of his age was damned as the profane equivalent of hell and believed a potential proletarian revolution would interrupt this infernal ever-the-same. The 'eternal reiteration' of the past does not foreshadow the coming of the Messiah; it is the hell His coming will annihilate. Indeed, as Michael Löwy has suggested, there is a precise correspondence in Benjamin's oeuvre between the Messiah's coming and the establishment of a classless society through revolutionary proletarian insurgence.[38] In its positive theological nuance, repetition does not deconstruct origin but leads to its reestablishment. As Löwy argues, the line 'Ursprung ist das Ziel' [origin is the goal] may be read as expressing a vision 'of the redeemed future as a restoration of paradise lost (*Tikkun*).'[39] Given his own obsession with the notion of redemption, the eschatological resonance in this verse constitutes a major reason for Benjamin's attraction to it.

Benjamin cites Kraus's line at the outset of the fourteenth of the historico-philosophical theses. In this thesis, Benjamin speaks of history as the object of a construction. Such a construction – the product of critical reflection – subverts the historicist articulation of history as a diachronic continuum, a linear succession of events that renders time empty and homogeneous. The antithesis of empty and homogeneous time is *Jetztzeit* ('nowtime'). The example of *Jetztzeit* mentioned by Benjamin in the fourteenth thesis attests that such time is indeed 'time as repetition,' as Miller states in 'Narrative and History' (472). Nowtime is present time fulfilled through its constellation with a past event or epoch. Thus, Robespierre appropriates antique Rome and reactualizes it by envisioning the French Revolution as its repetition. The French Revolution comes to see itself as the return of Roman Antiquity, thereby blasting this epoch out of the continuum of history (1:701). *Jetztzeit* is the configuration of two specific, concrete historical events, designed to subvert the linearity of a historicist mode of temporality in which all events and epochs are stripped of their unique, heterogeneous character – their alterity – by being cast into the void of a homogeneous, nondifferentiated continuum. *Jetztzeit*, like *Ur-*

sprung, is for Benjamin a historical construction and a historical category. Both *Jetztzeit* and *Ursprung* are inscribed by a dialectic. In the fourteenth thesis, the dialectic of *Jetztzeit,* as a 'tiger's leap into the past,' partakes of the revolutionary character of Marxist dialectics (1:701).

Benjamin was not strongly influenced by Marxist thought until after he wrote the *Trauerspiel* book, and the dialectic of origin described there is not invested with a revolutionary, political character. However, like the dialectic that informs *Jetztzeit,* the dialectic of origin is conceived as the product of a historico-philosophical reflection; it is by no means a 'natural history,' a modality Benjamin detested.[40] The antithetical poles of the dialectics of origin and of nowtime are the same; on the one hand, there is the presence of unique, noniterable historical events or epochs, resonant with the radical alterity of concrete historical facticity. The antithesis of this discrete element in the historical event is its repetition through the construct of a nowtime, in which it is reconstellated with an equally unique and heterogeneous moment. The paradox of iterating the nonrepeatable historical event through the interaction of a dialectic is as evident in Benjamin's delineation of *Ursprung* as it is in the fourteenth thesis: 'The guiding principles of philosophical contemplation are recorded in the dialectic that inhabits origin. From this dialectic, singularity and repetition show themselves to be conditioned by each other in all essentials' (1:226).

In all particulars, then, Benjamin's articulation of origin anticipates his delineation of nowtime, a circumstance confirmed by Habermas. Habermas interprets Benjamin's seminal definition of *Ursprung* in the *Trauerspiel* book as signifying the redemption of phenomena through their immersion into the world of ideas as they issue from the process of becoming and dying away. Phenomena are thereby stripped of their pre- and posthistory as of a natural-historical costume and penetrate the domain of the eternal. Later in Benjamin's career, nowtime is substituted for origin in this redemptive process: 'This constellation of natural history and eternity later gives way to the constellation of history and nowtime. The place of origin is taken over by the messianic arrestment of the event.'[41] Miller therefore errs in believing that the repetition inscribed in nowtime disrupts the 'continuities of origin.' Instead, Benjamin sees both *Jetztzeit* and *Ursprung* as historical modalities in which (1) an event or phenomenon is reconstellated (2) through the juxtaposition of its past history with a messianically charged present or in its pre- and posthistory (3) to explode the historical continuum or to subvert the linearity and reductionism of inductive and deductive approaches to literary form. As this threefold pairing suggests, the priorities of *Jetztzeit* and *Ursprung* are different. However, it also demonstrates that both *Jetztzeit* and *Ursprung* are historico-philosophical constructs designed to evoke the heterogeneity – the alterity – of critically reflected modes of form and time. *Both* origin and nowtime would explode the continuum of history.

Still, this does not precisely explain why Benjamin borrowed Kraus's verse for the fourteenth thesis. Wolin comments that Benjamin's 'use of the concept of "origin"' in the fourteenth thesis 'represents a secularization of its original employment in *Origin of German Tragic Drama,* in keeping with Benjamin's later interest in historical materialism.'[42] However, not only is the concept of origin *already* somewhat secularized in the *Trauerspiel* book, but Benjamin was certainly aware that the line 'Ursprung ist das Ziel' in Kraus's poem is uttered by God. In his essay on Kraus, Benjamin takes note of the theological nuance in Kraus's destructive-critical 'tact' (2:339). He cites Kraus's polemical verse, directed against Stephan George, whose theurgic impulses move him to seek the immediacy of divine plenitude through a hierarchic language that would deify the body and embody God. The theurgic movement toward such plenitude ignores the path of life. Thus, Kraus's George does not approach the goal from the origin: 'Und der das Ziel noch vor dem Weg gefunden, / er kam vom Ursprung nicht' (2:359–60) [and he who found the goal even before the path, / he did not come from the origin]. Benjamin compares this verse to the line from 'Der sterbende Mensch' ('The Dying Man') that he adopted as his motto for the fourteenth thesis. It is modified here by Benjamin from the original 'Du bliebst am Ursprung' [You remained at the origin] to read, 'Du kamst vom Ursprung – Ursprung ist das Ziel' [You came from the origin – origin is the goal].

Benjamin comments that this line represents God's comfort and promise, rewards presumably denied to those who, like Kraus's George, seek the goal through an immediacy that avoids the origin. Of the origin elucidated in 'The Dying Man,' Benjamin remarks, 'Dieser "Ursprung" – das Echtheitssiegel an den Phänomenen – ist Gegenstand einer Entdeckung, die in einzigartiger Weise sich mit dem Wiedererkennen verbindet' [This 'origin' – the seal of authenticity on the phenomena – is the object of a discovery, which is bound in a singular way to the act of re-cognition] (2:360).[43] For Kraus the locus of this scene of re-cognition is the rhyme, which finds the origin of its sacred fulfillment at the end of the poetic verse much as blessedness will occur at the end of days. In the rhyme, the child perceives the 'rustling of all sources in the origin.' Kraus, however, falls *at* the origin, as a demoniac hybrid of spirit and sexuality (2:360–61).

Benjamin's Kraus is a tragic figure. If origin is the goal, he does not reach it. He attempts to attain origin through the rhyme, but – a demoniacally cleft rhymester – he dies there. For Benjamin, the impulses in Kraus's line 'origin is the goal' are at once destructive, demoniac, theologically redemptive, and heuristic. As we have seen, Benjamin sees the *destruction* wrought by the Krausian quotation – taken out of context – as a return to origin. In the citation, origin and destruction are intertwined (2:363). The destructive character of the Krausian citation lends it its purificatory, redemptive quality – creaturely life is not pure 'im Ursprung' (2:365). Origin *and* destruction must also come together to master the demon (2:367) of Kraus's tortured persona. For Benjamin, the process of restoration and destruction inherent in the origin-inscribed Krausian citation is the same process invoked in the fourteenth thesis. A historical event is 'cited' in the construction of nowtime – wrenched out of its context and destroyed, renewed, restored, and redeemed in this fulfillment of present time. The origin becomes the 'seal of authenticity on the phenomena' because it is a discovery that is a rediscovery and recognition, just as nowtime stamps time with authenticity precisely through a heuristic iteration. 'Origin' in Kraus's poem makes the 'goal' an indefinitely deferred promise. Nowtime also holds out the promise of historical plenitude – the fulfillment of phenomena and events in the pre- and posthistory of their origin – by evoking for a fleeting moment the constellation of a historical totality. In his article 'Narrative and History,' Miller describes the time of nowtime as 'the eternal absence of any *locus standi*' (473).

In Kraus's poem, origin as the temporal and spatial displacement of the goal also subverts the attempt to posit a place of permanent standing. In the fifth of the theses, Benjamin describes the fleeting character of the true image of the past, an image that cannot be recaptured and that only flashes forth at the moment when it is capable of being recognized. Ironically, it is only at this transitory juncture that we are capable of holding on to the past (1:695). The *Passagen-Werk* refers to the authentic image of the past as the dialectical image. The dialectical image is the lightning-like ('blitzhaft') and leap-like ('sprunghaft') constellation of the then ('das Gewesene') with the now ('das Jetzt') (5:576–77). By citing Kraus's verse, Benjamin also imbues nowtime with this transitory, volatile, leap-like quality, with its destruction of temporal and spatial fixity. For Benjamin, Kraus's *Ursprung* clearly encompasses both destruction and redemption. As these forces constitute the dialectic of nowtime, Benjamin finds it useful to enact Kraus's destructive/redemptive citational poetics by wresting the line 'Ursprung ist das Ziel' from its context and making it the motto of the fourteenth of his historico-philosophical theses.[44]

In the addenda to his *Trauerspiel* book, Benjamin remarks on the theological-historical impulse inscribed in his concept of origin. This impulse infuses origin with dynamism and alterity. As in the *Passagen-Werk,* he defines *Ursprung* in the addenda as the Goethian archetypal phenomenon (*Urphänomen*) wrested from its heathen, nature-bound context and reconstellated in the Jewish contexts of history. The reason for this shift from a natural-historical to a Jewish-messianic domain becomes obvious when we realize, as Habermas already did in his relatively early essay on Benjamin, that the continuum Benjamin wished to explode through his redemptive criticism was rooted in the immutable character of natural history.[45] Only because *Ursprung* infuses *Urphänomen* with a theological disposition can it fulfill the concept of authenticity. As in the *Passagen-Werk*, Benjamin notes in the *Trauerspiel* book's addenda that his awareness of the Goethian archetypal foundation of his *Ursprung* concept came about as a result of his reading of Georg Simmel's 1913 study, *Goethe* (1:953–54). His realization of the theological cast of *Ursprung* also appears to be the product of a latent reflection, as this theological element is not foregrounded in the prologue to the *Trauerspiel* book. Nevertheless, the 1931 essay on Kraus also invests Kraus's notion of origin with a theological character, a character that helps allow *Ursprung* to act as 'the seal of authenticity on the phenomena' in Kraus's verse (2:360). Despite Benjamin's growing predilection for historical materialism in the 1930s, the theologico-messianic element in his thinking is never far from the surface of his later writing.[46] In his 1937 essay 'Eduard Fuchs, der Sammler und der Historiker' ('Eduard Fuchs: Collector and Historian'), however, he cites the *Trauerspiel* book's definition of the rhythm of origin in the context of assigning the explosion of the continuum of history and the dialectical subversion of the 'badly compiled findings of the actual' as tasks to be carried out by the historical materialist.

By recalling that the rhythm of origin concerns the pre- and posthistory of phenomena and not just their bare, obvious factuality, Benjamin would enable the historical materialist to overcome the reified (made 'thing-like') character of the historical continuum (2:468 and 468 n.4). In the *Passagen-Werk*, Benjamin associates the pre- and posthistory of the object of history – and the challenge it poses to the critical thinker to blast it out of the historical continuum – with its monadological structure (5:594). Because Benjaminian *Ursprung* adapts the monadological structure in order to inscribe the literary genre with its pre- and posthistory, this passage represents an invocation of origin similar to that of the *Trauerspiel* book but reconstellated according to the priorities of Benjamin's historical materialism.[47] As origin is called upon to subvert a linear and univocal reading of history in favor of a volatile, multivalent, and disruptive historiography, the fallacy of inevitably equating origin with 'illusory continuities' (Miller) and a 'reassuring foundation' (Derrida) is again obvious. Benjamin may have been evincing the hope for such a foundation by constantly evoking the possibility of a messianic age. He was, as he himself noted, 'Janus-faced' in his thinking, and the subversive cast of his ideas often reveals a longing for utopian reconciliation. His desire to disrupt the continuum of history cannot be separated from his wish to see history emerge as a totality in which everything that has been forgotten will be remembered. This telos of historical plenitude, however, does not render his *technique* of origin any less dynamic; as a *means* to an end, this technique remains consistent with poststructuralism's own methodological priorities.

The principle of origin elucidated in the prologue to the *Trauerspiel* book is also mentioned explicitly in the *Passagen-Werk*, in a previously cited fragment that repeats – (although not in all particulars) – the comparison of *Ursprung* with Goethe's *Urphänomen* made by Benjamin in the *Trauerspiel* book's addenda. In the *Passagen-Werk* fragment, Benjamin eliminates the references to the theological dimension of origin, although he repeats his belief that his *Ursprung* transposes *Urphänomen* from the heathen realm of nature to the Jewish historical sphere. He goes on to note that his work on the Parisian arcades is also concerned with a 'comprehensive exploration of origin' ('Ursprungsergründung') and defines this exploration as a historical research: 'That is to say, I am tracing out the origin of the configurations and fluctuations of the Parisian arcades from their ascent to their decline, and I am trying to grasp it through the economic data.' This procedural statement is followed by the assertion that such (historical) data cannot be viewed as archetypal phenomena when considered within a causal nexus. They can only be regarded as archetypal phenomena in the light of their fully unfolded articulation: as a 'series of concrete historical forms' (5:577). What is carried over from the methodology of origin in the *Trauerspiel* book to this fragment is Benjamin's concern to evoke phenomena in their historical totality while preserving the discrete character of their particular historico-philosophical constellation.

Although it might seem that these priorities are antithetical, their codependence becomes evident when one considers what Benjamin regarded as the alternative: the acceptance of a historicist methodology and the postulation of a historical continuum. Benjamin felt that the empty homogeneity of the historical continuum blocked the evocation of historical totality precisely by *denying* the individual phenomena, events, and epochs of history their concrete spatial and temporal specificity. Just as Goethe's archetypal plant ('Urpflanze') is a paradigmatic representation of all plants, so Benjamin's exploration of the *Ursprung* of the Parisian arcades' formations and transformations has as its telos the evocation through exemplars of an archetypal history ('Urgeschichte') of the nineteenth century (5:579). Benjamin viewed Goethe's 'Metamorphose der Pflanzen' ('The Metamorphosis of Plants,' where the 'Urpflanze' or 'archetypal plant' hypothesis is made) as a counterpart to the *Farbenlehre* (*The Theory of Colors,* where the 'archetypal phenomenon' concept is delineated) (3:149). He is undoubtedly thinking of the archetypal plant when he compares the development – through his originary praxis – of the arcades' economic data into archetypal phenomena with the leaf, from which develops 'the entire abundance of the empirical plant world' (5:577).[48]

Just as Goethe sought to create totalized representations of the natural world through the hypothesis of the archetypal phenomenon and the archetypal plant, so Benjamin hoped to glimpse modernity in its *historical* totality through his *Ursprungsergründung* of the Parisian arcades. Such a wish for 'full presence' (Derrida) could be viewed as an example of the bad metaphysics associated by deconstructionists with the notion of origin, although some of them – as Miller's article 'Narrative and History' attests – use Benjamin as an authorizing voice in their writing. As we will see, Adorno accuses Benjamin of collapsing history into an identitarian continuum in his critique of the Arcades Project. Such an accusation is comprehensible in light of Adorno's obsession with sustaining the alterity of historical phenomena against subjectivist authoritarian attempts to reduce history to the ever-the-same. However, one should keep in mind Benjamin's investment of historical objects with a monadological structure. It is the monadological structure of the historical object that lends it the character of an archetypal phenomenon. As each *idea* as monad contains the image of the world (1:228), so the historical object inscribed by an archetypal image attains a discrete but plenitudinous character that blocks its appropriation by and reduction to the historical continuum.

These qualities provide the historical object with its destructive character. It is not surprising then that only two fragments after adumbrating the monadological structure of the historical object, Benjamin notes, 'the destructive or critical moment in the materialist writing of history attains its validity, with which the historical object first constitutes itself, in the explosion of historical continuity' (5:594). The destructive or deconstructive impulse Miller identifies in Benjamin's oeuvre is concomitant with Benjamin's equation of the historical object under the sign of materialist reflection with a monad. This is evident even in one of the passages from the historico-philosophical theses cited by Miller in 'Narrative and History' (472 n.17). It is the monadological element in Benjamin's critical praxis that allows him to invest historical objects with both plenitude/archetypal totality and deconstructive volition/radical alterity. Moreover, as in the *Trauerspiel* book, Benjamin's appropriation of the Lebnizian monad in his later 'historical materialist' phase is central to his use of *Ursprung* as a heuristic technique, a technique consistent with his dialectic of destruction and redemption. The conflicted nature of such an approach lends validity to Habermas's characterization of Benjamin's hermeneutics as both conservative and revolutionary, as a decoding of the history of culture that would redeem that history only to enact its overthrow.[49] What Benjamin says of 'the destructive character' in his 1931 essay of the same name applies both to his own general praxis and to the way in which he employs the notion of origin: 'He reduces what exists to rubble, not for the sake of the rubble, but for the sake of the path that winds through it.' (4:398)

In the original version of the prologue to the *Trauerspiel* book, Benjamin describes the phenomenon of origin as antithetical to historical causality:

Nur ist das Phänomen des Ursprungs einer flachen, einzig dem Kausalverlaufe zugewandten Geschichtsbetrachtung nicht gegeben. Vielmehr gehört es einer solchen zu, deren Zentrum in der Untersuchung der historischen Zeit liegt und welche deren Epochen nicht als Gebilde subjektiver Anschauungsweise sondern einer objektiv und teleologisch bestimmten Rhythmik, in welche der Kausalzusammenhang unter moralischen Begriffen eintritt, zu erfassen strebt. Eine solche Konzeption der die Grenze zwischen Natur- und Weltgeschichte ernsthaft prolematisch werden müßte, würde Wiederholung als wesentlichstes Motiv jeder Periodisierung in beiden betrachten und die Frage, in welchem Sinne es in der Geschichte, einem als solchen unwiederholbaren Verlaufe, diese dennoch gibt zum experimentum crucis ihrer Geschichtsphilosophie machen. (1:935)

[However, the phenomenon of origin is not open to a contemplation of history characterized by flatness and attuned only to the process of causality. It rather belongs to a contemplation of history whose center lies in the investigation of historical time, whose epochs are not structures of subjective modes of perception but which strives to attain an objective and teleologically determined rhythm into which the causal relationship enters under the aegis of moral concepts. The boundary between natural and world history would appear seriously problematic to such a conception. It would regard repetition as the most essential theme of all periodization in both modes of history. It would make the question of the sense in which this repetition exists in history, in spite of history's character as an essentially unrepeatable process, into the *experimentum crucis* of its historical philosophy.]

A recent monograph by Thomas Dörr provides a valuable summary of the tendency in recent criticism, often influenced by the writings of Derrida, to assume that Benjamin's embrace of reproduction and repetition as both critical and aesthetic modalities *subverts* all origin-grounded thinking.[50] Derrida himself believes Benjamin's theory of mechanical reproduction, as delineated in his famous essay 'Das Kunstwerk im Zeitalter seiner technischen Reproduzierbarkeit' (1936; 'The Work of Art in the Epoch of Mechanical Reproduction'), deliberately bursts open the artwork's structure of origin ('Ursprungsstruktur').[51] Dörr accepts completely Derrida's general critique of origin and believes Benjamin's 'praxis of reproduction' anticipates it.[52] However, Derrida, Dörr, and other recent Benjamin critics overlook the earlier version of the *Trauerspiel* book's prologue, in which the technique of repetition is made a *corollary* to the phenomenon of origin. Benjamin's description of the phenomenon of origin as contrary to the flatness of historical causality is reminiscent of his later use of *Ursprung* to undermine the continuum of history. Benjamin's early and final versions of the *Trauerspiel* book's prologue regard origin as inscribed by the mutually conditioning dynamics of singularity ('Einmaligkeit') and repetition ('Wiederholung') (1:226 and 936).

This dialectic is reflected in the fourteenth of the historico-philosophical theses, where 'origin is the goal': the French Revolution attains its historically discrete, continuum-exploding character by self-consciously repeating the modes of ancient Rome.[53] Benjamin's definition of origin as the antithesis of causality-governed historiography and as the philosophical vessel circumscribing the dialectics of singularity and iteration is also consistent with his reinvocation of *Ursprung* in the *Passagen-Werk*. Here, too, Benjamin suggests that origin is antithetical to 'the point of view of causality,' and his Goethian leaf simile points to his inscription of the Parisian arcades with both repetition and concrete historical specificity (5:577). Benjamin's insistence on a critical perspective that applies moral concepts to the analysis of historical epochs is consistent with the redemptive impulse in his work. This consistency also obtains in Franz Rosenzweig's principle of origin, and in a note written sometime in the 1930s Benjamin states, 'The relationship of my concept of origin, as developed in the *Trauerspiel* book and in the essay on Kraus, to Rosenzweig's concept of revelation, should be investigated' (6:207).[54]

What we can say about Benjamin's concept of origin can also be partially applied to Rosenzweig: their concepts of origin evoke historical totality but are structured to reflect the concrete specificity of all historico-philosophical constellations. The concept of origin is calculated to redeem phenomena and to explode the historical continuum that reduces them to the ever-the-same. The monadological character of Benjaminian *Ursprung* invests it with a dialectic of repetition and singularity. It is easily adaptable to both the theological and materialist strands of Benjamin's destructive critical praxis. The phenomena and forms signified by Benjamin's *Ursprung* are inscribed by an allegorical character that elucidates their fundamental multivalence and fragmentary, open-ended quality. The deconstructive impulse inherent in such *allegoresis* helps to explain Benjamin's popularity with poststructuralist critics who nevertheless conveniently overlook the connection between alterity and origin in Benjamin's thought. This connection between philosophy and the principle of nonidentity is even more strongly manifested in the work of Theodor Adorno.

CHAPTER 3

The Principle of Origin
and the Philosophy of Origin:
Probing Theodor Adorno's
Antinomies

The emphasis Nietzsche's genealogical investigations placed on exposing the ignoble origins of such cherished institutions as religion and academic erudition was carried on in this century by Theodor W. Adorno. Like Nietzsche, Adorno tended to articulate the origins of various societal phenomena by dissecting them into the disparate and often antithetical elements by which they were constituted. In his essay 'Theorie der Halbbildung' (1959; Theory of superficial cultivation), for example, Adorno traces the crisis of contemporary elevated cultivation (*Bildung*) not just to the mass media's domination of all cultural trends but to the dual nature of *Kultur* itself. While culture's professed ideal at the height of its propagation in the eighteenth century was the cultivation of free and independent thinking, its consistent goal was always assimilation in the service of social harmony and order. Once the dialectical tension between freedom and assimilation was exhausted, assimilation became predominant, and superficial culture reigned supreme. The origin of *Halbbildung* is rooted in *Bildung* itself, that loftiest of German ideals. Adorno draws on Nietzsche to show that *Bildung* is rooted ideally in the principles of autonomy and freedom but consistently has reference to a uniform, dictatorial order for its formative foundation. Like so many of the ideals exposed by Nietzsche, the origin of *Bildung* is informed by an antisynthetic, self-canceling dialectic that already guarantees its dissolution: 'Daher gibt es in dem Augenblick, in dem es Bildung gibt, sie eigentlich schon nicht mehr. In ihrem Ursprung ist ihr Zerfall teleologisch bereits gesetzt'[1] [Therefore at the moment when 'Bildung' exists, it ceases to exist. Its decay is already teleologically fixed in its origin].

At the conclusion of his essay, Adorno enunciates an ideal circumstance where antitheses such as cultivation and its want ('Unbildung') or nature and culture are transcended. He then launches an attack on the philosophy of origin – a strategy quite characteristic of his praxis. In arguing that culture cannot be hypostatized as an inherently discrete and autonomous construct, Adorno criticizes the tendency to reduce historically developed phenomena to their origin. This trend is inherent in the articulation of another cherished German concept, spirit ('Geist'), which is often seduced into elevating itself to the status of *Ursprung* (8:120). This critique of the philosophy of origin in connection with a dissection of hypostatized concepts like 'spirit,' 'culture,' and 'cultivation' is a regular feature of Adorno's procedure, but so is his productive use of a Nietzschean dialectics of the interstice, dialectics that revolve around *Ursprung*'s employment as a heuristic concept. This use of *Ursprung* as a positive genealogical technique in Adorno's exploration of the self-destructive foundation of *Bildung* itself suggests that the principle of origin and the philosophy of origin constitute antinomies in Adorno's methodology. These antinomies will be the focus of this chapter.

Adorno's view of *Bildung* as driven by the hidden agendas of assimilation, social pacification, and uniformity is consistent with his view of humanity's relationship to nature. He discerned a broad tendency in all spheres of modern life – philosophical, political, cultural, and economic – to suppress the otherness of nature by obliterating it and bringing it under the suzerainty of man's universal subjectivity. Adorno and his Frankfurt School colleague Max Horkheimer characterized this process of domination as the 'Dialektik der Aufklärung' (Dialectic of Enlightenment) in their book (written between 1941 and 1944 and published in 1947) of the same title. Adorno believed that it was possible to illuminate – and thus resist – this process through a philosophy based on the principle of nonidentity and a dialectics, like Nietzsche's, that was resistant to the dominant postsocratic tendency toward universalization and synthetization.

These general principles of Adorno's thought have already been widely treated, and it is unnecessary to characterize them further with such broad strokes.[2] Less thoroughly examined, however, is the unique way in which Adorno employs the notion of *Ursprung* in upholding his fundamental principles. One of these principles has been adumbrated by Susan Buck-Morss's remark that history for Adorno 'unfolded in the spaces *between* subjects and objects, men and nature, whose very nonidentity was history's motor force.'[3] This observation captures Adorno's attempt to situate the dynamic force of history in a gap or interstice between antithetical poles. Buck-Morss's location of the generative element in Adorno's historical dialectics in the gap between subject and object recalls Nietzsche's dialectics of the interstice, the 'nonplace' where the *Ursprünge* of history are manifested.

In the *Negative Dialektik* (1966; *Negative Dialectics*), Adorno notes that the attempt to locate the reason for the existence of antagonism at the origin of human society does not involve merely idle speculation. This antagonism, Adorno believes, arose as a function of natural history, of man's predatory nature, or it first became something set down essentially as a theoretical postulate. The antagonism at the origin of society might have resulted from necessities tied to the survival of the human race or it may owe its existence to purely fortuitous circumstances such as when individuals and groups engaged in initial arbitrary attempts to attain social power and domination. Adorno surmises that if the origin of human antagonism was grounded in evolutionary necessities connected with the survival of the species rather than in archaic, arbitrary acts stemming from the lust for power, this explanation would suffice to undermine not only the construction of the world spirit of Hegel but also the systematic totality of Marx and Engels (6:315). Thus, Adorno devotes much of the *Negative Dialectics* to deconstructing the subjectivist universalism inherent not only in the dialectics of Hegel, Marx, and Engels but also in the ontology of Heidegger.[4]

Adorno, however, does not actually claim that the origin of antagonism is contingent or necessary, inhering in man as autonomous subject or natural object. Origin can only be in between, in that nonplace that alone upholds the principle of nonidentity. Adorno sees history itself as generated in this space. In a manuscript entitled 'Zur Philosophie Husserls' (1934–37; On the philosophy of Husserl), for example, he anchors history's origin at the point of divergence (the site of the dialectic) between the historical subject and object.[5]

Adorno criticized Husserl's phenomenology for its subjectification of history through the positing of absolute (subjective) reason. A postulation of Husserl's formulated in his *Ideen zu einer reinen Phänomenologie und phänomenologischen Philosophie* (1913; *Ideas Pertaining to a Pure Phenomenology and to a Phenomenological Philosophy*), that of a sphere of absolute origins, particularly irritated Adorno. In the introduction to the *Negative Dialectics,* he defines this realm as 'das Bodenlose' ('the abyssal'), which is the creation of a self-enclosed subjectivity that simply hypostatizes its own concepts rather than adhering to that which it is not. Thought achieves this adherence precisely through a break with Hegelian *prima philosophia,* which encompasses the dissociation of thought from the corporeal and binds thought to that which is nonidentical to it, thereby obliterating the Hegelian illusion of thought's absolute suzerainty (6:44). However, because Husserl is also caught up in the search for 'transcendental first principles,' his category of origins is absolute and purely an extension of the subject.[6] This subject thus becomes identical to its object, rather than hanging on to that which it is not. Later in the *Negative Dialectics,* Adorno is even harsher in his condemnation of the sphere of absolute origins, seeing its *autarky* as a metaphysical deadness (6:186). Indeed, this very sovereignty is upheld only by that which stands in a relationship of otherness to the subject:

> So wenig ist das Subjekt die 'Sphäre absoluter Ursprünge,' als die es sich philosophiert; noch die Bestimmungen, kraft deren es seine Souveränität sich zuspricht, bedürfen immer auch dessen, was ihrem Selbstverständnis nach bloß ihrer bedürfen soll. (6:222)

> [So little is the subject the 'sphere of absolute origins,' as one tends to refer to it in philosophical terms. Indeed, the very determinations through which it declares its sovereignty always need that which, according to their own self-understanding, should only need them.]

Perhaps the best statement of why it was precisely the concept of a sphere of absolute origins that Adorno found particularly troubling in Husserl's thought can be found in the opening lines of Adorno's study of Husserl's phenomenology, *Zur Metakritik der Erkenntnistheorie: Studien über Husserl und die phänomenologischen Antinomien* (1956; *Against Epistemology, a Metacritique: Studies in Husserl and the Phenomenological Antinomies*): 'The attempt to discuss Husserl's pure phenomenology in the spirit of the dialectic opens itself to the suspicion of arbitrariness. His program is based on a "sphere of Being of absolute origins," safe from the "organized spirit of contradiction," as Hegel once referred to his procedure in conversation with Goethe' (5:12). Despite the harshness with which he attacks the abstract universalism in Hegel's world spirit, Adorno recognizes that the power of contradiction immanent in his dialectics subverts the identity Hegel postulates between subject and object. He can thus appreciate the elements in Hegelian dialectics that, in spite of themselves, point toward his own negative dialectics, seeking to preserve the nonidentity between subject and object. However, as Adorno points out, Husserl attacks Hegel from the opposite angle; it is Hegel's *doubts* concerning *prima philosophia* and the choice of an absolute first principle ('eines absolut Ersten') to which Husserl objects. Husserl characterizes this skepticism as a 'plunge into the abyssal' (5:13), and it is precisely this term 'abyssal' – 'das Bodenlose' – that Adorno employs at the outset of the *Negative Dialectics* to describe Husserl's sphere of absolute origins (6:44). This sphere is abyssal for Adorno because it completely blocks the path leading toward the mediation of a nonidentity between subject and object. In spite of its shortcomings, the spirit of contradiction in Hegel's dialectics leaves this path open. The sphere of absolute origins is a sphere of absolute subjectivity devoid of all traces of entity. Indeed, although Adorno believes Husserl grounds his attempt to reestablish a *prima philosophia* through a reflection on the (Hegelian) spirit, he notes that Husserl would first wish the spirit to be *purged* of all traces of entity (5:13). Because Adorno wants to preserve the distinctness of the nonsubjective entity, the sphere of origins cannot be absolute – it is only an extension of pure subjectivity.

In the introduction to the *Metacritique*, Adorno also offers a general critique of philosophies of origin. He traces the attempt on the part of such philosophies to fill the gap between subject and object back to pre-Socratic thought. At all times, this dualism is intolerable to philosophers of origin because it admonishes them that their objectivity is based on a subjective arbitrariness that approaches tautology. This abyss within philosophies of origin promotes a fanatical intolerance (5:21–22), which can perceive only the enemy in the nonidentical. The postulation by the philosophy of origin of a seamless continuity in history allows for its appropriation by fascism: 'The oldest, that which has been there the longest, should literally and directly rule' (5:28). However, *Ursprungsphilosophie* – the philosophy of origin – fears not just the conditioned, the nonidentical it finds in the context of nature and from which it attempts to free itself. It also fears it will lose itself in the determinacy of the purely subjective. This fear leads to the regressive quality of the subjectivist philosophy of origin, the flight back to Platonism (5:29), which Adorno believes sacrifices genuine knowledge in its search for a knowledge of origins. Adorno anticipates the invective he directs at Husserl's 'sphere of Being of absolute origins' in the *Negative Dialectics* when he charges that the phenomenological reductions behind Husserl's sphere are completely arbitrary (5:29). The immanence in which the pure subjectivity of the philosophy of origin is grounded itself reveals the arbitrariness of this philosophy: 'Während die Idee der Ursprungsphilosophie monistisch auf die reine Identität abzielt, läßt doch die subjektive Immanenz, in der das absolut Erste ungestört bei sich selber sein will, sich auf jene reine Identität mit sich selbst nicht bringen' (5:30–31) [While the idea of the philosophy of origins monistically strives toward pure identity, subjective immanence, in which the absolute first would remain undisturbed and with itself, does not allow itself to be brought to that pure identity with itself].

In sum, Adorno accuses the philosophy of origin in general and Husserl's 'sphere of Being of absolute origins' in particular of arbitrariness, totalitarianism, groundlessness, lifelessness, and the regressiveness of tautological thinking. Nevertheless, fascism's appropriation of *Ursprungsphilosophie* is the underlying reason it be-

came anathema to Adorno. Before beginning work on the manuscript on Husserl at Oxford in 1934, Adorno wrote a brief essay
entitled 'Der Ur' (1932; The primal) that described the way in
which Nazism used originary thinking to give its barbarism a civi-
lized veneer. Fascism strives to awaken the chthonic forces inherited from primal man ('der Urmensch') in its modern subjects and
to use the modern technological apparatus at its disposal to achieve
the synthesis of the originary and civilization, a product promis-
ing both a superior warrior and a superior cultural individual
(20.2:562–64). Adorno was so appalled at fascism's manipulation
of the philosophy of origin that his reading of an obituary for an
'Uromi,' or 'great-grandma,' prompted him in 1967 to see in the use
of this nickname the traces of the most monstrous barbarity. The
seemingly harmless nickname becomes, in Adorno's view, an evil
mask. The great-grandmother, under the sign of this name, is, indeed, a 'prehistoric monster' (20.2:571). The concrete social and
historical implications of the philosophy of origin as it evolved
during the onset of fascism were uppermost in Adorno's mind
when he directed his attention to this aspect of the writings of Heidegger and Husserl.

As Heidegger's thought had a greater (and far more ominous)
sociopolitical resonance than that of his mentor, Heidegger is the
object of Adorno's most powerful vitriol. He judges Husserl's phenomenology to be 'harmless' (5:45) but believes that it served as
the prototype for the ideology inherent in Heidegger's illusory notion of concretion – the rendering visible of the spiritual (5:43). An
even more powerful denunciation of Heidegger's philosophy of origin is found in a lecture delivered on 10 July 1962, where Adorno
claims that Heidegger's recourse to a belief in an ultimate origin
represents a reification of that which it pursues. In this lecture,
Adorno finds in Heidegger's originary thinking a relativist pseu-
dodialectics, in which every so-called primal concept ('Urbegriff')
corresponds to its antithesis.[7] Adorno, in other words, discerns
in Heidegger's philosophy, as Hermann Mörchen notes, an undialectical counterposition to his own negative dialectics. Adorno asserted that one cannot abandon dialectics through a backward leap
because this leads to the danger of origin-based primal thinking

('Ursprungsdenken').[8] Adorno sees Heidegger's undialectical recourse to the principle of primal origins as falling into this trap. It leads to a privileging of a ground, of a first principle, that attempts to transcend the split between Being and the individually existent. In order to attain concretion in the realm beyond this gap, Heidegger uses terms such as *Ursprung*. Adorno notes, 'Ich meine nun allerdings, daß gerade in der deutschen Situation dieser Begriff des Bodens oder des Ursprungs eine besonders funeste Rolle spielt; daß hier wirklich etwas wie eine sehr schwere Schuld des Heideggerschen Denkens vorliegt' [Indeed, I believe that precisely in the German situation this concept of ground or origin played an especially deadly part and that Heidegger's thought is deeply implicated in it]. The pursuit of the absolute origin leads philosophy into an absolute relativism, into the (fascistic) glorification of internal human relationships and away from the recognition of external social realities.[9]

At the conclusion of the introduction to the *Metacritique*, Adorno notes that the trendy so-called *Seinsfrage*, the 'question of Being,' does not reveal originariness ('Ursprünglichkeit') but the exigency confronting the philosophy of origin, which needs but cannot grasp the ontic (i.e., what most fundamentally accords with Being) (5:43). As Gillian Rose suggests, 'Adorno argued that to make the question of Being irreducible and to grant it ontological primacy was to found another *Ursprungsphilosophie*, an absolute first.'[10] A philosophy of origin based on the chimera of Heidegger's facticity of Dasein, which seeks its ground in genuine historical existence, is understandably more ominous for Adorno than a philosophy of origin based, as in Husserl, on the self-enclosed realm of subjective intuition. However, Adorno condemns the identity principle of all phenomenology since Hegel, which uses the dialectic of the primal and the novel to establish the phantasmagoria of historical continuity, when he states, 'Since the preface of Hegelian phenomenology, whoever has refused obedience to the jurisdiction of the philosophy of origin has recognized the mediate quality of the old and, along with it, that of the new. It is determined to be already contained in the older form, as the nonidentity of its identity' (5:46).

Adorno not only wants to unmask the totalitarian face of the philosophy of origin but seeks to subvert the entire notion of *Ursprung*, associating it with the telos of identity and domination. Only by focusing resolutely on what escapes the spell of origin can one escape the jurisdiction of the bourgeois identity principle according to which the possibility of the new or novel is foreclosed and life is an eternal repetition of the same (5:46−47). On the other hand, although *Ursprungsphilosophie* in the *Metacritique* is virtually ubiquitous − Adorno identifies it not only with Hegel, Husserl, and Heidegger but also with the pre-Socratic philosophers as well as with Plato, Aristotle, and Kant (5:19−22 and 28−30) − Adorno is always quite specific in the *Metacritique* to associate it with an epistemology anchored in the will to power of a domineering subject. In the *Negative Dialectics*, Adorno uses the term *Ursprung* in a Nietzschean way − to signify the breach (indeterminately situated between man's qualities as autonomous subject and natural object) that designates the locus of social antagonism. In order to strip the principle of *Ursprung* from its false ideological character, it must be disassociated from its link to some starting point of history in the primal past.

In the *Negative Dialectics*, Adorno suggests that the return to a starting point ('Beginn') in Hegel's philosophy of origin was the means by which the seamless identity of subject and object was to be achieved. Indeed, origin itself is an ideological principle; as in the *Metacritique*, Adorno charges that it is used to establish the rights of the 'autochthon' against the newcomer to a place. Whatever or whoever is there longest has the right to dominate (6:158 and 5:28). However, the false ideology underlying this notion of *Ursprung* is governed by a backward-directed glance toward a point of genesis, a beginning, in which to ground itself. It was precisely in contrast to this form of historical thinking that Benjamin developed his principle of origin. Although Adorno is too suspicious of origin to use such a contrast, he, like Benjamin, borrows Karl Kraus's laconic line to indicate the possibility of using *Ursprung* in a way that subverts the phantasmic return to a prehistoric *Ur* used to justify authoritarian domination:

In dem konservativ klingenden Satz von Karl Kraus 'Ursprung ist das Ziel' äußert sich auch ein an Ort und Stelle schwerlich Gemeintes: der Begriff des Ursprungs müßte seines statischen Unwesens entäußert werden. Nicht wäre das Ziel, in den Ursprung, ins Phantasma guter Natur zurückzufinden, sondern Ursprung fiele allein dem Ziel zu, konstituierte sich erst von diesem her. Kein Ursprung außer im Leben des Ephemeren. (6:158)

[In the conservative-sounding line of Karl Kraus, 'origin is the goal,' something is expressed that could hardly have been meant in its place and context: the concept of origin must be stripped of its static excesses. The goal would not be to find a way back into the origin, into the phantasm of good nature, but origin would fall only under the domain of the goal, it would first constitute itself from this goal. No origin except in the life of the ephemeral.]

As Gerhard Kaiser has suggested, Benjamin and Adorno viewed the relationship between origin and history in fundamentally different ways: 'In Adorno's work, the origin is conceptualized from the otherness of history, which history can never reach. In Benjamin's work, origin is conceptualized from history, from which origin issues.'[11] Although this assertion represents a useful starting point for considering the divergences in the way in which Benjamin and Adorno treat the principle of origin, it is not entirely accurate. When Benjamin cites Kraus's line in the fourteenth of his historico-philosophical theses, he uses Kraus as an authorizing voice in the formulation of his principle of *Jetztzeit*. Benjamin demonstrates the potential of *Jetztzeit* to explode the continuum of history by showing through the example of the French Revolution's appropriation of ancient Rome how the empty and homogeneous time of the era of late capitalism can be radically subverted. Such a synchronous cut in the continuum of history is a 'tiger's leap into the past' (Benjamin 1:701) – that primal leap into a thereby actualized historical past signified by Benjamin's understanding of the term *Ursprung*. Origin does not issue from history, as Kaiser would have it, but provides history with a goal that activates its dialectical potential. However, Kaiser is correct in suggesting that Adorno has quite a different view of origin's positive potential. Under the sign of a Marxist dialectic, the tiger's leap into the past in an attempt to create a dynamic historical synchronicity would inevitably suggest to Adorno the principle of identity and the domination of the historical object by a manipulative subject, which he explicitly located in the philosophies of origin of Marx and Hegel.[12] Kaiser is quite correct in pointing out that Adorno attempted to mediate the principle of origin from the 'otherness' of history – only thus could he uphold the principle of nonidentity.[13]

Adorno's reception of Benjamin's early works, particularly *The Origin of German Tragic Drama*, was generally favorable. In the 1932 essay 'Die Idee der Naturgeschichte' (The idea of natural history), for example, Adorno discerned in Benjamin's concept of allegory, rooted as it is in the transitory character of natural life and the singularity of historical objects, a way to subvert the portentous mystifications in the popular myths of an 'Urgeschichte' (1:357–60). As we have seen, Adorno was appalled at the totalitarian ideology he saw lurking behind the idea of such an ur-history, and thus Benjamin's propositions concerning allegory were particularly welcome to him. In the *Negative Dialectics*, Adorno views the adulation of primal experience raised above the level of the historical. He attacks this adulation in 'Die Idee der Naturgeschichte' by drawing on Benjamin's concept of the ephemeral nature of life under the sign of allegory as 'also a piece of the philosophy of origin,' a philosophy of origin he examines here in its specifically Heideggerian manifestation (6:147). Moreover, as in 'Die Idee der Naturgeschichte,' Adorno invokes in the *Negative Dialectics* the *Origin of German Tragic Drama*, with its emphasis on the transitoriness of the conjunction between nature and history, to debunk the metaphysical concept of natural history he finds in contemporary ontology (6:352–53). However, as Rose has suggested, Benjamin's attempt to write an *Urgeschichte* of modernity in the Arcades Project aroused Adorno's antipathy, and this is understandable given Adorno's adverse reaction to the whole notion of conceptualizing a primeval history.[14] In describing Benjamin's Arcades Project in the 1950 essay 'Charakteristik Walter Benjamins' ('A Portrait of Walter Benjamin'), which was included in the collection of essays titled *Prismen: Kulturkritik und Gesellschaft* (1955; *Prisms*), Adorno noted that Benjamin's *Urgeschichte* of modernity 'did not intend to discover archaic rudiments in the recent past but would determine the newest, the most recent, to be itself an expression of what is oldest' (*Prismen*, 10.1:248). In the *Metacritique*, Adorno had characterized just such a procedure as a reification generated by the bourgeois dialectic he saw governed by the philosophy of origin (5:46–47). This charge of reification is, then, not surprisingly, leveled at Benjamin (*Prismen*, 10.1:243).

For Adorno, the attempt to view the newest as a figure of the most archaic is a principle of the law of identity, which collapses all of history into the continuum of the ever-the-same. He embraces Benjamin's *Trauerspiel* book precisely because it evokes the ephemerality of historical existence. By fixing the most modern as a figure of the most archaic, Adorno must have felt Benjamin betrayed that ephemerality and fell under the spell of the subjectivist attempt to dominate the object. This would explain Adorno's cryptic sentence in the *Negative Dialectics*, 'Kein Ursprung außer im Leben des Ephemeren' (6:158) [No origin except in the life of the ephemeral]. Only by envisioning *Ursprung* as anchored in ephemeral life can the retreat back to a primeval past, with its 'phantasm of a good nature' (6:158), be avoided. Moreover, by interpreting Kraus's maxim 'origin is the goal' to mean that origin constitutes itself *from* the goal – or, as Kaiser puts it, from the 'otherness' of history – Adorno seeks to uphold the principle of nonidentity by freeing this goal of subjectivist domination. If one thinks from the goal rather than toward it, then the goal itself, and not the thinking subject governed by the telos of mastery, will establish an ephemeral *Ursprung* free of the suprahistorical authoritarianism Adorno finds in *Ursprungsphilosophie*. However, this is only the subtext of Adorno's interpretation of Kraus's maxim. Adorno cannot describe how origin can constitute itself from the goal without some form of intervention by a prejudiced subject. To do so would mean engaging in the sort of mysticism he criticized in the philosophy of origin.

Nevertheless, a genuinely constructive and actualizable element inherent in the notion of *Ursprung* also presented itself to Adorno, an element that avoids the historicism he generally associated with the philosophy of origin. Buck-Morss identifies this element in her discussion of Adorno and Horkheimer's *Dialectic of Enlightenment:* 'To identify the historical "source" (*Ursprung*) or historical prototype (*Urbild*) or historical development (*Urgeschichte*) was to construct it from the perspective of the present, and for the purpose of criticizing the present.'[15] Indeed, the *Dialectic of Enlightenment* provides significant examples of the way in which Adorno is able to use the concept of origin as a positive heuristic tool. Written by Adorno with his friend and Frankfurt School colleague Max Horkheimer during their exile in California in the early forties, the *Dialectic of Enlightenment* outlines the mechanisms of domination that constitute the hidden, or what Nietzsche might call the 'shameful,' origins of 'enlightenment' thought and practice. These hidden origins are revealed to be man's fear of the subjection of the self *by* nature, which forces man to engage in the subjection *of* nature. This primal fear generates everything from ancient myth to the deceptions of the culture industry, both of which attempt to promote social conformity and the suppression of the passions in order to keep the chthonic forces of nature in check.

However, the *Dialectic of Enlightenment* does not describe the metamorphosis of myth-governed society into a society governed by an alienated ratio in a simple, diachronically linear fashion. Such a methodology would presuppose, à la Rousseau, some identifiable point at which this process began. However, as Fredric Jameson has stated, 'the peculiar originality of Adorno's and Horkheimer's conception of a "dialectic of enlightenment" is that it excludes any beginning or first term, and specifically describes "enlightenment" as an "always-already" process whose structure lies very precisely in its generation of the illusion that what preceded it (which was also a form of enlightenment) was the "original" moment of myth, the archaic union with nature, which it is the vocation of enlightenment "proper" to annul.'[16] This means that, like Nietzsche before them, Adorno and Horkheimer must make use of the peculiar dynamics of *Ursprung* to create the synchronic cuts necessary to demonstrate effectively how ancient and modern man feels and felt the same compulsion (grounded in the fear of the nonidentical) to use instrumental reason in order to dominate nature.

The technique of origin makes use of the volatile quality, rooted in the etymology of the German term, to 'leap' into, out of, and between seemingly discrete historical ideologies, constructs, and events in order to unmask the truth (concealed by the diachronic flow of history) of their genealogies. In the case of the *Dialectic of Enlightenment*, this means exposing the primal fear linking the most archaic magical rites with the most modern scientific or technological procedures. Without reflecting on the particular resonance of *Ursprung* tapped by Adorno and Horkheimer, Jameson confirms their reliance on the fusion of the primal and the kinetic inherent in this technique when he comments that 'a "scene of origins" will be necessary; so that the Ur-motivation of the mimetic is staged as fear and impotence before Nature, which ritual mimesis and, after it, science, are called upon to master.'[17] Adorno and Horkheimer must stage a scene of origins precisely because this procedure alone will allow them to evoke the fundamental unity between these respective forms of domination.

Jameson's expression 'scene of origins' accurately captures the affinity Adorno and Horkheimer seek to establish between ancient and modern efforts to control nature and shows that such a scene may disrupt history's linear narrative flow in order to reveal a synchronic cut. A scene of origins stages not just the first moments of a pathology; it evokes this pathology's most modern manifestations as well. Nevertheless, Jameson's description of Adorno and Horkheimer's scene of origins presents a somewhat distorted notion of how mimesis is articulated in the *Dialectic of Enlightenment*. Man's fear of nature is not presented in this work as ill-founded; the havoc wreaked on humanity by natural disasters of all kinds has engendered a legitimate dread of nature's caprice.

The vulnerability of the human subject in the face of such potential lethality creates an understandable desire to reduce the arbitrary character of natural disasters by dominating nature itself. Mimesis is the effort to adapt to nature, and so lessen its dangers, by becoming at one with it through mimicry and shamanistic magic. As an attempt to subdue and overcome nature's alterity, mimesis is radically distinguished from science. While ritual mimesis attempts to *close* the gap between subject and object, science develops an ever-increasing gap between itself and the objective natural world (3:27). In the *Dialectic of Enlightenment,* mimesis exercises a double function. The articulation of mimesis as a 'scene of origins' shows the absolute entanglement of primal fears with the most modern forms of domination. However, mimesis also constitutes a less oppressive and overbearing means of coming to grips with these fears and is held out in the *Dialectic of Enlightenment* as a telos to be realized in an unforeseeable future. In discussing this work, Miriam Hansen has noted that 'as a utopian category, mimesis prefigures the possibility of a reconciliation with nature, which includes the inner nature of human beings, the body and the unconscious.'[18] We must therefore amend Jameson's remark to note that the staging of a scene of origins in the *Dialectic of Enlightenment* is also meant to instill this work with an (albeit relatively faint) utopian dimension.

In spite of the synchronic element in their book, Adorno and Horkheimer are careful to document historical changes in the subjectivist perspectives that legitimize domination. For example, they see the industrialization of society and the repudiation of thought ('Denken') as simple ideology by world leaders (which frees them of the need to justify their actions by reference to legal discourses) within the context of a specific historical constellation. They note, 'At all times, the particular origin of thought and its universal perspective were inseparable' (3:55). In this case, the specific origins of contemporary thought are informed by the process of mechanization. Adorno and Horkheimer suggest that the process of industrialization has thoroughly eliminated thought's powers of reflexivity and led to intellectual passivity and the reification of society (3:55). This enables the authoritarian forces of domination to establish in the minds of their subjects that thought is mere ideology.

Thus, the sentence 'At all times, the particular origin of thought and its universal perspective were inseparable' acquires a twofold significance. On the one hand, particular historical conjunctions establish the horizons that shape thought contemporaneous with those conjunctions and govern its perspectives. This is a general postulate of all modern hermeneutic thinking, from Dilthey and Heidegger to Gadamer.[19] On the other hand, Adorno and Horkheimer are also at pains to show how the contemporary forces of domination, by identifying the origins of thought in their present-day particularity, are able to *intervene* on a universal basis in the historical process and *determine* thought's universal perspective. This aspect of the treatment of *Ursprung* in the *Dialectic of Enlightenment* avoids the false historical determinism ('Geschichtlichkeit') Adorno associated with Heidegger (6:134–36) and actualizes it in the manner described by Buck-Morss. Adorno and Horkheimer constitute *Ursprung* from the perspective of the present and as a way of unmasking and demythologizing contemporary authoritarian practices.

If 'origin is the goal' for Karl Kraus, Adorno and Horkheimer also suggest that it is the telos of the dialectic of enlightenment. However, origin is the goal of an administered world in precisely the ideological sense Adorno indicated in the *Negative Dialectics* did *not* apply to Kraus's maxim, namely, as the return to a phantasmic 'good' nature (6:158). This 'good' nature is revealed in the *Dialectic of Enlightenment* to be beyond the purview of a science that does not recognize it. However, the utopia of a nature beyond the purview of science is not a concrete historical goal. Instead, it represents an epistemological turn brought about by the fulfillment of the dialectic of enlightenment. Once nature falls completely under the domination of enlightenment subjectivity, it will be remembered in its now no longer threatening prescientific state of origin. This memory, a false construct of the dialectic of enlightenment, also represents enlightenment's culmination (3:60). The cognitive return to the *Ursprung* of nature is undoubtedly part of the fraudulent ideology of the philosophy of origin. Adorno believed such origins were established only through the dissolution of the nonidentity of nature and its thralldom to an authoritarian subject. By exposing this origin as a subjectively constituted chimera in the *Dialectic of Enlightenment*, however, Adorno and Horkheimer use it as a positive tool to expose enlightenment's mass deception.

Constructed from the perspective of the present and for the purpose of criticizing the present, the discrete historical origins of narrative modes such as epic and myth postulated by traditional anthropologists of culture like Rudolf Borchardt are collapsed. Both epic and myth are shown in the *Dialectic of Enlightenment* to be generated by the telos of domination and exploitation (3:63–64). The epic time of the Homeric narratives is shown to be simply the sequentialization of mythic time (3:66). However, mythological thought is shaped by the impulse to reify the forces of nature. This tendency is propelled by a concept of natural origin based on the divine and demoniac. In other words, mythology transforms both external and internal forces into anthropomorphic powers emanating from a divine or demoniac origin. Enlightenment makes a break with this view. Through enlightenment reason, the forces of nature are reconstituted as the simple and undifferentiated object that encompasses whatever resists the abstract power of the human subject (3:109). Particularly in works of art (the *Odyssey* is the operative example used in the *Dialectic of Enlightenment*), this resistance of nature manifests itself as the nonidentical. Thus, as Jameson tells us, the 'otherness of the work of art,' its 'truth-content,' is, for Adorno, 'identified as the *Ansich,* the in-itself of being or of nature.'[20] The discrete subject capable through its autonomous power to reason of transforming natural forces of magical origin into mere abstractions is itself constituted through the displacement of mythological thought by reason. This explains Adorno's description of the dialectic of enlightenment in the *Negative Dialectics* as an 'Urgeschichte des Subjekts' (6:186) [ur-history of the subject].

In the *Metacritique,* Adorno had already identified the abstraction mechanism through which the ratio dominates nature by reducing it to pure identity with the philosophy of origin. In approaching complete liberation from the context of nature, the philosophy of origin fears losing itself in pure subjectivity. For this reason, the abstraction mechanism turns toward the same ontology – an ontology *rooted* in the context of nature – it works to negate (5:28–29). This is perhaps the reason why, as Adorno suggests, fascism can so easily embrace the philosophy of origin; *Ursprungsphilosophie* is driven, through its regressive turn, to re-mystify nature as a chthonic realm inhabited by those same living forces of divine or demoniac origin that the abstract ratio had worked against. In the *Metacritique*, Adorno notes that, 'Thanks to this tendency [the inclination toward an ontology it strives to negate], the embattled philosophy of origin has fled from subjective reflection into Platonism and had to strive desperately, at the same time, to reduce such a relapse to a common denominator with the irrevocable, subjective-critical motif. This dates back to Kant' (5:29). It is of course ironic that Adorno traces the flight of the philosophy of origin away from the autonomy of subjective reflection back to Kant, for Kant's definition of enlightenment is the most concrete formulation of the independence of subjective ratio, of the 'abstract power of the subject,' described by Adorno and Horkheimer in the *Dialectic of Enlightenment*.[21]

The regressive recourse to myth-based thinking on the part of the autonomous 'enlightened' subject is explicitly described in Adorno's *Jargon der Eigentlichkeit: Zur deutschen Ideologie* (1964; *The Jargon of Authenticity*). Through a process initially discussed in the *Metacritique* but now specifically related to the recidivism exemplified by existentialist jargon, this subject reinvokes mythic thinking. The subject is driven to this act by the hidden dynamic violence that propels it. The reinvocation of the myth is evident in all 'dialectical theology' (6:434). In the jargon of authenticity, the mythological and the reified become entangled with the antimythological and rational element of language (6:442). This jargon does not concern itself with language's distancing of itself from its magical origins (6:441). Indeed, a passage from Karl Jaspers postulating a return to the origins from whence we grew suggests to Adorno an anti-Sophistic outlook that gives evidence of the final stage of mythological thinking in its processed state. Plato originally ridiculed the Sophists for hypostatizing thought. Sophism privileges an idealistic form of epistemology that eschews factual knowledge and a concrete awareness of the constitutive elements in the objects it examines, making it an easy target for Platonic invective. Adorno, however, criticizes anti-Sophism, which insists that thought must possess a foundation, for using this circumstance to bring thought itself into disrepute.

Adorno equates this anti-Sophistic point of view with a 'verhärtetes Ursprungsdenken' (6:443–44) [a hardened origin-based thinking] because it seeks such an absolutely primal foundation through a return to epistemological origins. Adorno sees Jaspers's advocacy of laying bare the 'root' of all opinions, modes of comprehension, and customs as an example of such jargon-inflected, anti-Sophistic mythology – mythology in its ultimate, modern form. The *Ursprungsdenken* described in the *Jargon of Authenticity* and the *Ursprungsphilosophie* identified in the *Metacritique* are both shown to be trapped in an endless back-and-forth motion between the abstractions of ratio-governed subjective reflection and the obscurantist mythological belief in reified natural forces of divine origin. Adorno asserts that if the word *Ursprung* had any meaning, it would go beyond the artificial oppositions created by the jargon of authenticity and recognize them as elements of one guilty fascistic whole (6:445–46). It is, of course, precisely the philosophy of origin, however, that fascism has appropriated and attempts to realize (5:28).

One of Adorno's strongest objections to what he identifies as the jargon of authenticity is its inclination toward pseudoetymologizing, particularly in Heidegger. Adorno is especially harsh in his critique of Heidegger's paronomastic tendencies, that is, his clustering of words sharing a common stem but distinguished by prefix and suffix variations. For example, he sees Heidegger's use of paronomasia in 'Über den Humanismus' (1949; 'Letter on Humanism') to elicit ontological nuances ('Sein,' 'Da-sein,' 'Seiende,' 'seinsgeschichtlich') as a philosophically banal attempt to conjure the absolute magically (6:447). Heidegger's investment of Dasein with a dual 'ontic-ontologic' character points ultimately to a philosophy of pure identity (6:493–94). Adorno also levels this charge of absolutism and identity against Heidegger's philosophy of origin, and, while an extended analysis of Adorno's critique will be offered in chapter 5, it is worth noting here that Herman Rapaport has described Heidegger's paronomasia as moving in a direction virtually opposite to the one described by Adorno. Rapaport, in examining this technique in Heidegger, concludes that it foregrounds Being's irresolvable antinomies and blocks the closure toward which all philosophies strive. With regard to Heidegger's recurrent use of the pronoun 'es' in the essay 'Zeit und Sein' (1969; 'Time and Being'), Rapaport believes 'one could say that the "it" is merely a marker standing in the origination of the saying of origin by means of enabling a rift in words through which temporality comes about by way of the interrelations of difference and identity.'[22] Intentionally or not, Rapaport here uses his discussion of paronomasia in Heidegger to reenact this technique and to elicit the same nuance his interpretation of Heidegger's 'es' evokes in 'Time and Being.' In using paronomasia to enable a rift in the word 'origin,' Rapaport shows the interrelation of difference and identity latent in the saying of origin itself. Heidegger employs this word-play repeatedly in connection with the term *Ursprung* in a manner calculated to elide its frequent affiliation with pure identity.

In the *Jargon of Authenticity,* Adorno identifies both Jaspers and Heidegger as representatives of the obscurantist mythic thinking he had associated in the *Metacritique* with the recidivist turn from absolute subjective autonomy, which is characteristic of the philosophy of origin. Adorno's conflation may appear unjust in light of the famous split between the two men over Heidegger's embrace of the national socialist program.[23] Jaspers himself criticized Heidegger's recourse to the concept of *Ursprung* as a way of avoiding an honest engagement with concrete historical realities.[24] However, in his *Vom Ursprung und Ziel der Geschichte* (1949; *The Origin and Goal of History*), Jaspers expresses his belief that mankind has a single, unknowable origin and goal. They are only capable of being perceived

> im Schimmer vieldeutiger Symbole; unser Dasein bewegt sich zwischen ihnen; in philosophischer Besinnung suchen wir uns wohl beiden, Ursprung und Ziel, zu nähern. . . . Im Ursprung war die Offenbarkeit des Seins in bewußtloser Gegenwärtigkeit. Der Sündenfall brachte uns auf den Weg, durch Erkennen und durch endliche Praxis mit Zwecken in der Zeit zur Helle des bewußt Offenbaren zu kommen.[25]

> [in the glitter of ambiguous symbols; our existence moves between them; in philosophical contemplation we seek to move closer to both of them, origin and goal. . . . In the origin,

the manifest nature of Being existed in a presentness without consciousness. The Fall set us on the path that led us to the luminosity of the consciously manifest through knowledge and through a finite praxis with temporal objectives.]

Here again, origin becomes the goal in precisely the way Adorno claimed it must not, as the phantasmic return to a 'good' nature (6:158), in this case, a nature where man and nature regain their prelapsarian identity. Adorno objected to a similar strain in Benjamin's thought.[26] In Adorno's view, theologically established prelapsarian origins are as informed by bad metaphysics as the transcendental origins postulated by Heidegger's ontology. For Adorno, the passage of Jaspers cited by Adorno that equates origin with the root ('Wurzel') out of which we and our thoughts have grown signifies the return to (Goethe's archetypal) mothers (6:443–44). In the *Negative Dialectics,* Adorno noted, 'The category of the root, of the origin itself is domineering.' It is tied to the dominion of the autochthon (6:158). However meaningful the post-thirties split between Heidegger and Jaspers may have been for historians of modern philosophy, Adorno identifies in the jargon of both men the dangerous totalitarian obscurantism he associated with the philosophy of origin.[27]

In order to be freed from such totalitarian conjunctions, origin has to bear the trace of the otherness of the object. This association situates origin in the nondeterminate space between subject and object. In one of the instances in which Adorno debunks the sphere of absolute origins in the *Negative Dialectics,* he demonstrates that the subject is not the locus of this sphere. He indicates that the ego's genuine sovereignty can only originate in relation to the nonego, the object. The sphere of origins is not absolute because it is not situated purely in the subject. Adorno implies that the origin of true autonomy in the subject inheres in the interstice between ego and otherness (6:222). Of course, this implication suggests as well that the sphere of origins also cannot inhere *in* the object, in the viscerally feared chthonic otherness of nature.

Adorno's critique of the sphere of absolute origins and his positing of origin in an indeterminate interstice between subject and object is related to his strongly negative attitude toward the concept of 'expressive' or 'genetic' totality. This Hegelian category of a metasubject that unites substance and genesis as manifestations of the Absolute Spirit was adapted in subsequent Marxist theory to signify the proletariat – the collective subject of history and the determinant motor force of its objective outcome. The issue of the legitimacy of a notion of expressive or genetic totality has constituted a major dilemma for most Marxists, as Martin Jay has shown in his study *Marxism and Totality* (1984). The problem it poses for any Marxist who wishes to articulate a nonhegemonic principle of origin becomes evident through Jay's reading of Louis Althusser's later epistemology: 'For at the same time that he staunchly denied any origin or genetic center in the structural totality, he contended that everything in it, including theoretical practice, was somehow "in the last instance" a function or expression of class struggle. Thus he began surreptitiously to reproduce that very expressive concept of totality that he had been at such pains to exorcise from Marxism.'[28] The denial of origin cannot simply 'exorcise' metaphysical totality from epistemological theory. Although Althusser's notion of 'structural causality' bears a certain resemblance to Heidegger's 'simultaneity of origins,' his attempt to divorce structure from origin does not eliminate a tendency toward projecting hegemonic causality in his writing. Adorno categorically rejected the concept of expressive totality because of its tacit linkage of thought to causation in the social sphere.[29] This rejection is reflected in his decoupling of origin from genetic agency, a decoupling he enacts by situating origin in an indeterminate region between subject and object.

While Adorno's refutation of expressive totality encompasses the rupture of an unmediated bond between subject and object, he cannot completely elide their affiliation. When he wishes to demonstrate evolutionary continuity between characteristics in man and forces in nature prior to its domination by man, Adorno, like Nietzsche, uses the word *Herkunft*. For example, in the *Dialectic of Enlightenment*, Adorno discerns in the stereotyped character of the Jewish physiognomy a stimulation to fascists to commit manslaughter. This urge results from the shameful recollection, inspired by viewing such a face, that human ancestry ('Herkunft') lies in nature, in a natural condition from which the human subject has degenerated (3:290). Elsewhere in the *Dialectic of Enlightenment*, Adorno and Horkheimer cite example after example of the evil 'other' side of progress, negative phenomena concomitant with man's self-proclaimed march toward freedom, health, and justice. They remark, 'The spirit and all that is good in its origin and existence is hopelessly entangled in this horror' (3:253). The origin of all genuinely existent historical phenomena, in other words, is caught up in the interstice between good and evil.

The distinction between the evolutionary continuity designated by *Herkunft* and the more critically productive dialectics of the interstice gleaned from the examination of the genuine *Ursprung* of a phenomenon also carries over into Adorno's aesthetics. In his essay 'Über Jazz' (1936; On jazz), Adorno is willing to grant that the *Herkunft* of this musical form may be traced back to Africa. Contemporary musicologists, however, tend to focus on the African roots of jazz as a way of defending their argument that the powerful, primal unmediated forces it thereby inherits can be used to revitalize European music. Adorno equates such thinking with a 'recourse to false origins' (17:82). He finds that the African elements in jazz are, at best, parodistically compromised in what is an utterly commodified form of entertainment. He situates the true origins of jazz in the locus between salon music, with its false patina of an obstreperous individuality that really masks social domination, and the military march, which does not even hide its authoritarian character.

Even the form of jazz most effusively praised for its individualism and primal immediacy, 'hot music,' reveals, in Adorno's view, an enslavement to social conformity. With such a revelation, according to Adorno (particularly in the form of the symphonic jazz march),

> hat der Jazz nach den Polen seines Ursprungs sich aufgespalten, während in seiner Mitte die hot music, zu verfrühter Klassizität verdammt, ihr schmales Spezialisten-Dasein führt. Dann aber auch ist der Jazz nicht mehr zu retten. (17:100)

[jazz has split along the poles of its origin, while in its midst 'hot music,' condemned to a premature classicality, leads its narrow specialist existence. But then jazz can no longer be saved].

Hegel's dialectics, according to most of his interpreters, would show how the antithetical poles of a historical phenomenon are resolved into a synthesis. Adorno's negative dialectics, on the other hand, suggest how a historical phenomenon such as jazz obliterates itself when it moves out of the interstice that shapes its origin as a concrete entity and divides itself back into the antithetical poles of that *Ursprung*.[30]

Adorno's essay on jazz contains in miniature the two theories of the notion of origin evident in his aesthetic magnum opus, the comprehensive but never completed *Ästhetische Theorie* (*Aesthetic Theory*), which was first published in 1970. Briefly stated, Adorno views origin as a misguided aesthetic tool when it is used to trace a genre or movement such as jazz back to an ontically privileged primordial epoch. Origin attains a positive critical status when it is used to mediate dialectically within the constellation of elements that give rise to artistic manifestations. This mediation frees art from its historicist imprisonment and allows insights with genuine contemporary relevance. The recourse to false origins condemned by Adorno in the jazz essay is shown in the *Aesthetic Theory* to govern the aesthetics of both the classicists and the late romantics. Adorno notes, 'Art has its concept in the historically changing constellation of moments; it does not allow of a definition. Its essence cannot be deduced from its origin, as though the origin was a foundational stratum upon which all that follows builds up and collapses as soon as the foundation is unsettled' (7:11).

In the jazz essay, Adorno had exposed this sort of historicism as governed by a false ideology; here, he is content to attack its imprecise methodology, which combines positivism and vague speculation. However, he is equally averse to the philosophical tendency to divide the *Ursprungsfrage*, or question of origin, into two separate spheres, one treating origin as an ur-historical problem and one defined by the problem of ontological essence. If the former sphere is a false ideological construct that imprisons aesthetic origins in the incomprehensible recesses of prehistory, the latter would be reminiscent for Adorno of Husserl's ahistorical 'sphere of Being of absolute origins,' purely subjective and lacking any methodological foundation. Adorno claims that the strict separation of these aspects of the question of origin contradicts the essence of the word *Ursprung*, presumably because the word conveys both historical dynamism (*Sprung*) and fundamental primalness (*Ur*). Adorno goes on to suggest that art is governed by the dynamics of its past, present, and future, by its (nonidentical) relationship to its otherness. Aesthetics must take this into account (7:11–12).

By suggesting that philosophy has lost sight of the true meaning of the word *Ursprung* by separating the ur-historical and the ontologically essential and by rooting the concept of art in a historically changing constellation of moments dynamically linking art's past, present, and future, Adorno hints at a view of aesthetic origin reminiscent of Benjamin's use of the term 'Konstellation.'[31] It appears in the *Origin of German Tragic Drama* in connection with ideas as unchanging arrangements of phenomena. Of course, Benjamin had viewed phenomena under the sign of origin as governed by the dynamics of their pre- and posthistory, but ideas themselves are 'eternal constellations' (1:215) of phenomena and reach historical plenitude in the totality of their phenomenal history. This is a fundamental aspect of Benjamin's definition of *Ursprung* (1:226). Adorno invested the Benjaminian term 'Konstellation' with a temporal dimension; for Adorno, constellations are historically dynamic.[32] The same is true of the term 'Konfiguration,' used by Benjamin and Adorno interchangeably with 'Konstellation.' In his *Trauerspiel* book, Benjamin notes that,

> Die philosophische Geschichte als die Wissenschaft vom Ursprung ist die Form, die da aus den entlegenen Extremen, den scheinbaren Exzessen der Entwicklung die Konfiguration der Idee als der durch die Möglichkeit eines sinnvollen Nebeneinanders solcher Gegensätze gekennzeichneten Totalität heraustreten läßt.

> [Historical philosophy as the science of origin is the form that allows the configuration of the idea to emerge from the re-

mote extremes, the apparent excesses of the course of development. This idea is to be characterized as the possibility of the totality of a meaningful juxtaposition of such opposites.]

Revealed in this way, the configuration of the idea achieves a redeemed stasis in which its past and present history is no longer pragmatically real (1:227). Adorno uses the device of the configuration to redeem the use of *Ursprung critically,* but because his aesthetics is never informed by the theological telos of an eschatological plenitude, his configurations and constellations are resolutely historical. In the first appendix to the *Aesthetic Theory,* Adorno rejects as dubious all attempts to interpret art from the perspective of its origin. He views crude biography, the history of ideas, and the ontological sublimation of the concept of origin as aesthetic approaches tainted by a false recourse to the principle of origin. He nevertheless sees some value in this principle when its application is governed by an aesthetics that treats the work of art as a historically dynamic configuration:

> Gleichwohl ist der Ursprung auch nicht radikal außerhalb der Sache. Daß die Werke Artefakte sind, ist ihr Implikat. Die Konfigurationen in einem jeglichen sprechen zu dem, woraus es hervorging. In jedem hebt sich, worin es seiner Herkunft gleicht, ab von dem, wozu es wurde.

> [However, the origin is not entirely irrelevant. Works imply their status as artifacts. The configurations in each one address that from which it emerged. In each work, that which approximates its provenance distinguishes itself from that which it became.]

He goes on to note that artworks can only resist the destructive power of concrete historical pressure if they can maintain their monadological unity (7:446).

As in the *Dialectic of Enlightenment,* Adorno makes a Nietzschean distinction here between *Herkunft* ('provenance') and *Ursprung.*[33] As historically configured artifacts, mediated by a notion of origin free of historicist thinking, artworks are freed from the historicist imprisonment that views their *Herkunft* as inevitably governing that which they become in the course of history. As monadological configurations, artworks resist such pressure. By treating artworks as monads, Adorno, like Benjamin, attempts to accomplish two seemingly antithetical objectives. In the above-cited fragment, he attempts to show how artworks can resist 'genuine historical pressure' (7:446) as monads. Elsewhere in the *Aesthetic Theory*, Adorno says that the artwork's relationship to history is mediated through its monadological core. However, in both cases, he is trying to show that the artwork as monad resists the continuum of history while retaining its historical dynamism. As with Benjamin, establishing the immanent history of the monadologically structured artwork's process of becoming ('Werden') leads to the 'explosion' (7:132) of the continuum of history. Nevertheless, Adorno's aesthetic monadology was somewhat more extreme than Benjamin's in its rejection of literary typologies. While Benjamin refuted Croce's complete abnegation of theories of genre, Adorno's greater emphasis on the windowless character of the artwork as monad led him to use Croce as a starting point for highlighting what he saw as the completely discrete, individuated quality of each genuine work of art.[34]

Adorno was strongly critical of the notion of going back to the origin of art in order to find some mysterious primary layer that gave rise to all succeeding artistic products. In the *Negative Dialectics*, he had tied the search for such an irreducible essence to Heideggerian ontology. He noted there that Heidegger's glance toward origin is directed so far backward that he can establish it as magically omnipresent (6:113). Presumably, it is the displacement by the late romantics of the origin of art into some pristine foundation that allows them both to postulate that this foundation is resonant in all subsequent works and that the earliest works of art are of the purest and most elevated quality (7:11). Adorno himself is not above discussing the 'magical origin' of artworks (7:210). One of Adorno's aims in using such an expression, however, is to 'disenchant' this magical origin. He treats it not as a fount of primeval purity lying at the root of art and subsequently tainted by history as would his late romantics. Instead, the magical origin of artworks is tied to their initial purpose: to have an impact on nature. Art in its origin is tied to the subjective domination of nature. Subsequently, art was displaced in this endeavor by rationality, but traces of this repressive mode are still evident in art's form; form as sedimented and modified content can never deny art's origin (7:210). Art's magical origins are really art's *pudenda origo*. Art is rooted in an attempt to overcome natural domination as ancient as man himself. Even classicism – the locus of a second *Ursprung,* namely, art's autonomy from nature – is rooted in repression, which effectively cancels that autonomy (7:243). Origin thus appears in works of art as a trace that denies the exalted status of the self-referentiality, elevation above the mundane, and autonomy traditionally ascribed to them by bourgeois aesthetics.[35]

Adorno attacks those aesthetic methodologies that treat the question of the origin of art as a substantive problem. Those aesthetics that examine art's origin in terms of essence ('Wesen') even overlook the etymology of the word *Ursprung* (7:11). His critique of such essentialism is articulated in the draft introduction to the *Aesthetic Theory* as a critique of phenomenological approaches to this question. Adorno notes that phenomenological aesthetics opposes both conceptual approaches and abstract generalizations. It is concerned to capture art in its essence, an essence held to be both its origin and that which judges what is true and what is lacking in verity within it. Adorno objects that there is no sense in searching for the individual origin of artworks because these works' objectivity subsumes their subjective moments. It would be equally futile to search for the essential origin of art, as it is not accidental that art has freed itself from its origin. This act of liberation is a law ('Gesetz') of art (7:522). It is quite likely Adorno had Heidegger's essay 'The Origin of the Work of Art' in mind when he equated phenomenological approaches to the question of the origin of art with the search for art's essence or *Wesen* because this is precisely what Heidegger does at the outset of his work: 'Here origin means that from which and through which a thing is what it is and how it is. That which something is and how it is we call its essence [Wesen]. The origin of something is the provenance [Herkunft] of its essence. The question concerning the origin of the work of art inquires into its essential provenance [Wesensherkunft] . . . the question concerning the origin of the work of art becomes the question concerning the essence of art.'[36]

By equating *Herkunft* and *Ursprung* here, Heidegger postulates an essential continuity between an artwork's subjective origin and its ultimate concretion as a physically complete object. Adorno views as misguided the notion that an artwork is locked within a historical continuity from its point of origin. This would explain his comment that art mocks all attempts to reduce it to its essentialness ('Wesenhaftigkeit'), that it is not what it has always been but what it has become, and that art inevitably frees itself from its origin (7:522). Like Benjamin, Adorno felt the question of origin in art was only productive when it dealt with art as historically realized – its present-day status – not what it was at its point of inception. As Buck-Morss puts it, origin for Adorno 'really meant the appearance of something in history in a particular social constellation through which its present meaning could be deciphered.'[37] This commentary is substantiated by Adorno's remark later in the draft introduction concerning aesthetic objectivity: 'its truth constitutes itself in its development, in what is subsequent rather than in what comes first' (7:530).

Adorno wrote an excursus to the *Aesthetic Theory* entitled 'Theorien über den Ursprung der Kunst' ('Thoughts on the Origin of Art') that provides an added dimension to his position on aesthetic origin. He begins with an attack on the extreme positions found in aesthetic treatments of the question of origin, namely, the ontological and the historically positivistic approaches. Similar to the critique of these positions at the outset of the *Aesthetic Theory* (7:11), the excursus attacks ontology for its insubstantial metaphysics and the purely historical approach for its failure to realize art is only what it has become (7:480). Like Benjamin in the *Trauerspiel* book, Adorno discusses the strengths and weaknesses of Croce's argument that the question of aesthetic origin is irrelevant. Unlike Benjamin, however, he finds that Croce's position is essentially valid; subsequent empirical investigations into the problem of aesthetic origin have failed to seriously challenge Croce's view (7:481).

Adorno devotes most of the rest of the excursus to dismantling such scientific research. He is particularly concerned to show that aesthetic mimesis is not to be equated simply with animistic super-stition, as many of these investigations claim. On the contrary, from its outset there is a rational component to aesthetic mime-sis. Adorno views aesthetic behavior as a dynamic process that sets mimesis into motion and modifies it. Aesthetic behavior is informed by subjectivity, but it is also characterized by its sense of being touched by the Other. This sense is called a shudder ('Schauer') (7:489–90). Given that this excursus is devoted to a discussion of the theories of the origin of art, it would not be unrea-sonable to surmise that this shudder itself defines the origin of art. If so, it stands as a metaphor for the nonspace between a purely subjective consciousness caught in its own reification (7:490) and complete immersion in the Other, which is impossible outside the erotic sphere.

Aesthetic consciousness is, in its origin, a premonition of the Other, a premonition that momentarily frees the perceiving sub-ject from the need to grasp cognitively, and thereby repress, the object in its otherness. Cognition, however, is not simply sus-pended but is joined to the erotic. Adorno equates the ability of artworks to pass over into their Other ('in ihr Anderes überzu-gehen') with erotic behavior (7:263). The origin of aesthetic con-sciousness is in the interstice between the cognitive and the erotic, between self-enclosed subjectivity and the orgasmic merging into the Other; or, as Adorno puts it in the last sentence of the excursus, 'Such a constitutive orientation on the part of the subject toward objectivity in the aesthetic mode of behavior conjoins eros and knowledge' (7:490).

What unites Adorno's comments on the notion of *Ursprung* in the many diverse contexts in which they are found is essentially the common thread running through his entire oeuvre: the princi-ple of nonidentity. To be more precise, Adorno is 'the philosopher of Identity in a very special sense,' as Jameson puts it; he articu-lates, in short, the drive toward domination latent in all concep-tual, scientific, and systematic thinking in the 'enlightenment.'[38] In Adorno's vocabulary, this term is not restricted to the eighteenth-century movement normally associated with it. The 'dialectic of enlightenment' is a universal process. It signifies reason's attempt to overcome nature's resistance to human control, although Adorno and Horkheimer express the hope that their work will free 'enlightenment' as a concept from an inevitable association with this domineering tendency and allow it to be seen in a positive light (3:16). 'Nonidentity' is the term Adorno uses to indicate the presence of nature, the nonsubjective and nonsubsumable, in a world dominated by instrumental reason. If Adorno's philosophy may be said to have a goal, then, it is to foreground such nonidentity in historical artifacts, works of art, and society itself.

To enact such revelations, Adorno had recourse (like Benjamin) to *Ursprung* as a technique to show how these phenomena resist human history through their ineradicable alterity and yet are resolutely historical, inscribed by the chronology of the efforts to master them. Whether he attacks Husserl's sphere of absolute origins, Heidegger's recourse to a primal origin lost in the course of history but resonant in all of it, the use of origin as the basis of the ideology behind fascistic authoritarianism, or the use of origin by positivistic and ontological aestheticians as a means of conceptually grasping the essence of art – in all these cases Adorno is attacking the subjective attempt to overcome, and thereby dominate, the otherness of the object. Such attempts manifest themselves in all areas of human endeavor, from epistemology to aesthetics, from politics to industry. Given Adorno's wide-ranging critique of the notion of origin, it is easy to see him – as in Foucault's interpretation of Nietzsche – as an ally in the general poststructuralist attempt to deconstruct it.[39] As with Nietzsche, however, such a view is misleading. Like Benjamin and Nietzsche, Adorno finds in the principle of origin a critically constructive element, both 'for the purpose of criticizing the present,' as Buck-Morss suggests,[40] and as a nondiscursive way of evoking that gap between the subject and object that upholds the principle of nonidentity. This means that one must conceive of origin as constituting itself from the goal, from the object – from the Other.

CHAPTER 4

Theism, Temporality, and Origin:
Franz Rosenzweig

In Franz Rosenzweig, it would appear that we are confronted with a thinker whose philosophy illustrates Edward Said's dictum that 'origins are divine.'[1] As Alan Udoff has suggested, in Rosenzweig's oeuvre origin is inevitably bound up with the attempt to 'think God back into creation.'[2] Rosenzweig's use of the term is resolutely linked to his Jewish theology, particularly as it is developed in his magnum opus *Der Stern der Erlösung* (*The Star of Redemption*), which was written during the years 1918–19 and published in 1921. Unlike Adorno, Rosenzweig did not live to see the philosophy of origin manipulated by national socialism to favor the domination by an 'autochthonous' people of their ancestral homeland. Thus, he saw no need to establish the principle of origin as a radically ephemeral category, free of the possibility of appropriation by totalitarian thinking. In approaching the problem of origin from a theological perspective, Rosenzweig appears to have posited a seamless continuity between the primal postlapsarian past and the present day, a view that would, of course, have been anathema to Adorno.

Nevertheless, *The Star of Redemption,* as Buck-Morss has suggested, undoubtedly impacted Adorno's thinking, even if its influence was mediated through Benjamin and Gershom Scholem. Both Adorno and Rosenzweig opposed the totalistic system they believed was evident in Hegel's philosophy with an emphasis on the fragmentary nature of reality. In addition to this mutual opposition to Hegel, Buck-Morss notes that, for Rosenzweig, 'Knowledge was "revelation" which "looks back into the past. . . . But the past only becomes visible to revelation when and as revelation shines into it with the light of the present."' Buck-Morss cites this passage from *The Star of Redemption* to support her thesis that the theories of Adorno and Rosenzweig share important characteristics.[3] When we recall Buck-Morss's insightful comment that

Adorno equates the identification of *Ursprung* with its construction 'from the perspective of the present,' we see possible affinities in Adorno's and Rosenzweig's positions on origin.[4] As the passage cited by Buck-Morss indicates, the past for Rosenzweig is only illuminated through the revelatory light of present-day perspectives.

Rosenzweig's most extensive commentary on Hegel is found in his doctoral dissertation, developed under the direction of Friedrich Meinecke and published under the title *Hegel und der Staat* (Hegel and the state, completed in 1913 but not published until 1920). While engaged in research for this dissertation, Rosenzweig, in a letter dated 26 September 1910 and addressed to his good friend Hans Ehrenberg, makes the following remark concerning Hegel's early theological writings: 'Much of the metareligious is hidden in all of these questions concerned with the origin of evil, with God and history. The religious itself is always positive religion. It begins with the fact, not with the origin and essence of the fact' (BT 111). As Alexander Altmann has noted, this passage suggests that 'from the very start' Rosenzweig is 'troubled by such metaphysical questions' related to problems of origin.[5] However, it also militates against any tendency to see Rosenzweig's views on origin as informed entirely by a metaphysical perspective. He has difficulty accepting what he believed was Hegel's metareligious approach to such questions as the origin of evil, God, and history because of its supposedly totalistic idealism. Like Adorno, Rosenzweig objected to what he perceived as a lack of attention by Hegel to the individual, the particular, the transitory, and the specific historical detail.[6] This indifference is based on the supposed irrelevance of these concretions for Hegel's allegedly systematic philosophy or perhaps, more ominously, on their potential force as a subversive counterweight to what Rosenzweig believed was Hegel's abstract idealism. By shifting the locus of religious thought from the origin and essence of the factual to the factual itself, Rosenzweig points toward his later anchoring of *Ursprung* in facticity, in the 'fragmentary' nature of reality and the discrete nature of the individuated spheres of man, world, and God.

In his book on Hegel and the state, Rosenzweig develops the critique of Hegel that he hinted at in his letter to Ehrenberg. Examining some of Hegel's youthful sketches, Rosenzweig discusses Hegel's early views on the connection between religion and the state. He finds it particularly noteworthy that Hegel determines the origin of polytheism from the perspective of the state's historical development (HS 1:16). This connection between the state and religion points toward what Rosenzweig refers to as the 'living totality' informing Hegel's concept of *Volksgeist*. This spirit of the people is rooted in the totality of national life. Hegel's adaptation of the romantic notion of a *Volksgeist* to evoke a sense of the organic totality of the relationship between the people, its state, and its religion is given impetus by what Rosenzweig describes as Hegel's 'impulse towards unity.' By positing an organic totality underlying collective national life, the youthful Hegel is able to arrive at the formulation of a universal reason (HS 1:24–25). As Buck-Morss notes in elucidating the common elements of Adorno's and Rosenzweig's thinking, Rosenzweig 'rejected Hegel's closed system, his metaphysical identity of the totality of reality with truth.'[7] Rosenzweig sees in Hegel's evocation of such concepts as universal reason, the spirit of the people, the collectivity of national life, and the inevitable link between religion and the history of the state an early attempt to arrive at such a closed metaphysical system, at the union of truth and a totalized reality.

Buck-Morss's remark helps to explain Rosenzweig's rejection of the metareligious element underlying the concept of origin in Hegel's early theological writings, a rejection suggestive of Adorno's critique of the absolutism he perceived in what he would come to term Hegel's 'philosophy of origin.' Rosenzweig concludes his paragraph on Hegel's metareligious tendencies in the letter to Ehrenberg by contrasting Hegel's theology with that of Luther. Rosenzweig notes that Luther disregarded the sort of speculative theological contemplation later engaged in by Hegel in order to focus on God as the ultimate dispenser of blessings (BT 111). Hegel's emphasis on the organic totality grounding theological elements in a metareligious origin effaces the sense of God as mankind's benefactor. This emphasis also blurs the distinction between the three spheres of man, world, and God, uniting them under the aegis of universal reason. The attempt to establish these spheres as the interlocking but highly discrete facets of existence was to become the telos behind *The Star of Redemption*. In discussing the triadic arrangement of Rosenzweig's cosmogony, Nathan Rotenstreich has suggested that 'Irreducibility is the negative presentation or assertion of the particular and unique sphere with which the system is concerned. With respect to the world, the core of metalogic is thus that "disconcerting fact about the world" that, after all, "it is not spirit."' Rotenstreich correctly notes that Rosenzweig's emphasis on the irreducibility of each individual sphere is distinctly anti-Hegelian.[8]

Rosenzweig wrote his letter to Ehrenberg and his book on Hegel and the state before he underwent the profound experience, on the day of Jewish atonement in 1913, that turned him into a committed Jew and set him decisively on the path leading to the creation of *The Star of Redemption*.[9] As Otto Pöggeler has suggested, however, the recent publication of Rosenzweig's letters and diaries no longer allows one to treat the book on Hegel and *The Star of Redemption* as essentially the work of two distinct authors.[10] Even more importantly, Rosenzweig's brief critique of the allegedly all-encompassing, metareligious nature of the principle of origin in Hegel's early theology points toward Rosenzweig's own avowedly anti-Hegelian and anti-idealist notion of origin in *The Star of Redemption*.

As Else-Rahel Freund has noted, Rosenzweig is primarily indebted to Hermann Cohen's logic of origin for the foundation of his own principle of origin as it evolved in *The Star of Redemption*.[11] Rosenzweig wrote a review (first published in abridged form in 1937) of Cohen's *Deutschtum und Judentum, mit grundlegenden Betrachtungen über Staat und Internationalismus* (1915; The German way of life and the Jewish way of life, with basic observations concerning the state and internationalism). This review provides both a clarification of some of the positions elucidated by Rosenzweig in his book on Hegel and the state and points toward Rosenzweig's adaptation and modification of Cohen's logic of origin in *The Star of Redemption*. At the outset of this review, Rosenzweig refers to the historical myth underlying the fate of the Jewish people, a myth beyond time and yet regulating the course of Jewish existence up to the present day: that the Jewish people are eternally a nation of immigrants, never completely at home in the lands in which they reside. The myth flatly denies the Jewish people recourse to the principle of autochthony. Rosenzweig anchors the Diaspora not in the fall of the Second Temple but in the Adamic past. While Adam is born of the earth, the Jew is the eternal immigrant, the new-comer. The myth of the Jewish people is grounded in a sequence of immigrations dating back to the time of Abraham. The land of the Jews is always held in abeyance; it is never the 'land of birth' (z 169). Rosenzweig has recourse in this review to a principle fundamental to *The Star of Redemption* and many of his subsequent essays: the Jews as a unique nation are bonded together not through an autochthonous link to a given piece of land but through ties of blood and the promise of God. The rights of the autochthon never fall to the Jews, whereas it is precisely such rights that provide other peoples with the imprimatur of distinct nationhood. Adorno's objection to the philosophy of origin on the grounds of its possible appropriation by fascistic thinking thus can never apply to Rosenzweig because he deliberately forswears any recourse to the element of autochthony in discussing the origins of the Jewish people.

Because the roots of the Jewish people can never be anchored in a specific autochthonous homeland, Rosenzweig is led to see Cohen's work under the sign of a fundamentally dualistic origin. He says of Cohen's book on the German and Jewish ways of life: 'From the beginning, this work was anchored in two origins: on the one hand, in a strongly rooted Jewish sensibility and a broad knowledge of Jewish things, on the other hand, in a powerful relationship with German idealism, which led to an effective engagement with the philosophical movement' (z 171). But can Rosenzweig ground his own work in one unified, discrete origin? The opening passages of his review of Cohen's book point to the inevitably dual nature of all Jewish thought. Living in the Diaspora, even the avowedly Jewish thinker's work will be partially rooted in the culture of the alien people among whom he happens to reside. Although Rosenzweig is far more self-consciously critical than Cohen – in *The Star of Redemption* and elsewhere – of the basic tenets of German idealism, his oeuvre, too, is anchored in the same double origin as that of the founder of Marburg Neo-Kantianism.

Nor can one view the individual components of this double origin as mutually exclusive or even discrete. It is certainly true that, unlike Cohen, Rosenzweig decided (after completing *The Star of Redemption*) to drop his pursuit of a career in the mainstream of German academia in favor of a life devoted to the promotion of Jewish education among the assimilated German-Jewish community. However, as Paul Mendes-Flohr has noted, this decision 'did not mark a break with the ideals of German philosophical culture to which he so passionately subscribed. Indeed, both ideationally and spiritually there is a continuity between his deep involvement in the philosophical tradition of German idealism and his later theocentric affirmation of Judaism.'[12] Undoubtedly, this sense of the double origin at the base of their thinking helped inspire Cohen and Rosenzweig to articulate the principle of origin itself as a fundamentally dualistic construct. In spite of Rosenzweig's avowed rejection of a dialectical approach in his theology,[13] the dualistic nature of Rosenzweig's concept of origin is reminiscent of the Nietzschean dialectics of the interstice explored in chapter 1.

Rosenzweig naturally saw the influence of Kant behind Hegel's proclamation of a universal reason underlying national spirit. However, he detects already in Hegel's youthful thought a move away from what Hegel saw as the limitations of the purely moral and ethical foundation Kant provides to his 'religion of reason.' Hegel's merging of national spirit (*Volksgeist*) and universal reason has an obvious political and social dimension; it allows him to conceive of a 'nationales Gesamtleben,' a 'totalized national life' (HS 1:25). Although we might expect it, this notion of a totalized national life does not lead Hegel to call for the union of church and state, as Rosenzweig makes clear in the second volume of the work on Hegel and the state (HS 2:187). Nevertheless, the religious impulses of the individual are intimately tied to the origins of the state in Hegelian political philosophy: 'The will of the individual soul, embattled by the world and by fate to attain religious salvation, requires the concept of the authoritarian and ethically self-regulated state. However, while we perceived this in the consummated system as the key to the entire organization of the system, we saw it in the course of development as the origin of the conception of the state' (HS 2:188). This formulation of the origin of the conception of the state indicates what Rosenzweig terms the 'cornerstones' of the entire Hegelian system, which is the absoluteness of the individual and the absoluteness of the totality. The glue that bonds the part (the individual) to the whole (the totality) is destiny ('Schicksal') (HS 2:188).

Rosenzweig's positive reception of Cohen's book on the German and the Jewish ways of life partly derives from Cohen's radically different use of reason in addressing the use of origin. In an introductory essay to Cohen's Jewish writings (written in 1923 and first published in 1924), Rosenzweig notes that the centerpiece of Cohen's philosophy of history is the history of unindividuated human reason. This same history constitutes, for Rosenzweig, the essence of Hegel's system. Rosenzweig notes the way in which Cohen's thoughts return to Hegel again and again (Z 181). However, the foundation of Cohen's thought is Kantian. What appears to distinguish Cohen from Kant and his followers, and from Hegel and his followers, is his anchoring of the origin of reason and nature in God:

> But there have been enough Kantians. Why hasn't the protest in any of their works against the 'great thought of immanence' attained that tone that has really come from the 'beyond,' a tone that has come from a genuine beyond and thus cannot be ignored? This voice has such a tone, when it asserts the one and only God, the origin, incomparable to all creation, of nature *and* reason, against all the magic of a still highly spiritualized pantheism, when it asserts the inalienable rights of the soul against all the claims of culture. (Z 183; Rosenzweig's emphasis)

The subtext of this passage is actually a description of the Kantian Cohen's theistic turn. In Hegel's evocation of the origin of what Rosenzweig terms the 'authoritarian and ethically self-regulated state,' the individual soul allegedly loses its independent integrity. The individual soul's religious impulses serve merely as the origin generating the concept of the state. Rosenzweig sees in Cohen's theism, which establishes God as the origin of both nature and reason, the liberation of the individuated soul from the aegis of culture, a liberation no prior Kantians had been able to achieve. When Rosenzweig speaks of the inalienable rights of the soul against the claims of *Kultur* – that loaded term suggestive in German not only of 'culture' but also of Germany's attempt to establish a discrete social and (later) national identity – there can be little doubt that he saw these ominous claims embodied in the political philosophy of Hegel, whom he sees as responsible for the false concept of immanence that Cohen alone dared to oppose (z 183, 209).[14] Buck-Morss is correct to assert that in opposing to Hegel's 'totalistic view' an insistence on the fragmentary, individuated nature of reality, Rosenzweig's thought can be linked to Adorno's theory.[15] However, unlike Adorno, Rosenzweig found it necessary to turn to theology to preserve the integrity of the individual against its dominance by the 'totality,' that is, *Kultur* and its institutional embodiment, the state.[16] Rosenzweig's theological orientation is reminiscent of Benjamin's, whose attempt to highlight the discrete nature, the specificity of phenomena, is grounded in a resolutely antitranscendental form of messianic thinking. As with Benjamin, the nonidentitarian, nonsynthetic character of Rosenzweig's theological turn is largely attributable to the pervasive presence of origin-based thinking in his work. Of course, in positing three all-encompassing cosmographic spheres – man, world, and God – Rosenzweig is prevented from focusing as obsessively as Benjamin on the fragmented and conflicted nature of phenomena, phenomena under the sign of allegory. Instead, Rosenzweig's chief ally, and the source of inspiration for his particular linkage of the redemption of the individual to the originary, was Hermann Cohen.

According to Rosenzweig, after Hegel's abstract idealism has made the individual irrelevant as a philosophical entity, Cohen turns to God to make the individual once more comprehensible within the realm of philosophy. However, God and man are only two elements in Cohen's cosmology. The other is nature, and because man is also a part of nature, a correlation between God and nature is also established. This in turn allows one to perceive the concept of creation (z 209). Rosenzweig, however, elides here an important marker in the path toward the concept of creation opened up by Cohen's theology. Cohen also used the principle of origin to arrive at creation. Analyzing Cohen's two most significant theological works, *Der Begriff der Religion im System der Philosophie* (1915; The concept of religion in the system of philosophy) and the *Religion der Vernunft aus den Quellen des Judentums* (1919; *Religion of Reason out of the Sources of Judaism*), Eliezer Berkovits has given a trenchant summary of this aspect of Cohen's theory of origin. Berkovits notes that for Cohen, 'Religion must find the origin of Becoming, and finds it in Being that is identified as God. God is the precondition of Becoming, which is the world of nature and of man. God as Being is the explanation of Becoming.'[17]

Berkovits's explanation allows us to comprehend how it is possible for Rosenzweig, in his introduction to Cohen's Jewish writings, to so casually note that man is a part of nature, a casualness surprising in view of the enormous energy Rosenzweig devotes in *The Star of Redemption* to establishing the independent integrity of the three realms of man, world, and God. Seen from the perspective of origin, God is the sine qua non of Becoming. Man and nature exist in an a priori relationship to Becoming, while God is Becoming's a priori ground. These relationships allow for the positing of creation. As Berkovits puts it, 'since God is thus conceived as the origin of Becoming, he is of necessity the source of all activity. This yields us the idea of creation.'[18] Nature and man are on one side of the equation of creation, and God is on the other. Using Cohen's infinitesimal analysis to refute the doctrines of emanation and idealism, Rosenzweig implicitly came to similar conclusions, in *The Star of Redemption*, concerning God's relationship to the origin of the world (SE 150–53). In the introduction to Cohen's Jewish writings, Rosenzweig notes that the 'Individuum quand même' is philosophically comprehensible only through God (z 209). Seen in this light, Cohen's theological concept of origin provides for Rosenzweig a positive counterweight to Hegel's supposed vision of an immanent origin generative of political, social, and religious institutions that reduce the individual to an abstraction subject to historical destiny, a vision described by Rosenzweig in his book on Hegel and the state.

Cohen's most well-known articulation of a theory of origin occurs not in his theological writings but in the form of a previously mentioned 'logic of origin' in his *Logik der reinen Erkenntnis* (1902; Logic of pure cognition). It is this work's principle of origin that Rosenzweig implicitly cites in *The Star of Redemption* as a foundation upon which he would build. An examination of the theory of origin in *Logik der reinen Erkenntnis* will thus provide a useful introduction to Rosenzweig's own views on origin in *The Star of Redemption*. At the outset of his book, Cohen attempts to establish the criteria of 'pure cognition.' He traces the history of this concept from its roots in mythology through a variety of stages still tinged with the impure affects of human consciousness. He sees such impurities in the conflation of the realms of logic and metaphysics, the blending of the logical and ethical spheres, and the inability of the romantic school to differentiate between pure cognition and the intuition of the genius. Such confusion results when one seeks the origin of thought in realms external to thought itself. Thus, Cohen uses an immanent approach in addressing the problem of pure cognition. In doing so, he finds logic to be the only epistemological system that can generate pure cognition: 'Thinking may not have any origin external to itself, if its purity must be otherwise unlimited and unobscured. Pure thinking, within itself and exclusively, must beget exclusively pure cognitions. Consequently, the theory of thinking must become the theory of cognition. *We are attempting to organize logic as such a theory of thinking which is in itself the theory of cognition.*'[19] Cohen goes on to demonstrate that the logic grounding pure cognition is the logic of mathematics. It is in the realm of mathematical science that thinking breaks free of its mythologico-psychological substrates.[20]

Having established that mathematical logic is the ground of pure cognition, Cohen devotes a chapter in the introductory portion of his book to illustrating what he terms the 'logic of origin.' He opens this seminal chapter by citing Nicholas of Cusa's dictum that mathematics is the only certainty we possess. He credits Cusa with making the mathematical concept of infinity the fulcrum of scientific knowledge. Cohen goes on to discern two fundamental schools of thought in the search for the epistemological foundation of scientific reason: atomism and infinitesimal analysis. The ancient atomistic doctrine holds that atoms are the ground of Being, as they form the smallest indivisible totalities. According to this hypothesis (the basic presupposition of chemistry), atoms are the origin of Being. The other school of thought finds the origin of Being in emptiness ('das Leere'). This is the postulate of infinitesimal analysis, the path taken by physics and the 'legitimate instrument of mathematical science,' although neither logic nor mathematics is fully aware of the centrality of this principle as a heuristic tool.[21]

The analysis of the infinite achieves this status by virtue of its ability to ground the problem of origin. Cohen goes on to speak of 'the principle of origin.' He states that the principle is cognition ('Erkenntnis') and that principle now signifies origin.[22] This equation of principle, origin, and cognition is quite obscure, but it is clarified by Walter Kinkel's explanation of Cohen's use of the term 'Prinzip' ('principle'). According to Kinkel, Cohen employs this term to indicate the method by which pure cognitions are themselves to be devised. Reflecting Plato's conception of origin ('Ursprungsgedanke'), which ascribes to thinking alone the task of generating Being, Cohen's principle of origin ('Ursprungsprinzip') is characterized by an exclusively immanent epistemology.[23]

As principle – that is, as a means of articulating pure cognition – origin becomes the ground of thought, as *Ursprung* is the sole category capable of the engendering of thought in a purely immanent way. Although Cohen does not say so directly, this immanence must be tied to *Ursprung*'s evocation of a 'leap into being' without any reference to external categories. Thinking for Cohen must have no origin external to itself if it is to produce the pure cognitions he associates with logic. Thus, Cohen must find a zero point – what he later calls a Nought ('das Nichts') – capable of giving pure thought a basis in reality. He is here forced into what appears to be a tautology, as only an immanent origin itself is capable of giving rise to such pure thought, the thought of logic, in Cohen's system. What obviates the tautology of this move somewhat is Cohen's investment of *Ursprung* with endlessness, rendering it 'new' and 'genuine.' This infinite quality in the category of origin was not evident in Cohen's earlier definition of pure thought. It becomes the fulcrum of Cohen's logic of origin. The anchoring of logic's fulcrum in the pure cognition of origin, and the concomitant investment of the task of logic with an infinite quality, allows Cohen to claim he has broken new ground.[24]

I noted in chapter 3 that Adorno criticized Husserl's sphere of absolute origins for the pure subjectivity, devoid of all traces of nonidentical externality, in which this sphere finds its ground. Cohen seeks to base his principle of origin on the pure cognition he finds in infinitesimal analysis precisely to avoid the taint of irrational subjective psychology he finds in other epistemological systems. Nevertheless, his attempt to establish a purely immanent origin, stripped of all influences external to subjective cognition, renders it as identitarian as the philosophy of origin Adorno identified in the works of Hegel and Husserl. We have established the validity of Buck-Morss's claim that Adorno and Rosenzweig shared an aversion to closed systems and totalistic thinking, particularly as they found such tendencies manifested in the philosophy of Hegel. Thus, it must surprise us when Rosenzweig in *The Star of Redemption* accepts Cohen's logic of origin as a foundation for his own thought largely because it is devoid of all Hegelian tendencies: 'Though the master may thoroughly deny it, we are continuing to build upon the great scientific achievement of his logic of origin, the new concept of the Nought. Though he may be otherwise more a Hegelian than he conceded in the execution of his thoughts – and thus as much an "idealist" as he asserted – here, in this foundational thought, he made a decisive break with the idealistic tradition' (SE 23). In its immanence and mathematical certitudes, Cohen's logic of origin would appear to be as Hegelian as any other element Rosenzweig might have identified in his thought. Indeed, Benjamin, despite the immanence of his own principle of origin, quite explicitly identified a Hegelian cast of thought in the abandonment of historical fact for logical certitude in Cohen's logic of origin:

> Contrary to Cohen's belief, the category of origin is thus not purely logical, but historical. The Hegelian dictum 'so much the worse for the facts' is well known. In principle, it signifies

that the insight into the relationships between essences lies within the philosopher's purview and that the relationships between essences remain what they are, even when they do not imprint themselves in a pure form in the world of facts. This genuinely idealistic attitude purchases its certainty by abandoning the core of the idea of origin. (1:226)

Cohen's logic of origin seeks to abandon the historically constituted real world in favor of an inner realm of mathematical abstractions and would eliminate the disturbing but genuine psychological cast of human thought in favor of the lifeless perfections spun out by pure cognition. In this sense, Benjamin is correct to see in Cohen's logic of origin a 'Hegelian' desertion of the world of facts.

Before we examine precisely what it is that Rosenzweig finds revolutionary and distinctly nonidealistic in Cohen's logic of origin, it is important to point out that Rosenzweig, at the very outset of *The Star of Redemption,* exhibits as strong an aversion to the abstract universalism he finds in German idealism as Benjamin and Adorno do. As surprising as it may seem in the light of Benjamin's apparently sound critique of the logic of origin, it is precisely the ability of this logic to be used as a means to undermine idealist universalism that makes it valuable in Rosenzweig's eyes. The opening line of Rosenzweig's book appears to contradict Cohen, who established mathematics as the basis of pure cognition. According to Rosenzweig, 'Vom Tode, von der Furcht des Todes, hebt alles Erkennen des All an' (SE 3) [All cognition of the All commences with death, with the fear of death]. Thus, absolute human cognition is rooted in the fear of absolute emptiness, absolute nothingness. Idealistic philosophy seeks to ignore this circumstance – it turns its back on the a priori of cognition, on the 'dark precondition of all life' (SE 5) in its search for the All. Just as Benjamin foregrounds the theme of death and looming nullity in the baroque allegory to subvert the lifeless unitarianism of the classical symbol and as Adorno asserts the ephemerality of origin over against the hermetically sealed, subjectively constituted timelessness of the philosophy of origin, so Rosenzweig confronts idealism's search for a universal and presuppositionless cognition of the All with the agony of the human death cry. It is precisely in Cohen's logic of origin that Rosenzweig finds a philosophical ground to sustain his principle of the Nought as a weapon against what he finds to be the empty abstractions of idealist philosophy.[25]

What allows Rosenzweig to do this is Cohen's discussion of the *judgment* of origin in *Logik der reinen Erkenntnis*. Remaining faithful to his earlier thesis that cognition is pure only when the origin of thought is immanent and seeks no ground outside itself, Cohen characterizes the belief that one can add an Aught ('Etwas') to thought as an error. Only that which thought finds out for itself can be established as a given. An Aught such as that symbolized by the letter 'A' already signifies a certain value. Given the externality of this value to thought, which only gives rise to genuine cognition when it is immanently generated, there is no hope of discovering the origin of the Aught. To be more precise, one cannot find the origin of the Aught in the Aught itself. Cognitive judgment must make a detour to establish the origin of the Aught, and this detour can only be constituted by the Nought.[26] At the outset of his chapter on the judgment of origin, Cohen had found the question of origin to be directly connected to the question of chaos; the transformation of the problem of origin into the question of the origin of spiritual Being disguises and represses this chaos.[27]

By making the Nought into the a priori of the origin of the existent, Cohen once again confronts philosophy with the looming abyss of chaos inherent in the concept of origin. Cohen sees Anaximander as responsible for shifting the question of origin to the question of the origin of spiritual Being by equating origin with the eternal. Eternality (or infinity) and immortality are, of course, proximate concepts. Cohen believes immortality is an example of infinite judgment, the antithesis of the judgment of origin. Just as the origin of the Aught can only be ascertained by the judgment of cognition through a detour into the Nought, so the principle of the spirit is arrived at by passing through the shadow image both of life and all those concepts life holds dear: soul, immortality, and eternality. That shadow image is death. The origin of the Aught is anchored in the Nought. The origin of the spirit in the human soul is anchored in man's creaturely mortality.[28]

Cohen comes very close here to embracing fully what we saw characterized by Nietzsche in an entirely different context as the theory of the *pudenda origo*, the view that mankind's noblest and most ethereal precepts are rooted in dark or shameful notions, in fear of death, in the chasm of nonexistence, and in physical ephemerality. Cohen tries to pull back from this chasm by drawing on Leibniz's mathematical principle of continuity as a law of thought, reinvoking his own postulate that thought generates origin, and then turning the Nought (as the fulcrum of the judgment of origin) into a principle of benign harmonious epistemological continuity: 'Kein Schreckbild des Nichts unterbricht diesen Zusammenhang der zu erzeugenden Ursprungseinheiten. Nirgend darf ein Abgrund gähnen. Das Nichts bildet überall den wahren Übergang'[29] [No bogeyman of the Nought interrupts this cohesion of the units of origin that are to be generated. Nowhere can an abyss be allowed to yawn. The Nought constitutes everywhere the true transition].

It is, of course, too late. Cohen's anchoring of the question of origin in the thought of chaos, his establishment of the Nought as the sole detour leading to the Aught, and his discovery of the origin of spirit in the seed of death rooted in man's animal Being has opened an abyss so wide that not even the authorizing voice of a Leibniz can close it. However, the abyss that Cohen has opened only to draw back from is rediscovered by Rosenzweig, who uses it as a dump site for the lifeless and deathless chimeras he finds in German idealism. In accusing Cohen of betraying an idealistic attitude, Benjamin clearly comprehends Cohen's own conception of his project: at the conclusion of *Logik der reinen Erkenntnis* Cohen characterizes pure cognition as a 'triumph of idealism' and notes that the logic of origin turns the logic of science into the logic of idealism.[30] However, Benjamin only follows Cohen's exploration of pure logic *as far as* the latter's establishment of a logic of origin. He does not consider Cohen's further journey into the dark and hidden recesses of this cognition, which must be explored in order for Cohen to articulate the judgment upon which this logic is based. Rosenzweig did follow Cohen to the precipice, but, while Cohen draws back from this seeming aporia, Rosenzweig welcomes it and turns it into a foundation upon which he can build. Rosenzweig clearly perceived Cohen's reticence; this is why he notes that Cohen would reject his attempt to build upon Cohen's logic of origin by further elucidating the new concept of the Nought and characterizes Cohen's methodology as essentially idealist (SE 23).

Where does the fruitful originality of Cohen's turn of thought lie? All traditional philosophies are confronted with a Nought, if only as the zero point from which they must build their systems. Certainly German idealism is no different in this regard. However, Rosenzweig credits Cohen with replacing idealism's general, undifferentiated Nought with a particular Nought. By postulating an undifferentiated zero point, idealism immediately makes the leap to Being, as pure cognition in its idealist form offers nothing to stand in the way of such a leap. Cohen creates a *particular* Nought by refusing to see in the Nought the simple a priori from which Being emerges and instead treating it as the detour ('Umweg') through which judgment must pass in order to arrive at the origin of the Aught. As we have seen, this detour also leads through chaos, ephemerality, contingency, and death, precisely those realms that Rosenzweig's idealists would avoid. Cohen's particular Nought – the Nought emerging from the judgment grounded in the logic of origin – can thus be utilized by Rosenzweig in order to confront idealism with its aporias.

Throughout the *Aesthetic Theory*, Adorno uses a similar formula, 'determinate negation' ('bestimmte Negation'), to show that crises, conflicts, and dilemmas belie the seeming continuity of artistic, social, and technical progress and harmony. However, determinate negation is also part of a harmonizing dialectical process in the aesthetic realm. For Adorno, determinate negation alone allows art to sustain its promise of reconciliation. The irresolvable antinomy existing between all works of art provides the sole basis for the unity of art history. Such unity is thus illusory unless we regard it as the 'dialectical figure of determinate negation' (7:59–60). Moreover, there is more utility in the logic of origin for Rosenzweig than is suggested by a merely negative application. As Rosenzweig reminds us, Cohen's Nought does, after all, point to the Aught, just as

Adorno's principle of determinate negation would allow aesthetics to mediate (though not identify) the genuine truth character of artworks (7:195). The Nought springs from the mathematical differential of Cohen's infinitesimal analysis rather than from idealism's single and undifferentiated zero point. Thus, the differential contains within itself the qualities both of the Aught and the Naught. It constitutes, indeed, both of these antipodes at once (SE 23).

Taking Cohen's differentiated Nought as a point of departure, Rosenzweig envisions a triple Nought, a Nought he already vaguely discerns in Cohen's 'Nichts des Wissens' ('Nought of knowledge'). Rosenzweig is hesitant to credit Cohen fully with having evolved a triple Nought because he is only able to clearly differentiate two discrete 'Noughts of knowledge' in Cohen's epistemology. These two Noughts apply to the 'metalogical' and 'metaethical' spheres (SE 24). As Rotenstreich has noted, Rosenzweig 'refers to *meta*physics in the context of his discussion of God and His being, to *meta*logic in the context of the world and its meaning, and to *meta*ethics in his consideration of man and his self.'[31] It was Rosenzweig's primary telos in writing *The Star of Redemption* to establish the spheres of man, world, and God as the interlocking yet discrete nodes of the existent (i.e., nonideal) universe. As *Logik der reinen Erkenntnis* was written prior to Cohen's theistic turn, Rosenzweig is reluctant to credit him with formulating a Nought of knowledge in the metaphysical realm – the realm of God. As we have already seen, Rosenzweig would later come to praise Cohen's principle of 'metaphysical' origin in his introductory essay to Cohen's Jewish writings.[32] In *The Star of Redemption*, however, Rosenzweig is already able to see in Cohen's logic of origin a useful epistemological foundation – with its universal yet differentiated principle of the Nought – in which to ground his universal yet differentiated planes of man, world, and God.

The influence of the logic of origin is evident throughout the course of *The Star of Redemption* almost every time some aspect of the principle of origin is addressed. For example, shortly after his elucidation of Cohen's Noughts of knowledge, Rosenzweig makes the leap into the metaphysical realm he saw only dimly outlined in

Logik der reinen Erkenntnis – he establishes God as, initially, a Nought. It is through a Cohenian detour into God as Nought that Rosenzweig arrives at the Aught of God, which is God in his internal fullness. Rosenzweig describes the evocation of the Aught of God from what we perceive as the Nought of God as an act of liberation, but, adhering to Cohen's principle of purely immanent cognition, he emphasizes that God cannot be acted upon from outside. It is action through which the action of the Aught of God breaks forth, but this very action can never be related to something outside of God. It is the shattering ('Zerschlagen') of the All into an All for itself – in other words, the establishment of God as a particular Nought – that renders this action possible (SE 27–28). The establishment of particular Noughts allows for the emergence of differentiated origins in the still stream of essence (SE 27). Essence is bound to origin, while action is bound to beginning (SE 26). Insofar as Cohen noted that essentiality is activated with the emergence of the question of origin, the derivation of essence from origin is consistent with Cohen's principle of origin.[33] The derivation of differentiated origins from particular Noughts is related to Rosenzweig's discovery of discrete Noughts of knowledge in *Logik der reinen Erkenntnis;* as all origin is grounded in the pure cognition of immanent thought, differentiated origins must be possible if this knowledge can be bi- or trifurcated.

However, the equation of beginning and action is tied to Rosenzweig's conception of the logos rather than what he learned from Cohen; positive affirmation – 'das Ja' – is 'in the beginning.' It is the point of departure, the archetypal word that sets creation into motion. It is the first step in the path toward the perfection of God (SE 28–29). The action implied in 'Anfang' ('beginning') is this first step, the step that sets in motion the evocation of God in his immanent fullness. However, even this first step partakes of Cohen's technique of infinitesimal analysis.[34] In a reversal characteristic of Cohen's logic of origin, Rosenzweig postulates that the detour of the negating predicate ('x') must be taken to arrive at the affirmative subject ('y') or the 'Yea' that is to be found in the beginning, insofar as the beginning is only arrived at through the establishment of origin; or, as Rosenzweig puts it, this algebraic reversal – which is necessary to evoke the Yea – must take place precisely because it is here that we are dealing with the question of origins (SE 29).

Another important element in Rosenzweig's distinction between origin and beginning has been elucidated by Stéphane Mosès. Mosès notes that Rosenzweig both encompasses and generates the proper name as the absolute origin of the coordinates of the world. The proper name is used by the 'I' as a means by which to affirm, on a personal basis, the revelation of the creation of the world, of which the 'I' is the center. However, whereas the human experiences him- or herself in this way as the founder of the coordinates of space and time, the Judeo-Christian vision of the world undermines the unmediated link between space and time. Time has a beginning; indeed, Mosès, with perhaps unintended irony, refers to this beginning ('commencement') as the origin ('origine') of time. Only space has a center; this center is space's origin. Jewish mythology is linked to the spatial dimension, as Jews experience origin as a center outside of time, a center itself anchored to the timeless concept of a 'holy land.' Christians experience origin as a beginning anchored to the birth of Christ. As Christian experience is anchored in the temporal dimension, the Christian concept of history evolves indifferently in all directions of space. The two dimensions – center and beginning, space and time, Judaism and Christianity – define the world of revelation in Rosenzweig's system. However, Mosès hints without explicitly stating that these dimensions are only arrived at for Rosenzweig through the negating predicate of the origin, in this case the name of God. The name of God is a particular Nought, the Nought through which the Yea at the beginning must pass to attain its status as an Aught. Mosès notes that Rosenzweig's use of the proper name as the absolute origin of the coordinates of the world is derived from the Jewish tradition that saw in the revelation at Sinai the revelation of the name of God. It should be added that Rosenzweig sees revelation, springing as it does from the moment, as being able to free creation from its fear that it will sink back into its origin in the Nought (SE 180). Revelation, however, is anchored in creation, as creation is the keystone of revelation. Only divine love allows the latter to emerge from the former (SE 174). In this sense, both revelation and creation stand under the sign of the Nought. Both Jewish and Christian mythologies must take the Cohenian detour through the Nought of the revelatory 'name of God as the name of origin' (Mosès) in order to become the Aughts of space and time.[35]

Rosenzweig was opposed to what he perceived to be Hegel's closed system, which was allegedly grounded in universal reason and a univocal view of origin. Cohen's particular Noughts allowed for the positing of what Rosenzweig termed the 'verschiedene Ursprünge des Bestimmten' (SE 27) [different origins of the determinate]. The concept of different origins of the determinate helps to ground Rosenzweig's discussion of reason in the world. He notes that thought ('Das Denken') pours into the world as a variegated system of individual determinations. The unity inherent in this system is not based on the sort of universal reason that evokes the world in abstract and undifferentiated thought. Rather, its unity derives from its discrete sphere of application – the world – and not from a uniform origin. As in our relationship to God, we know nothing of the world and we arrive at knowledge of the essence of the world – its Aught – only through the detour of the Nought (SE 45). A uniform origin is postulated prior to the application of thought, but the definite application of thought to Being makes this postulate impossible to prove. Rosenzweig adds, 'as this uniform origin did not lie in the world, the path from the "pure" – which had to be presupposed – to "applied" came to lie outside the realm of power of applied thought' (SE 46).

The knowledge of the world engendered by thought directed to Being-in-the-world (Dasein) is a discrete Nought of knowledge. Rosenzweig does not undermine the idealistic concept of universal reason by dismissing the possibility that it is informed by a uniform origin. Indeed, he is quite unequivocal in his postulation of a uniform and unifying *aesthetic* origin at the core of every work of art (SE 216). By creating a trifurcation of knowledge, however – knowledge of man, world, and God – cognitive reason (thought) is forced into specific spheres of applicability and thus must forego the possibility of actually demonstrating the unity of its origin (SE 46). The articulation of these three spheres creates differentiated origins.

Rosenzweig's concept of origin not only undermines the idealist concept of universal reason, it also fractures the unity of the idealist All. Quite early in *The Star of Redemption*, Rosenzweig attacked this ethereal realm by confronting it with the fact of human mortality, a fact Rosenzweig's idealists wished to skirt. However, this was only a starting point, as Rosenzweig's retrospective glance at the first part of his book makes clear. He notes that he has smashed the cosmic All by dividing it into the spheres of man, world, and God. This fracturing takes place as we search for the origin of the Aught upon its emergence from out of the Nought: 'The more deeply we descended into the night of the positive in order to seize the Aught directly at its origin from the Nought, the more the unity of the All shattered for us' (SE 91). The origin of the positive – the Aught – in the Nought belies the idealist concept of the All. The All is shattered precisely at the interstice between Aught and Nought, as the former emerges from its origin out of the latter.

What is revealed to us of the essence of man-world-God is manifested at the site where the subjective Aught makes its primal leap – its 'Ur-sprung' – from the predicative Nought. As with Nietzsche and Adorno, then, what emerges into perceived essence – as idea, as historical phenomenon, or, in Rosenzweig's case, as the revelation of one of the three cosmic spheres – occurs at the interstice governed by origin. The destruction of the unity of the All through the origin of the Aught from out of the Nought results in a scattered mass of disconnected elements, unrecognizable to us because they are torn out of their familiar, everyday constellation. In the subtitle to this discussion, Rosenzweig refers to this condition as 'The Chaos of the Elements' (SE 91). The influence of Cohen is undoubtedly reflected in this formulation, as it was Cohen who noted the relationship between the thought of chaos and the earliest historical interest in the question of origin. Cohen finds that with the progressive abstraction and spiritualization of Being, and after Anaximander's postulation of the infinite, the interest in the question of origin disappears.[36]

When Rosenzweig smashes the abstract, infinite All, the primal chaos of the elements attains once more its central ontological force, and the question of origin becomes paramount once again.

The chaos of the elements is ontological, a newly emergent fact of Being. Origin is preontological, anchored in the Nought of knowledge. The elements, having become factual results through Rosenzweig's smashing of the All, must themselves become origins in order for the spheres of man, world, and God to become reconstituted as a genuine constellation.[37] This is the gist of Rosenzweig's position on the question of origin in the transition of part 1 of *The Star of Redemption*, entitled 'The Elements or the Perpetual Pre-World,' to part 2, 'The Path or the Eternally Renewed World.' Having emerged from their origin in the Nought of knowledge, the purely factual of the elements reconstitutes itself as 'the origin of real movement' (SE 97). As origin, it thus itself attains preontological status, generating the emergence into Being of the eternally renewed world.[38]

The All is shattered, and its elements reconstituted, at the site of an interstice governed by origin. The reconstituted elements form a beginning or passageway between two seemingly antithetical poles, the Nought and the Aught of knowledge (SE 96–97). Nevertheless, Rosenzweig might object to describing the two movements – from the All to the elements, from the elements to the renewed world – as a 'dialectics of the interstice,' the term we used in connection with Nietzsche's concept of origin. In explaining that the Nay and the Yea stand in an unmediated relationship to their origin, Rosenzweig expressly rejects the use of a dialectical model that would see the Nay as the antithesis of the Yea (SE 124–25). What, however, do Yea and Nay signify? The context in which Rosenzweig comes out against a dialectical interpretation of the Yea and the Nay is a discussion of God as creator. Freund notes, 'With respect to God the Yea affirms something infinite, His essence, and the Nay negates something finite, His freedom. The And joins freedom and essence together into living unity. Strictly speaking, this union results not from the two extremes, but rather from two points that already have been modified by each other.'[39] It is important not to conflate the Yea with the Aught and the Nay with the Nought. The bond between freedom and essence attains an a priori status by virtue of the mutual and contemporaneous origin of freedom and essence in the Nought. Were this not the case, freedom unfettered by the facticity of the essential could be evoked as absolute spirit, and then we would arrive at Hegel's dialectically mediated realm. The mutual and contemporaneous origin of the Yea and the Nay in the Nought had been established at the outset of *The Star of Redemption* (SE 30–31). In rejecting a dialectical model as a means of interpreting their relationship, Rosenzweig merely confirms what he has already asserted. However, the Aught and the Nought are anchored in no such Leibnizian prestabilized harmony. The Nought is the precondition of the Aught, and like Judaism and Christianity, they exist in a relationship of dynamic tension. In the gap between them, governed by the origin of the Nought, the elements emerge, reconstitute themselves, and become origins in turn. In this sense, it is possible to speak of a nonsynthesizing yet productive dialectics of the interstice in Rosenzweig's concept of origin.

Rosenzweig's belief that origins lack a unified point of departure and are only manifested in an interstice is also reflected in his language theory. He emphasizes that the origin of speech is grounded in a separation, the division between an 'I' and an Other. The 'I' cannot constitute a homogeneous beginning for speech; speech only exists because another lives. Speech is contingent upon a separation that it can bridge but never close. As relationships are time-bound, so too is speech. Language, according to Rosenzweig, is for-the-Other, and, before it comes into being, the 'I' and the Other must be aware of the gulf between them.[40] But what about language's theological dimension? Rosenzweig characterizes the logos of God as a beginning – God's archetypal word sets creation into motion. In his discussion of God as the creator, Rosenzweig clarifies his position on the archetypal word of God as the beginning of creation. The actual beginning ('Anfang') is the fact that God created. God's having spoken is but the audible fulfillment and the first great miracle of the silent beginning, the act of creation (SE 124). Rosenzweig also speaks of God's creating as the beginning of his self-expression (SE 125). God's creation of the world springs from the primal 'Yea' as a beginning, not as an origin. Also, as Udoff has argued, God's revelation is not to be treated in Rosenzweig's theology as an origin.[41] Origin is prior to revelation and redemption, although both the creation and the subsequent destiny 'of the People' (the Jews) is latent within it. Indeed, origin as the site of the creation of the Jewish people conceals revelation and final redemption (SE 353).

Is any element of Rosenzweig's hypercosmic scheme anchored in an origin springing directly from God? Our question receives a positive response toward the close of *The Star of Redemption:* 'Die Wahrheit ist von Gott. Gott ist ihr Ursprung. Wenn sie selber das Leuchten ist, so ist er das Licht, von dem ihr Leuchten urspringt.' [The truth is from God. God is its origin. When it is itself the illumination, then God is the light from which its illumination primally leaps]. God is the truth (SE 432), and the truth is its own final presupposition (SE 431). God as the origin of the truth, with the related postulates that God Himself is the truth and that the truth as a privileged ground is not subject to subversion or even limitation because it forms its own ultimate presupposition – all this seems to undo the view that origin finds its ground in the particular Nought, although God Himself is the particular Nought. Worse, positing God as the unmediated origin of truth appears to be an example of 'the metahistorical deployment of ideal significations and indefinite teleologies' Foucault objected to in the 'search for "origins"' (NGH 140).

Such a judgment is mitigated by a description of trust in the truth that actually seems to confirm it: 'All trust in the truth is thus based on an ultimate trust that the ground upon which the truth places itself with its own feet is able to support it' (SE 431). What is this 'ultimate trust'—seemingly privileged over the experience of the factual – Rosenzweig refers to? According to Michael Theunissen, 'the *Star of Redemption* develops the thesis that, in the fundamental dialogical comportment, in hoping trust, the future is present' and that 'Rosenzweig distinguishes reality from essence, that is, from truth.'[42] The ultimate trust in the ground of truth and the assertion that God is truth are themselves simply the ground of faith and hope rather than teleological postulates or ideal significations. Man's dialogical openness to God is also an openness to the future, not a premonition of some ultimate universal truth that the future may hold in store for us. Truth may have its origin in God, but it is far from being a universal concept (SE 432). Moreover, Rosenzweig suggests at the conclusion of *The Star of Redemption* that our cognition of God's truth – the countenance He turns upon us – is only partial (SE 465). Human cognition can only conceive of, but cannot grasp, ultimate, divine truth. The idealistic, epistemological embrace of the All could never become an actualizable telos for Rosenzweig, for whom cognition is rooted in – has its origin in – the finitude of mortality and the fear this finitude generates within us.

Theunissen's attempt to pose reality and truth or essence as antitheses in Rosenzweig's thought is somewhat misstated. Rosenzweig notes, 'Thus, if God is truth, this is no less the case with reality. Even reality's ultimate essence is the truth. Next to the proposition "God is truth" stands, with equal validity, the other proposition: "reality is truth"' (SE 429). What allows this fusion of essence, reality, and truth? What establishes the eternal truth, the enduring Being of God? It is the trust and faith of the human soul (SE 190–91). What is the origin of the soul? This origin is reached only by a detour into the Nought of man's defiant individuality. Defiance itself is the secret origin of the soul, providing it with steadfastness, the ability to maintain a strong and independent character (SE 190). The *Ursprung* of truth is anchored in God; God both encompasses and generates the 'primal leap' of truth's illumination (SE 432).

This illumination does not reveal an abstract, universal realm. God's revelation is always only partial and particular. Moreover, the enduring Being of God Himself is only instantiated through man's soul, itself anchored in the origin of the particular Nought of man's defiance. The truth may contain its own ultimate presupposition, but it is not detached from the particular essence of the individual human soul. This leads us to the conclusion that Rosenzweig does not privilege the divine or metaphysical realm, a charge Said, Foucault, and others have leveled at the principle of origin and its adherents. Certainly, Rosenzweig's postulation of God as the origin of truth is a postulation of metaphysical origin. However, each man's perception of God's truth is radically ephemeral, individual, and particular: 'Daß Gott die Wahrheit ist in jenem

Sinne, in dem wir es nun festgestellt haben: Ursprung der Wahrheit, – ich kann es nur erfahren, indem ich erfahre, daß er "mein
Teil" ist, "der Anteil meines Kelchs, am Tag da ich ihn rufe."' (SE
437) [That God is the truth in that sense we have established: origin of truth – I can only experience it by experiencing that He is
"my share," "the portion of my chalice on the day I call upon Him."]
The attempt to perceive God in the infinity of His creative acts
reduces Him to the mere 'origin' of creation and conceals Him
from man (SE 179). His countenance is revealed to the individual
only as the origin of a finite and individually mediated truth. Indeed, only by virtue of the radical ephemerality and particularity
of what inheres in origin is one permitted a sense of created life in
its totality (SE 181).

Rosenzweig is the only thinker discussed in this book whose
principle of origin is rooted in an unequivocal theism. He is un-
apologetic in his evocation of a metaphysical sphere, the very notion of which is anathema to poststructuralist philosophy. He was a
fervent believer in the messianic idea. Indeed, the ardentness of his
messianism, with its promise of eternal redemption, led to a heated
argument with Cohen.[43] It is ironic, then, that origin in Rosenzweig's thought is tied more emphatically to the qualities of particularity, ephemerality, alterity, plurality, and antiuniversalist fi-
niteness than it is with any of the figures treated thus far. These are
the characteristics most critics miss in the principle of origin. With
its own origin anchored in the mortality of the individual human
being and springing from death, Rosenzweig's philosophy was
perhaps bound to find them.

CHAPTER 5

Origin's Pluralistic Simultaneity:
Martin Heidegger

No modern philosopher has staked out more controversial positions on the principle of origin than Martin Heidegger. I have already noted the powerful denunciations of Heidegger's *Ursprungsphilosophie* by Adorno and Karl Jaspers. In this chapter, I will return to their arguments as well as examine attacks on the part of other leading twentieth-century thinkers. Certainly, Adorno, Jaspers, and others have presented a powerful case for the belief that Heidegger's philosophy of origin lends explicit support to subjectively constituted totalitarianism and indeed to fascistic dogma. More contemporary poststructuralist critics have accused Heidegger of engaging in (to use Jacques Derrida's well-known term) a 'metaphysics of presence,' which is to say that Heidegger attempts to overcome alterity, ephemerality, and the limits of conceptual finitude.

The ambivalence in Heidegger's evocation of origin is particularly acute in the political sphere. Derrida has shown that Heidegger's favoring of the German term *Geist* as a means of conjuring up the most preoriginary event in the metaphysical tradition ('pré-archi-originarité') – the event Heidegger would bring forth by summoning the modern (i.e., the German 1930s) spirit – tacitly underwrites Nazi claims to philosophical and political superiority. Adorno's critique of Heidegger's *Ursprungsphilosophie* as the attempt to render spirit visible is also quite cogent in placing Heideggerian spirit, origin, and the legitimation of Nazi metaphysics and politics into the same constellation. Heidegger's glorification of inner Being and internal relationships and his concomitant neglect of the social fabric (except at a highly abstracted level) are also convincingly tied by Adorno to Heidegger's obsession with origin. The consequences of these priorities for Heidegger's initial embrace of Nazism, as well as for his strained postwar apolitical stance, are obvious. Derrida, Adorno, Jaspers, Habermas, and others have made their case against Heidegger's intertwining of *Ursprungs-philosophie* with a dangerous politically tinged metaphysics quite well. My highlighting of counterinstances in Heidegger's work in this chapter is not an attempt to refute categorically their accusations nor to justify Heidegger's political tendencies (or, after World War II, his unconvincing lack thereof). I do so primarily to emphasize his productive contribution to a theory of radical origin.

The apparently surprising contiguity between Heidegger's philosophy and that of the subject of the last chapter, Franz Rosenzweig, is perhaps the best place to begin. On the surface, few modern thinkers appear more dissimilar. Rosenzweig, after all, adhered to a resolutely Jewish theism after his famous 'reconversion' to Judaism after his experience at Yom Kippur services in 1913. Heidegger not only consistently avoided all traces of theism, but his infamous embrace of Nazism in the 1930s has left him open to the charge – still hotly debated – of at least tacit anti-Semitism. Nevertheless, both Karl Löwith and Alan Udoff have convincingly argued that there are strong affinities between the views of Heidegger and Rosenzweig. In an essay originally written as a postscript to Heidegger's most influential work, *Sein und Zeit* (1927; *Being and Time*), Löwith notes that both Rosenzweig and Heidegger 'took the "facticity" of human Dasein as [their] common starting point.'[1] For Rosenzweig, the assumption of this facticity of human Dasein attains fundamental significance in diverting his philosophy of origin away from a complete adherence to the transcendent foundation of the metaphysical realm. What Heidegger came to call the 'thrownness' of Dasein's facticity creates a primal fear of transience in man, according to Rosenzweig. It is precisely this circumstance, however, that roots man in the world, so that man, world, and God become interlocking but discrete and coequal points of the triangle on Rosenzweig's star of redemption. We will see that the charge of 'metaphysics' leveled at Heidegger must be tempered by the fact that Heidegger never wavered from his adherence to this facticity. Indeed, as Löwith shows, this adherence can be taken as a positive sign that 'each man directed his thought away from the metaphysics of consciousness of German idealism.'[2] The refusal on the part of both men to adhere to the path of metaphysical idealism is rooted in their acknowledgment that death stands at the center of human existence and must ground philosophy, although Löwith accurately contrasts the purity of Heidegger's acceptance of existential finitude with Rosenzweig's affirmation of an eternity linked to the metaphysical realm of God.[3] Of course, the charge of metaphysical totalitarianism is generally not directed at a teleological *forward* thrust in Heidegger's philosophy of origin but at an apparent *backward leap* into a suprahistorical primal realm.[4] Thus, Heidegger's resolute commitment to the principle of human finitude does not alone absolve him of the charge of engaging in a pernicious transcendentalism.

Udoff opens his essay 'Rosenzweig's Heidegger Reception and the re-Origination of Jewish Thinking' by recognizing the inevitable gulf that separates Heidegger and Jewish writers such as Paul Celan and Rosenzweig, a gulf created by Heidegger's Nazi past. However, Udoff insists that one can – indeed must – articulate a common ground for Rosenzweig and Heidegger and that the two meet in 'the space of originative thinking.'[5] He concludes his essay by noting that it is the space of interrogation both encompassed and generated by the question of origin in which 'Rosenzweig and Heidegger may be found to meet.' Udoff suggests that this space of originative interrogation is tied to the 'radical questioning' of Being that informs the discourse of both men. This questioning challenges the validity of the nominal 'dividing lines,' artificially distinguishing between the phenomenal and the noumenal, through which philosophy has isolated and marginalized Being within a recondite metaphysical sphere.[6] In the last chapter, we discovered that it was Cohen's logic of origin – tied to a principle of cognition that only opens up a space for epistemology by first placing it under the sign of the Nought – that forced Rosenzweig to recognize the aporia of Being under the sign of the German idealists' abstract universalism. Partly through the influence of the judgment underlying Cohen's logic of origin, Rosenzweig stripped Being of the twin idealistic comforts of immortality and subjective control. This inspires him to consistently underscore Being's factical and finite dimensions. The space of origin is thus, as Udoff suggests, the instrument that leads Rosenzweig to rethink the question of Being by transcending the 'metaphysical stasis' that informs traditional ontology.[7]

For Heidegger, as well as for Rosenzweig and Cohen, the Nought invokes a principle more originary ('ursprünglicher') than negation or the use of the syntactic negator (the 'Nicht,' the simply 'Not') themselves: 'Wir behaupten: das Nichts ist ursprünglicher als das Nicht und die Verneinung' [We assert: the Nought is more originary than the 'Not' and negation].[8] This claim is found in the essay 'Was ist Metaphysik?' (1929; 'What Is Metaphysics?'). In the fifth edition of 'What Is Metaphysics?' (1949), Heidegger revised this passage by making the Nought the very order of origin ('Ursprungsordnung') (GA 9:108). Moreover, as with Rosenzweig and Cohen, it is human dread ('Angst') through which the Nought reveals itself to Heidegger (GA 9:113). All three thinkers believed that dread propels man to confront the Nought as the originary ground of the facticity of Dasein. Dread brings man into the space of the Nought as the order of existential origin. This results in the stripping away of Being's abstract, cogito-based universality. Being must reveal itself through Dasein. Dasein always serves Sein as the locus where Sein shows itself. However, Sein thus manifested as Being-in-the-world (Dasein) is devoid of metaphysical comforts. By placing Heidegger within the boundaries of *this* originative space, a space we have seen occupied by Rosenzweig and – with less resolution – by Cohen, the demystifying strain in Heidegger's 'philosophy of origin' begins to emerge. Undoubtedly, this element in Heidegger's *Ursprungsphilosophie* would be denied by Adorno and Jaspers, who tie Heidegger's treatment of origin to dangerously obscurantist aspects of his thought.

Of course, as my chapter on Adorno made clear, the critique of the Heideggerian principle of origin by Adorno and Jaspers has merit. However, when Jaspers calls Heidegger's move toward *Ursprung* an 'evasion into the before and after' and an 'appealing to the most extreme,' he overlooks the way in which Heidegger brings human dread and the order of origin into contiguity.[9] Such a move is no evasion into the before and after but the most direct confrontation with what we saw Rosenzweig refer to in *The Star of Redemption* as the 'dark precondition of all life' (SE 5), namely, death and the foreboding it generates. Even prior to addressing such issues in *Being and Time*, Heidegger made an attempt to connect origin to the facticity of existence, to the Being of Being-in-the-world as care (*Sorge*) and to evade the evasions of what Heidegger refers to as *Scheinursprünglichkeit*, the 'illusion of originariness.' Perhaps ironically, Heidegger's most significant effort to deal with these issues in his pre–*Being and Time* writings is found in his 'Anmerkungen zu Karl Jaspers "Psychologie der Weltanschauungen"' (1919–21; Notes on Karl Jaspers's 'Psychology of World Perspectives'). In previewing the methodological orientation his examination of Jaspers's work will take, Heidegger rejects the use of such criteria as 'absolute truthful authority,' 'relativism,' and 'skepticism.' By going back and examining the motives at the origin ('Ursprungsmotiven') of such terminological conventions, Heidegger would call attention to their own earliest self-understanding and attempt to undermine their philosophical validity (GA 9:3).

Heidegger's critique of what he believes are idealized epistemological formulations is significant as an example of his early use of origin-grounded thinking to call the tradition-encrusted clichés of philosophical categories into radical question. It is true that the examination of *Ursprungsmotiven* proposed by Heidegger implies a backward-directed glance at the cognitive idealization of these categories. However, far from being an 'evasive leap into the beforehand,' as Jaspers puts it, Heidegger's historical probing would lay bare, in the manner of Nietzsche's genealogy, the hidden, perhaps 'shameful,' origins, of contemporary hypostatized philosophical classifications. Heidegger refers to his procedure as the history of ideas-grounded destruction of the transmitted, which would stand in contrast to yet another 'invention' of a new philosophical program. It gains its destructive power by examining the originary ground of primary philosophical experiences and, in the manner of Plato and Aristotle, would trace the sense-making character of 'theory' back to its origin (GA 9:3–4). Heidegger undertakes this careful explication of his methodology largely in order to forestall the charge of the 'Scheinursprünglichkeit' that might be directed against his approach, a feigned originariness he associated with 'life philosophy' (GA 9:4).

What does Heidegger mean by the feigned originariness of life philosophy? A possible answer is suggested by Paul Ricoeur's summary of the psychological element in Dilthey's hermeneutics because, together with Nietzsche, Dilthey can clearly be taken as the leading representative of life philosophy. According to Ricoeur, 'Dilthey sought the distinctive trait of understanding in psychology. Every science of the spirit – and by this Dilthey meant every knowledge of man implying some historical relation – presupposes a primordial capacity to place oneself into the psychical life of others.'[10] To such a transpersonal and transhistorical approach to a primordial psychology, Heidegger opposes a notion of primordiality (or, as I would prefer to put it, originariness) rooted in the factical, the historical, and the self: 'The significance of originariness [Urspründlichkeit] is not as an idea external to or above history. Rather, this significance reveals itself in the circumstance that the absence of presupposition itself can only be won in a factically, historically oriented *self-criticism'* (GA 9:5; my emphasis).

The importance of originariness for Heidegger is not rooted in the desire to transcend metaphysically the bounds of history and achieve an empathetic awareness of prior thinkers, although Heidegger is unquestionably indebted to Dilthey for some of his insights into the nature of hermeneutic understanding. Instead, the term *Urspründlichkeit* suggests to Heidegger the capacity to explore the self in its historical facticity. Once again, Heidegger's embrace of originary thinking, contrary to the critiques of Jaspers and Adorno, is not simply an evasive leap backward or forward or a search for some primal ground that allows Being to glow with a metaphysical splendor. The lack of philosophical presuppositions suggested to Heidegger by the principle of *Urspründlichkeit* does not provide one the license to transcend the self and history; precisely the opposite is the case. Moreover, in attempting to trace philosophical classifications and theory back to their cognitive origin, Heidegger is far from legitimizing a *prima philosophia*. Instead, he is engaged in the very *destruction* of traditional philosophical structures.

Heidegger's attempted destruction of metaphysics is carried out in the attempt to recuperate Being from oblivion. This clearly differentiates Heideggerian 'destruction' from contemporary 'decon-struction.' However, as Herman Rapaport has argued, there is a complex filiation between the two approaches; both would subject the history of ontology to a critique rooted in the problematic of temporality. This is why Derrida never allows himself to be pinned either to a categorical embrace or refutation of *Destruktion*. As Rapaport puts it, 'Derrida plays with the "difference" of such a choice and thereby allows himself to pursue simultaneous perspectives or directions which would appear to be merely incompatible or un-tenable. In this way he disarticulates the decidability of any intel-lectual "event" that would constitute the historical difference be-tween deconstruction and Heideggerian thought.'[11] What was said earlier of Benjamin is also true for Heidegger: regardless of any ultimately nostalgic, recuperative purpose inherent in their ide-ologies, the *methodological* element in their philosophies of origin is clearly compatible with poststructuralist praxis.

Heidegger's essay on Jaspers's study of the psychology of world perspectives anticipates his explication of the order of Dasein's ori-gin as rooted in human care, dread, and the feeling of affliction:

> Traced back to its origin and its genuine foundational expe-rience, the meaning of existence is precisely *the* meaning of Being. It cannot be attained from the 'is' of the specifically cognating, explicating, and at the same time somehow objec-tivating 'is.' Rather, it must be won from the foundational ex-perience of the *afflicted* possession of itself, which is fulfilled *prior* to any possible subsequent 'is'-like objectivating cogni-zance, a cognizance irrelevant to the fulfillment. (GA 9:30; Heidegger's emphasis)

Heidegger adumbrates the origin of existential meaning by way of discussing how the ego is experienced. The ego is experienced as the self, not as the individuation of a generality or as a part of a whole. Existential meaning cannot be derived through a process of objectification whereby the ego is made to seem alienated from itself. Instead, its origin is anchored in personal experience. Like Adorno, Heidegger refutes the attempt to view the ego's originary experience of its existence as reducible to the concept of a disinterested subject striving toward 'objective' cognition. Instead, the originary signification of existence is rooted in the afflicted ('bekümmert') possession of itself. In this context, the ego reveals itself to be the fully concrete, historically factical self.[12] It is accessible in historically concrete self-experience ('Eigenerfahrung,' GA 9:30). This self-oriented view of the origin of existential meaning is far from Adorno's attempt to project an ephemeral origin from the discrete otherness of the object in the subject/object relationship. Nevertheless, it suggests at least an early good faith effort to avoid the sort of 'objective' thinking, grounded in an alienated ratio, that Adorno associated with the 'enlightenment' philosophy of origin. Moreover, Heidegger warns that tracing the ground of experience back to its origin does not involve a simple historical probe into the past of the ego (a sin of the 'objective' psychology Heidegger would call into question) but is based on the ego's own experiences of the past as revealed in the ego's horizon of expectation (GA 9:31). However, Heidegger certainly reveals himself to be still under the ban of Husserl's intuitive phenomenology when he credits his former mentor with making it possible for philosophy to take possession of this affliction-grounded radical origin of signification (GA 9:36).

One of Jaspers's more insightful recent interpreters, Elisabeth Young-Bruehl, implies that when Jaspers refers to clarity as the faculty that 'gives certainty in the practice of life,' he is pointing only toward what the self can experience and not toward 'objective' criteria established by a scientific psychology: 'But again, this is not objective certainty; it is the certainty of self-being, of the human *Ursprung*.'[13] At least in part, Heidegger's discussion of Jaspers's book suggests that the human *Ursprung* and true *self*-being – Being as rooted in the concrete personal experience of affliction and not as the construct of 'objective' psychological or philosophical categories – are one and the same. This is not to assert that Heidegger and Jaspers are fully in accord over the relationship between psychology and the origin of psychical Being. As Young-Bruehl suggests, Heidegger's analysis is critical of what he sees as a lack of methodological rigor in Jaspers's analysis of 'fundamental concepts' of philosophy, concepts both men would call into question.

Young-Bruehl goes on to note that *Being and Time* was Heidegger's *own* 'effort to look back through the history of philosophizing in the West to its origins and to ask how the basis of all concepts, intertwined in the roots of all conceptualization – Being, *Sein* – had been misunderstood or neglected, forgotten.'[14] Of course, the tracing of Western philosophy back to its origins is only part of the telos underlying *Being and Time*. Heidegger also wishes to show how Being in its genuine temporally conditioned facticity is a Being-in-the-world, a Dasein rooted in the dread caused by the awareness of its own finitude. As with Rosenzweig and Benjamin in his *Trauerspiel* book, exposing the origins of Western conceptual thinking is only a prelude for Heidegger to elucidating a more temporally legitimate principle of origin. In the case of Heidegger, Dasein's true origin is found to be dread (*Angst*). The dual nature of Heidegger's treatment of origin in *Being and Time* is largely responsible for the incredible frequency with which the term *Ursprung* or its derivatives – *ursprünglich* ('originary'), *gleichursprünglich* ('simultaneously originary'), *das Ursprüngliche* ('the originary'), and so forth, appears in its pages.

As we might expect, Heidegger's attempt to get at the conceptual root of Western philosophizing and his desire to evoke a principle of Dasein distinguished from the sort of thinking characterized by these concepts often causes him to make use of the term *Herkunft* (ancestry) rather than *Ursprung*. This use of *Herkunft* is similar to Nietzsche's genealogical procedure and is especially prevalent when Heidegger attempts to examine a concept or idea in a historically linear, diachronic fashion. For example, he attempts to illustrate the ancestry of the idea of transcendence, which holds that man is more than an understanding being ('Verstandeswesen'), by directly citing (respectively) Latin and Renaissance German passages from texts of Calvin and Zwingli (GA 2:66). By doing so, Heidegger demonstrates a direct continuity between early Protestant and contemporary understandings of this idea. At the very outset of *Being and Time*, Heidegger notes that the Being of the individually and factically existent ('Das Sein des Seienden') is not to be determined through such a diachronic procedure, that is, by recourse to another individually existent entity ('Seiendes') in its ancestry ('Herkunft') (GA 2:8). However, Heidegger does not appear to be consistent in equating *Herkunft* with ideas, concepts, or existent Being in their historical linearity. For directly after examining both the Greek and early Protestant (Calvin, Zwingli) roots of the idea of transcendence, Heidegger notes, 'Those origins relevant to traditional anthropology, the Greek definition and the theological guide, demonstrate that beyond the attempt to reach the essential determination of the individual human entity, the question concerning his Being remains forgotten. This Being is rather conceived as "self-evident" in the sense of the *present-to-hand Being* of the other created things' (GA 2:66; Heidegger's emphasis).

The lineage of what is defined as human, shown in its transcendental aspect to be established through ancestral continuity, is seen here as tied to origins relevant to traditional anthropology. Perhaps more importantly, however, is that these origins are deemed relevant *only* to traditional anthropology and not to Heidegger's own prefatory analysis of Dasein. For traditional anthropology, as the cited passage indicates, determines the essence of the human as an individually existent entity to be contiguous with the present-to-hand Being of the rest of created existence. What for traditional anthropology are the relevant origins necessary for the determination of the essence of the human as individually existent are, in reality, false ancestral criteria. In the attempt to show the human as ontologically self-determining, traditional anthropology does what Heidegger claims one must *not* do in making such a determination – it makes use of a linear recourse to other, present-to-hand manifestations of the individually existent, a recourse Heidegger associates with the examination of ancestry. The establishment of *genuinely* relevant *Ursprünge* must be governed by a different procedure.

How does Heidegger begin to enunciate such a procedure? The heuristic principle that allows one to overcome the linearity of traditional anthropology and other branches of science governed by the historicism of *Herkunft* is encapsulated by the word *Gleichursprünglichkeit*, which evokes a *simultaneity* of origin. In a discussion devoted to being within Being (*In-Sein*), Heidegger reiterates and develops further his opposition to a linear, ancestry-based methodology. He notes that a thematic questioning of being within Being does not allow the derivation of the originality or originariness of one phenomenon through others. This reiterates the rejection of linear derivation at the outset of *Being and Time* (GA 2:8). He emphasizes that the task of thematically analyzing the *In-Sein* is *not* related to the existential a priori of philosophical anthropology but is governed by a fundamentally ontological telos. Finally, Heidegger underscores the incompatibility of the ontological principle of the simultaneity of origin with a procedure based on the demonstration of (diachronically continuous) ancestry:

> Das Phänomen der *Gleichursprünglichkeit* der konstitutiven Momente ist in der Ontologie oft mißachtet worden zufolge einer methodisch ungezügelten Tendenz zur Herkunftsnachweisung von allem und jedem aus einem einfachen 'Urgrund.' (GA 2:175; Heidegger's emphasis)

> [The phenomenon of the *simultaneity of origin* of the constitutive moments has often been neglected in ontology due to a methodologically unrestrained tendency to demonstrate the ancestry of one and all from a simple 'primal ground.']

Heidegger's explicit equation of the neglect of the phenomenon of *Gleichursprünglichkeit* with the ontological attempt to situate ancestry in an undifferentiated 'primal ground' demonstrates that he wants to differentiate this phenomenon from any link to the historically primordial. This indicates the fallacy of the neologism used heretofore to translate the term – 'equiprimordiality.' This English word resonates with the temporally aboriginal overtones Heidegger disliked in the term *Urgrund,* a disinclination highlighted by his apostrophizing of it.

I noted in a previous chapter that Nietzsche opposes the principle of *Ursprung* to the linearity – grounded in a single root – of a primal will to knowledge. Such linearity is suggested by Nietzsche's use of the term *Herkunft.* The above-cited passage suggests Heidegger's embrace of a similar opposition. Even more importantly, Heidegger's rejection here of an ontology based on an *Urgrund* undermines Adorno's accusation that the search for such a dangerous primal ground underlies Heidegger's philosophy of origin. Hermann Mörchen has noted that Adorno's many analyses of

Heidegger completely ignore his use of the concept of *Gleichur-sprünglichkeit,* and he argues that Heidegger might have derived the notion of simultaneous origin from Max Scheler.[15] In *Die Wissens-formen und die Gesellschaft* (1925; The forms of knowledge and society), Scheler notes that the harmony between a given epoch's dominant theoretical image of the world and the respective political, economic, and social realities coexistent with this image do not exist in a causal relationship. Instead, they are determined through a simultaneous origin governed by the unity of the epoch's ethical and dynamic structures.[16]

Scheler provides an example of such a simultaneity of origin by elucidating early capitalism's relationship to nature. Early capitalism's desire to dominate nature expresses itself in both a technical will to power and in a new way of thinking about and viewing nature, a theoretical dimension encapsulated in a new system of natural categories. The technical will to power and the new framework of (theoretical) categories manifest themselves simultaneously – they are '*gleich* ursprünglich.'[17] Scheler's postulation of a simultaneity of origin in early capitalism's technical and theoretical attempt to establish hegemony over nature is reminiscent of Horkheimer and Adorno's efforts in the *Dialectic of Enlightenment* to show how enlightenment philosophy and technology work hand in glove to bring about the subjective domination of the natural world.

From a historical perspective, the use of the principle of the simultaneity of origin lends to the procedure of Scheler and Heidegger the character of a Nietzschean-Foucauldian genealogy, which eschews tracing the linear development of phenomena and ideas in favor of charting their simultaneous epochal eruptions. Adorno might have deliberately overlooked Heidegger's embrace of *Gleich-ursprünglichkeit* because it contradicts his consistent attempt to paint Heidegger as a philosopher who espouses the continuous, unbroken authority of first principles and primal, autochthonous grounds. Indeed, reacting to this sort of critique in his *Zur Sache des Denkens* (1969; *On Time and Being*), Heidegger denied that *Being and Time* attempted a 'Rückgang in den Grund, den Ursprung' (ZSD 33) [retreat into the foundation, the origin].

Heidegger makes use of the notion of a simultaneity of origins on numerous occasions in *Being and Time* and in other works, which suggests an attempt to avoid the metaphysical favoring of any one dimension of his ontology. In a discussion of care as the Being of Being-in-the-world ('Sein des Daseins'), Heidegger cites an ancient fable, according to which Saturn gives Jupiter possession of the human body when the human being dies but commends the creature to care while it lives. Heidegger interprets the fable as fixing the origin of the Being of the individual entity in care, an origin that imbues and dominates the individual entity as long as it 'is in the world' (GA 2:263). Heidegger uses this fable to underscore his belief that the origin of Being as Being-in-the-world is care, a conception of origin that leads to the marginalization of Being by robbing it of its metaphysical assurances. However, even this emphasis on man's subjugation to care as the origin of his individuated Being-in-the-world, which would appear to damn him to a comfortless facticity, is too one-sided for Heidegger. He thus draws on Konrad Burdach to assert that care also encompasses and generates the possibility of *perfectio*, the development of the individual toward his greatest possibilities. Heidegger then uses the term 'gleichursprünglich' to show the simultaneity of origin of both this dimension of Dasein's Being and that dimension that incorporates man's deliverance to a care-ridden world – his state of thrownness ('Geworfenheit') (GA 2:264). To use a term we have employed often in this book, Being as Being-in-the-world is shown to dwell in the interstice. However, this nonplace is generated in Heidegger's ontology not by antithetical origins but by the simultaneity of origins determined by care.

Heidegger's emphasis on the possibility of *perfectio* counterbalances the thrownness of existence by demonstrating the simultaneous origin of both elements of human Dasein in care. In a related move, Heidegger attempts to subvert the overemphasis placed by philosophy on the purely factical – what traditional philosophy defines as *Sein* – by demonstrating that what traditional philosophy derides as mere appearance (*Schein*) provides a legitimate ontological equilibrium to the 'real.' In his *Einführung in die Metaphysik* (1953; *An Introduction to Metaphysics*), Heidegger finds a

profound but as yet inaccessible connection between the dichotomous pairings of Being and Becoming, on the one hand, and Being
and appearance, on the other. It is the simultaneity of origin of
these divisions that points to this deep, hidden coherence (GA
40:105). In order to evoke the *Sein/Schein* dichotomy in its original
Greek sense, Heidegger claims the very originary ('ursprünglich')
nature of their division points to an underlying cohesion between
the two spheres (GA 40:106). The simultaneity of origin in the division between Being and Becoming, on the one hand, and Being and
appearance, on the other, grounds this cohesion because Being discloses itself and becomes factical only as appearance ('Erscheinen').
This circumstance leads the Greeks to see a fundamental unity between nature and truth (GA 40:109). By resorting to the principle
of the simultaneity of origin, Heidegger attempts to establish a
philosophical equilibrium in the respective dichotomous pairings
of *perfectio* and facticity, and the truth of ontological reality and the
appearance of individuated Being in nature.

Ultimately, Heidegger shows that the supposed dichotomy between a concretely real external world and the illusory nature of
our perception of this world's appearance is based on a false presupposition, namely, that the perceiving subject who attempts to
overcome this dichotomy is ontologically isolated. Heidegger sees
the false a priori of an isolated subject who confronts the reality of
a world external to himself as especially acute in Kantian philosophy.[18] In *Being and Time,* Heidegger closely examines the famous
postulate in the *Critique of Pure Reason* that the empirical consciousness of one's own Dasein is proof of the Dasein of objects in
the realm *spatially* external to this self-aware subject. Heidegger
uses the principle of the simultaneity of origin to demonstrate that
a valid *temporal* proof underlies Kant's axiom: 'The proof for the
"Dasein of things external to myself" is supported by the circumstance that change and steadfastness, in a manner simultaneously
originary, belong to the essence of time' (GA 2:270). The postulate
that change and steadfastness are governed by a temporal simultaneity of origin is a necessary corollary to Heidegger's refusal to
favor either an (ontologically fixed and stable) *Urgrund* or the historicist notion of linear, diachronic change. Heidegger notes, how-

ever, that the correctness of this temporal postulate does not support the connection between the external (objective world) and internal (consciously perceiving subjective consciousness) realms upheld by Kant. Dasein is always 'too late' with such subject/object dichotomies; as an entity always already thrust into a world, Dasein cannot uphold the chimera of a discrete, isolated, subjective consciousness (GA 2:271–73).

In his *Phänomenologische Interpretation von Kants Kritik der reinen Vernunft* (Phenomenological interpretation of Kant's 'Critique of Pure Reason'), consisting of lectures delivered around the time of *Being and Time*'s appearance (1927–28), Heidegger continues his recourse to the principle of the simultaneity of origin in exploring cognitive dualisms in Kant's epistemology. Kant argues in the introduction to the *Critique of Pure Reason* that there are two trunks of human cognition – sensuality ('Sinnlichkeit') and understanding ('Verstand') – that may share a common, unknown root. Heidegger asserts that Kant's true intention here is to show the independent nature of these modes of cognition and hence their simultaneity of origin ('Gleichursprünglichkeit') from a common root (GA 25:90–91). The two trunks of cognition are subsequently equated with visual contemplation ('Anschauen') and thought ('Denken'), both of which are synthesized as an a priori 'verstehende Anschauen' ('comprehending contemplation') by virtue of their original ('ursprünglich') unity (GA 25:161). However, thought itself is governed by a simultaneity of origin encompassing both a unification of perceptions and its relationship to objects within this unified perceptual field (GA 25:182). Finally, in discussing the origin of epistemological concepts in the ability to understand ('Verstandesvermögen'), Heidegger draws on Kant's analysis of pure concepts of understanding to deduce not a simultaneous but a double origin ('Doppelursprung') in their categories. As reflective notions, they are derived from their unifying function, but as types of Being they stem from the pure image of the temporally sensual (GA 25:253).

What unites these scattered remarks in this study of the *Critique of Pure Reason* is Heidegger's recourse to Kantian thought as a way of demonstrating that cognition is not purely a function of an isolated and alienated reasoning subjectivity but is in equal measure governed by nonrational, sensual modes of perception that are conditioned by the temporality of Dasein. To establish this dualistic view of cognition, Heidegger turns to the principle of the simultaneity of origin as well as to the notion of a dual origin. This is further evidence that Heidegger's 'philosophy of origin' is rooted neither in a unitary view of subjectivity nor in a favoring of metaphysical timelessness. Even when Heidegger opens his treatise on *Kant und das Problem der Metaphysik* (1929; *Kant and the Problem of Metaphysics*) by noting his intention in this work is 'die Ursprünglichkeit des Ursprungs der Metaphysik an den Tag zu bringen' (KM 14) [to bring to light the originariness of the origin of metaphysics], he is pointing toward his attempt in this further exploration of the *Critique of Pure Reason* to evoke the relationship between the self and the finite nature of 'original' time. As Werner Marx puts it in his comments on this treatise:

> Kant's 'unsaid' for Heidegger lies especially in Kant's 'wish' to give time the decisive role within the primal occurrence of transcendence, not because it forms the movement of the 'sequence of nows' but because as pure intuition it carries out the movement of a 'self-affection.' The pure intuition affects itself, in that it 'preforms the aspect of sequence and holds it as such *to itself* as the forming reception.' Accordingly, this 'original' time constitutes the 'self' as 'related to reception,' thus as 'finite.'[19]

'Original time' for Heidegger is not to be equated with an infinite realm beyond temporality but as the fundamental heuristic principle for establishing Dasein as a *historically* constituted Being-in-the-world. The fundamental characteristic of the 'field of origin' ('Ursprungsfeld') can only be established by focusing on the finitude of perception as man's essential epistemological attribute (KM 28). However, precisely this finitude problematizes any methodology that would lead to the 'revelation of origin' ('Ursprungsenthüllung'), particularly with respect to Kantian metaphysics (KM 42–45).

Heidegger's *Phänomenologische Interpretation von Kants Kritik der reinen Vernunft* is not only of interest because of its employment of such principles as the simultaneity of origin and the double origin but also because of its brief but trenchant critique of Cohen's logic of origin. He remarks that the 'logic of pure cognition' favored by the Marburg School is actually a logic of thought ('Denken') insofar as sensual or visual intuition ('Anschauung') is left out of account in its epistemology. Because Heidegger sees cognition as grounded in *both* visual contemplation and thought, which are themselves rooted in a simultaneous origin, he would naturally find this exclusion of 'Anschauung' unacceptable. He goes on to note Cohen's discussion of a logic of origin in connection with the logic of pure cognition and finds that Cohen's logic of origin is actually related to what Kant sees as a problem of transcendental logic. Citing a passage from the *Critique of Pure Reason,* Heidegger objects that pure logic is not concerned with the origin of thought's determination of objects ('Ursprung der Denkbestimmungen der Gegenstände') but only with the principles by which understanding ('der Verstand') uses mental images ('Vorstellungen') in their relationship to each other. It is irrelevant whether these mental images are empirically given or are generated a priori in the cognating subject (GA 25:185).

Heidegger is certainly correct to note that the logic of origin would be a problem of transcendental logic for Kant. In the *Critique of Pure Reason,* Kant terms transcendental all cognition that is not concerned with objects but rather with the a priori nature of our cognition of objects. Heidegger cites this passage shortly after adumbrating Cohen's logic of origin, and my discussion of this logic in the previous chapter suggests that in attempting to establish the immanent, a priori nature of pure cognition, Cohen's views point toward Kant's *transcendental* philosophy. In the introduction to the *Critique of Pure Reason,* Kant makes a clear distinction between cognition of an empirical origin and cognition of a transcendental origin.[20] What is of greatest interest for my purposes, however, is the nature of Heidegger's objection to Cohen's logic of origin.

As I noted in chapter 4, Benjamin had called the logic of origin into question because it suppresses the historical element in the category of origin (1:226). Heidegger, on the other hand, remonstrates against Cohen's principle from a phenomenological perspective. Simply put, Heidegger implies that the logic of origin bears no relationship to objects themselves; it is not 'gegenstandsbezogen' (GA 25:185). That Heidegger points toward *this* weakness in Cohen's logic of origin reveals a foreshadowing of Heidegger's views on origin after the so-called *Kehre*, or 'turn.' One of the most significant dimensions of Heidegger's later works is their *Gegenstandsbezogenheit*, their shift away from an emphasis on human Dasein and toward the 'Being' (*Sein*) of the objects of the phenomenal world. More specifically, Heidegger wrestles with the problem of creating a language that would allow the concealed Being of the phenomenal world to emerge in its concealedness by overcoming its oblivion, by confronting the metaphysics that have led to the oblivion of Being, to 'Seinsvergessenheit' (VA 72).

Despite rejecting Cohen's logic of origin as a misguided foray into the realm of Kantian transcendental logic and attacking the metaphysics leading to the oblivion of Being, Heidegger does not actually reject transcendental logic itself. In his treatise *Vom Wesen des Grundes* (1929; *The Essence of Reasons*), Heidegger equates Being-in-the-world with transcendence (GA 9:156). By its very definition, transcendence is the Being-in-the-world of Dasein (GA 9:163). We have seen that human Dasein for Heidegger signifies factical Being, Being in its temporal finitude. Again working with Kantian principles, Heidegger defines the ideal of transcendence as the representation of human finitude *in its totality* (GA 9:152). This totality circumscribes discrete Being, individual human Dasein, the Dasein of others, and the nonhuman presence ('Vorhandensein') of objects. The elements in this totality are, not surprisingly, informed by a simultaneity of origin, allowing for the inner possibility of transcendence as a genuine foundation (GA 9:163).

The exhaustive character of the genuine foundation must also allow for the ontologically marginal; to try to reduce it to something 'basic' does not lead to its origin but to the end of inquiry. Freedom must therefore provide the origin of the transcendental foundation. Freedom becomes the foundation *as origin* ('*als Ursprung*') when the transcendentally issuing foundation ('der transzendierend entspringende Grund') falls back upon it (GA 9:174;

Heidegger's emphasis). This claim synthesizes earlier assertions concerning freedom as transcendence as the '*origin of foundation in general*' (GA 9:165; Heidegger's emphasis) and on freedom as the origin of the (Leibnizian) 'principle of sufficient reason' ('Satz vom Grunde') (GA 9:172).[21] Finally, Heidegger's use of the principle of the simultaneity of origin in this treatise to distinguish between transcendental origin with its unified, tripartite grounding, and the nonunified character of privileged (first and highest) beginnings must be noted:

> Die Ursprünglichkeit der transzendentalen Gründe und ihr spezifischer *Grund*charakter bleiben noch unter der formalen Charakteristik der 'ersten' und 'obersten' Anfänge verdeckt. Deshalb mangelt ihnen auch die Einheit. Sie kann nur in der Gleichursprünglichkeit des transzendentalen Ursprungs des dreifachen Gründens bestehen. (GA 9:171; Heidegger's emphasis)

> [The originariness of the transcendental grounds and their specific *foundational* character remain hidden under the formal characterization of the 'first' and 'highest' beginnings. They thus also lack unity. This unity can only consist in the simultaneity of origin of the transcendental origin of the threefold grounding.]

I noted that the ideal of transcendence for Heidegger is not to be equated with some metaphysical 'going beyond' of Dasein but, on the contrary, signifies the composite representation of temporally circumscribed human finitude (GA 9:152). The tripartite structure of this all-encompassing transcendental grounding is shown to consist of that which goes to project the horizons of Dasein's historically confined frame of reference ('*Weltentwurf*'), Dasein's rootedness in the individually existent ('*Eingenommenheit im Seienden*'), and the ontological foundation of the individually existent ('*ontologische Begründung des Seienden*') (GA 9:171; Heidegger's emphasis).

In sum, Heidegger draws on the principle of the simultaneity of origin in this treatise to establish transcendental origin neither as a foundation metaphysically beyond the resolutely circumscribed contours of Dasein's facticity nor as the means for evoking a first and highest *prima philosophia*. Instead, transcendental origin is shown to be the ground for establishing the integral framework of finite human Being-in-the-world. The inclusive nature of this framework causes Heidegger to rely on the two heuristic postulates that allow for such an all-encompassing existential horizon: freedom as the origin of the principle of sufficient reason and the simultaneity of origin of the transcendental origin. The subsumption of the ontologically marginal by the principle of sufficient reason is a necessary corollary to addressing the question of its origin. Such a subsumption also, of necessity, rejects as exclusionary the equation of the principles of identity and contradiction with the principle of sufficient reason. This conflation leads to an epistemological dead end and not to origin, because it is equated with the cessation of all further questioning. Heidegger qualifies this assertion by noting that the principles of identity and contradiction point toward something more originary than the merely 'also transcendental,' namely, to the temporality of the event of transcendence (GA 9:173). Nevertheless, he clearly rejects the principle of identity as linked to the exploration of the origin of a principle of sufficient reason. All of these circumstances allow us to take note of elements in Heidegger's thought that contradict Adorno's equation of Heidegger's *Ursprungsphilosophie* with a philosophy of identity and demonstrate once again that qualities such as alterity, finitude, marginality, and freedom are not incompatible with the principle of origin.

Heidegger's remark that the principles of identity and contradiction point toward something more originary than that which is characterized by a principal character and belong to the temporality of the event of transcendence can best be understood in connection with his writings on poetry and art. In his discussions of Hölderlin's poetry, Heidegger translates the problems of originary identity and contradiction into the polarities of wandering and remaining, absence from and proximity to the transcendent homeland, and the self-concealment and disclosure of Being. These three closely related sets of binary oppositions are characteristic of Heideggerian thought after the 'turn,' when, as Löwith has noted, Heidegger stops seeking to make 'sense' of Being and instead seeks to evoke its discrete (as 'seiend,' that is, grounded in the individual entity) yet identitarian (as '*aller*seiend,' that is, equated with the comprehensiveness of the individual entity) modality. In making this assertion, Löwith also refers to the deceptive 'overgrown' and 'seldom tread' paths ('Holzwege') evoked by Heidegger, paths that may yet lead toward the homeland of Being.[22] This is an allusion to Heidegger's collection of essays published under the title *Holzwege* (1950), but his comments are equally applicable to the terrain described by Heidegger in Hölderlin's poetry.

One of the apparent contradictions confronting those who would journey to the transcendent homeland of Being is the juxtaposition of willing and forgetting, events that propel one along the path. In his interpretation of the poem 'Andenken' ('Remembrance') in the *Erläuterungen zu Hölderlins Dichtung* (1936–44; Commentaries on Hölderlin's poetry), Heidegger sees the poetic spirit evoked in the poem as coeval with the origin of the homeland: 'Die Heimat ist der Ursprung und der Ursprungsgrund des Geistes' (GA 4:92) [The homeland is the origin and the foundation of origin of the spirit]. The spirit resides in its beginning in the open, and in the beginning the homeland approaches the knowing will. However, *because it is origin*, the homeland necessarily conceals itself from this will. In its relationship to the poetic spirit, then, the homeland is a site neither of absolute presence nor absolute absence. At the outset of and the conclusion to the 'Andenken' essay, Heidegger refers to the condition of habitation of the site of origin ('Ortschaft des Ursprungsorts') of the poet, made fertile by the current that runs through it and that contains the riddle of origin (GA 4:79). Remembrance ('Andenken') thinks of the habitation of the site of origin while thinking of the journeying of the journey to the foreign (GA 4:150). The riddle of origin is revealed to be the '*purely-sprung-from*,' ('*das Reinentsprungene*') (GA 4:151; Heidegger's emphasis), which remains at the origin. It is a riddle because although origin shows itself as its springing or generating ('Entspringen'), it doesn't show itself in the 'sprung-from' but hides and withholds itself in the 'sprung-from's' appearance.

The poetic spirit as knowing will remains turned toward the homeland (GA 4:92–93), but the poet's origin-directed thinking is made timorous by the knowledge that origin cannot be directly experienced (GA 4:131). Gallantry comes in the form of a forgetting (Hölderlin's 'tapfer Vergessen') that loves the origin (GA 4:94). The holy festival ('Fest') celebrated by the poet is the essential origin of history, and the poet who issues from this festival becomes the founder of a history of humanity (GA 4:106). Moreover, although it is grounded in a nonplace between presence and absence, concealment and disclosure, origin in its self-stabilizing character is a foundational stabilization ('Erfestigen des Grundes'). This is a precondition of origin's allowing-to-spring or generate ('Entspringenlassen') (GA 4:146).

In examining Heidegger's use of the principle of origin in his writings on Hölderlin, particularly in his treatment of the poem 'Andenken,' we see it acquire an irreducible multivalence. This rich multivalence has been noted by Andrzej Warminski, who draws on mentors such as Jacques Derrida and Paul de Man to evoke the disjunctive sense of history, the rupture between semantic and syntactic structures, and the chiasmic reversals of this reading.[23] What even Warminski overlooks, however, is the role of *Ursprung* in generating this multivalence.[24] Origin in Heidegger's reading of Hölderlin does not simply subsume the binary oppositions of diachronic history and transcendent presence, revelation and concealment, gallantry and timidity, forgetting and remembrance. Instead, it points to their entanglement. Being as presence is Being-in-the-world, Being in its history – only thus is the origin of history 'the festival first transmitted by the sacred' (GA 4:106).

Origin as the revelation of the springing or generating ('Entspringen'), which yet hides in the appearance of the sprung from ('Entsprungene'), and the notion that poetry is remembrance that is foundation ('Stiftung') (GA 4:151), a remembrance yet mediated by the 'gallant forgetting' of the poet who loves the origin – all of these entwined polarities point toward Heidegger's establishment of the emergence of the work of art in the nonplace between the *unconcealedness* of Earth and the *concealedness* of World in 'The Origin of the Work of Art,' a dichotomy I discussed in chapter 1. The holding in unresolved suspension of these polarities can be tied to a fundamental axiom of Heidegger's post–'turn' thought, namely, that the work of art points neither to Being's concealment nor to its unconcealment but rather to the *unconcealment of its concealment* (see especially GA 5:25–44). This is the revelation yielded by the origin of the work of art. Although facing the homeland and possessed of a knowing will, the poet who forgets out of a love of origin is the instrument of this disclosure (see especially GA 5:44–66).[25] His timidity in the face of origin's unexperienceable nature and his gallant forgetting out of a hidden love of origin – these qualities make the poet the priest of the origin of history, a history founded by art (GA 5:65).

What does it mean to speak of a history founded by art? Heidegger does not intend history to be understood here in its traditional sense, as the descriptive chronicling of the past, the narration of past occurrences. History as a diachronically progressing series of events is termed 'Historie' by Heidegger, in contrast to the history art can generate, which is 'Geschichte' (GA 5:65). Chronological history, the narrative of the past, is inevitably intended as a pure disclosure. It is a revealing sanctioned solely in terms of its comprehensiveness, its ability to unconceal as much as possible about prior events and periods. The revelatory character of the artwork, on the other hand, reaches its apogee only when it manifests Being's originary concealment. If the artist is a historian, he is a historian who must forget. Otherwise, the art he generates cannot be situated between Earth and World as in the interstice between unconcealedness and concealedness. The concealed essence of Being is anchored in its dynamic quality; it is always new, always changing. The history of Being generated by art is therefore not the history *of* change but history *as* change. History as transformation founded by the artwork is informed by origin's volatility. In a discussion of 'The Origin of the Work of Art,' Reiner Schürmann writes that in an artwork,

> truth sets itself into work with a leap. The artwork founds a constellation of references and thereby brings truth into being. This rise of truth in a constellation is always other and always new. *The origin is always other and always new.* As such it requires a decision from man: Do we give heed to the sway of the origin or not? In the earlier writings an either/or is

urged upon our existence: whether the origin appears as manifold origination or as first causation is decided by a way of
existing. Heidegger wants us to exist according to the rise of
truth which is historical, that is, ever new.[26]

However, history itself is ever new only when it is founded by art,
an art inscribed by origin. In 'The Origin of the Work of Art,' origin
is evoked as manifold by virtue of the dialectic that defines it, a
dialectic of forgetting and remembering, revelation and occlusion.

It is the entanglement of these qualities that establishes the poet
as one who unconceals Being but only unconceals its concealment.
The knowing will would force Being's disclosure and open the
doors to the transcendental homeland, but the poet's gallant forgetting, his role as priest of the origin of a history that temporalizes understanding and induces forgetting, and origin's occultation in the
sprung-from – all ensure that only Being's concealment will be
unconcealed. Both the search for origin and its self-concealment
underlie the dynamics of human Being-in-the-world and the poet's
search for the divine. Thus, Heidegger notes in his expanded treatment of Hölderlin's poem, *Hölderlins Hymne 'Andenken'* (1941–42;
Hölderlin's hymn 'Andenken'): 'Einwiegen ist in die Wiege bergen
und da geborgen halten, ist Seinlassen im Ursprung. Der Ursprung
ist das Eigenste der Menschen und Götter, was sie als ihr Wesen
mitbringen' [Bringing to repose is a bringing to concealment in the
cradle and sheltering there, is letting-be in the origin. The origin is
the most characteristic aspect of the humans and the Gods, that
which they bring with them as their essence]. The bringing to repose is not a lulling to sleep or numbing, and the human is fundamentally alienated from his essence (GA 52:105). These circumstances assure that the search for origin will remain dynamic and
cannot be associated with stasis.

Heidegger's treatment of the concept of origin in his writing on
Hölderlin is closely connected to the poet's river imagery. The journeying in 'Andenken,' after all, is circumscribed by the course of
the Garonne and the Dordogne Rivers. In his discussion of Heidegger's interpretation of 'Der Ister' and 'Der Rhein,' Otto Pöggeler has
noted an interesting distinction in these two rivers' relationship to
the origin. The Ister flows *toward* the East but appears also to be

flowing *from* the East, as though it was going backward. The current lingers near its origin because even at its source a mingling of foreign and domestic waters takes place. The Ister thus flows past its origin only with difficulty. Its sadness is the holy sadness of knowing that a tarrying at the site of origin is necessary. The Rhine, on the other hand, rejoices and leaps. Having originally ('ursprünglich') inclined toward the East, it soon makes a turn and disappears into the distance. It is the Ister, however, that fulfills the law of historicity by incorporating the unity of the condition of habitation and condition of wandering as the river that remains at the origin and yet flows forth. This lingering at what Heidegger refers to more precisely in the 'Andenken' essay (but in connection with the hymn to 'Der Ister') as the 'condition of habitation of the site of origin' (GA 4:79) – this lingering while yet wandering forth, the intermingling of the waters of the homeland and the not-homeland, make the essence of the river the essence of the poet and the poetic dwelling he must transmit to humanity.[27] One might add that Heidegger establishes here through the principle of origin a dynamic and creative tension between identity and difference, both within his thinking through of the significance of Hölderlin's 'Ister' and in pondering the polarity between the Ister and the Rhine when they are viewed at their respective sites of origin.

As I noted in my discussion of the essay *The Essence of Reasons,* Heidegger views the principles of identity and difference as pointing to something more originary ('Ursprünglicheres') than the simply 'also transcendental,' namely, to what grounds the event of transcendence as temporal (GA 9:173). Heidegger takes up the problem of the relationship between identity and difference in his 1957 treatise *Identität und Differenz (Identity and Difference)*. As Mörchen has noted in his refutation of Adorno's critique of Heidegger's principle of origin as a philosophy of identity, Heidegger's concept of the simultaneity of origin foreshadows his interpretation of identity in *Identity and Difference*. This interpretation holds that identity is the 'appearance of the different in the same.'[28] Much of this treatise is a critical engagement with Hegelian metaphysics. Like Adorno and Rosenzweig, Heidegger rejects Hegel's alleged cancellation of the historically discrete and his concomitant suspension of the distinction between the universal and the particular in favor of a *return* to the historical character of thought and a radical differentiation between universal and individuated Being – 'Sein' and 'Seiendes' (ID 45–46).

In his 1930–31 lectures *Hegels Phänomenologie des Geistes (Hegel's Phenomenology of Spirit)*, Heidegger equated Hegel's use of the word 'Seiende' with what he refers to as 'das Vorhandene' – that which is present-to-hand. He saw Hegel's 'Sein' as equivalent to 'Vorhandenheit,' the quality of being present-to-hand (GA 32:59). Because Heidegger sees the presence of 'Vorhandensein' as equipmental nonhuman presence (in contrast to the human presence of 'Dasein'), he asserted in these lectures that Hegel's highly restricted use of 'Sein' and 'Seiendes' was a response to the *objective* ('*sachliche*') (GA 32:60; Heidegger's emphasis) problem of Being as it presented itself to antiquity.[29] Heidegger noted that his own use of these terms in their broadest possible sense represents an attempt to address the problem of the 'Seiende' in its relationship to Dasein. He argues that he treats the question of individuated Being in connection with 'the necessities of *our* Dasein,' in which the history of the problem of Being becomes reality, while noting that Hegel's treatment of the question of individuated Being inevitably led to its sublation (GA 32:60; Heidegger's emphasis).

Although Heidegger does not divulge here what these necessities entail, the basis of his rejection of Hegel's treatment of the *Sein/Seiende* dichotomy in *Identity and Difference* is clearly anticipated by his earlier confrontation with Hegel on this point. In contrasting his approach to Hegel's, Heidegger suggests that his elucidation of the question of individuated Being ('das Seiende') must be 'more originary' ('ursprünglicher'). He is far from proposing a backward-directed search for a *prima philosophia*, however. Instead, he suggests the need for a renewal based on the specific needs (whatever they may be) of contemporary human Dasein.

In sum, Heidegger's endeavor in *Identity and Difference* to sustain the discrete character of Being as 'seiend' in opposition to Hegel's alleged sublation of the *Sein/Seiende* distinction has a twofold purpose in light of the earlier lectures on the *Phenomenology of Spirit*. First of all, Heidegger wants to recuperate the historical character of thought itself.[30] Second, he wants to redirect philosophy toward an engagement with the genuine problems of Dasein as they manifest themselves in their present-day facticity. Contrary to Adorno's objections that Heidegger uses the philosophy of origin to establish an authoritarian first principle, Heidegger sees an originary approach to the *Sein/Seiende* dichotomy as concomitant with looking at Being's differentiated, historically factical, and contemporary character. Mörchen is therefore correct in defending Heidegger against Adorno's charge of an *Ursprung*-based authoritarian philosophy of identity.

Mörchen engages in this defense immediately after his assertion that Heidegger's interpretation of identity in *Identity and Difference* as being the 'appearance of the different in the same' is a logical corollary to the principle of simultaneous origin. Mörchen notes that Heidegger rejects the manipulation of an 'ultimate foundation' as the ground of our experience of phenomena, and he thus resists the sort of authoritarian 'fundamental ontology' that Adorno locates in his thought without ceasing to '*pose the question*' of origin.[31] In light of Heidegger's comments on the *Sein/Seiende* dichotomy in the lectures on the *Phenomenology of Spirit*, I should add that Heidegger feels the need to continue an originary questioning precisely to *avoid* the metaphysical pitfalls of a philosophy of identity.

Heidegger's principle of simultaneous origin bears a close resemblance to the concept of 'structural causality' developed by Althusser and Étienne Balibar in *Reading Capital* (1968), their attempt to rethink Marx's position on social totalities. This concept is placed in opposition to traditional philosophical formulations of systemic causality. Althusser finds the Cartesian model of a transitive, mechanistic cause-effect relationship inadequate for expressing the interaction between the whole and its parts. The Leibniz-Hegel proposition that the visible expression of a totality can be tied to an inner essence provides this totality with an adequate formulation but denies the whole a structure by creating a disjunction between an internal 'spiritual' core and its outward, phenomenal manifestation. The creation of the concept of structural causality to pose the condition of Marxist totality allows for the positing of a dominant structural determinant, namely, the economic. Because the whole is seen as structured, however, its causal elements can be posed as synchronic and therefore as temporally simultaneous.

This expression of totality thus overcomes both the non-holistic linearity evident in the Cartesian model and the static character Althusser associates with the Leibnizian-Hegelian concept.[32] Like *Gleichursprünglichkeit*, which is implicitly antihistoricist in its refutation of a causal chain of development emanating in a linear fashion from a single site of origin, structural causality poses a constellation of *simultaneous* origins. Neither the Althusserian nor the Heideggerian concepts, however, are antihistorical. Nor do they eschew chronology. They simply refute the notion that historical development must be anchored in a discrete, unconflicted point in time. The dilemmas generating their formulation are also contiguous. Althusser and Balibar want to account for the existence of contradictions within the whole, and Heidegger's *Gleichursprünglichkeit* concept is intimately tied to his postulation of identity as the appearance of difference in the same.[33]

Both postulates are designed to steer between the antithetical aporias of mechanistic linearity and metaphysical stasis, but their synchronicity does not place them outside the bounds of history itself. In comparing Adorno's figure of the constellation to Althusserian structural causality (a comparison that could be extended to *Gleichursprünglichkeit*), Jameson notes that their 'synchronic' nature 'does not imply any stasis of time or history, but rather a thinking which does not involve the temporal as such.'[34] This assertion should be modified: the bracketing out of the temporal here really represents both the liberation of the chronological from a *mechanistic* concept of time and the avoidance of its metaphysical suspension.

Heidegger's confrontation with Western metaphysics is, of course, at its most controversial in his writings on Nietzsche, particularly because of their attempt to use Nietzsche to show that this metaphysics has reached the terminal stage of its development. I have already touched on Heidegger's views on Nietzsche, and a return to his image of Nietzsche is unnecessary for my purposes. Nevertheless, Heidegger concludes his two-volume work on Nietzsche with an exploration of general metaphysical problems not specifically related to the figure of Nietzsche, and this excursus demonstrates more clearly than Heidegger's other works the self-consciously pre-Socratic resonance of his notion of origin. He traces the conflation of *archē* (origin) and *aitia* (*Ur-sache*, literally 'primal/originary thing' but actually meaning 'cause') back to the Platonic idea. Heidegger notes, 'Soon the equation of *archē* and *aitia* becomes self-evident, already, to a degree, in the works of Aristotle. Being shows the essential aspect of the rendering possible of presence, that is to say, the securing of determinancy or permanence' (N 413–14).

By uncoupling *archē* and *aitia*, *archē* once again emerges in its indeterminacy, in its finitude and lack of constancy, as the origin of Being's *dissemination* as *das Seiende – individuated* Being – and loses its character as a stable point of reference grounding a metaphysics of presence. If *archē*, in its pre-Socratic inception as the first term in the history of Western philosophy to signify origin, is truly void of any traces of a link to causality, to *aitia*, then a philosophy of origin like Heidegger's, conscious of *archē*'s discrete resonance, cannot be inevitably associated with the search for an absolute ground. Prior to Plato, Heidegger tells us, *archē* is *not* metaphysical, not the signifier of a numinous ideal outside of yet regulative of Being in its physical facticity. Thus, we can already see that Derrida's attempt to bring Heideggerian *archē* into inevitable contiguity with 'history,' 'cause,' and 'telos' and Habermas's interpretation of Heidegger's philosophy of origin as the search for all-powerful, foundational truths are somewhat misguided. Reading the *archē/aitia* uncoupling backward into the earlier texts of Heidegger I have examined, *archē/Ursprung* becomes liberated from its function as that which determines, stabilizes, and dominates – the authoritarian characteristics, that is, that Foucault and Adorno associate with philosophies of origin. It is this uncoupling that allows *Ursprung* to function in Heidegger's work as a ground, albeit as a ground for Dasein's indeterminacy, destabilizing thrownness, alterity, and dissemination.

In the penultimate chapter of his work on Nietzsche, Heidegger speaks of *aletheia* – the unconcealment of Being's concealment – as

only a faint presencing that does not return to a (privileged) beginning but only to pure unconcealedness. However, *aletheia* comes
under the yoke of the (Platonic) idea, and the *Seiende* – seen from
the perspective of the *archē* – is thereby released to an initial establishment of presence ('Anwesenheit,' N 458). The *archē* referred to
here is the uncoupled *archē*, and observing the subjugated *aletheia*
from its perspective should be seen as an attempt to achieve one of
Heidegger's fundamental goals – the *liberation* of *aletheia* from
metaphysical presence. This metaphysics is equated by Heidegger
with the will, the origin (*Ursprung*) of which is truth as certainty.
However, will has its *essential* origin ('Wesensursprung') in the lack
of knowledge of the essence of truth as the truth of Being. Through
forgetting – the sort of 'gallant forgetting' we saw evoked in Heidegger's treatment of Hölderlin – will leaves the beginning ('Anfang') it has never actually possessed. By locating will's essential
origin in an ignorance or incomprehension ('Unwissenheit'), Heidegger consigns metaphysics as 'Gewißheit' (certainty) to the
'Vergessenheit' (oblivion) of the not-remembered (N 467–68). By
attempting to write the end of the metaphysics of the will, Heidegger would liberate *aletheia* from its function as a 'first beginning'
and *archē* from its metaphysical character as a 'dominating [herr-
schend] beginning' (N 473–74). Metaphysics as a history of Being
is the 'going-forth from the beginning' (N 486), and by showing it
at the terminal stage of its linear development from a fixed beginning, the essence of Dasein as *unfixed* and *indeterminate* – and thus
as encompassed and generated by the *archē/Ursprung* – is revealed.

In my treatment of Heidegger's principle of origin I have highlighted elements in his work that call certain positions enunciated
by his most prominent recent critics – namely, Habermas and Derrida – into question. I will conclude this chapter by briefly examining their critiques of Heidegger's notion of *Ursprung*. In *Der philosophische Diskurs der Moderne* (1985; *The Philosophical Discourse of
Modernity*), Habermas accuses Heidegger after his 'turn' of engaging in a temporalized philosophy of origin. He sees Heidegger's
telos in the volumes on Nietzsche as a *return* to the origins, particularly to the pre-Socratic origins of metaphysics.[35]

Despite Habermas's accurate insight into Heidegger's predilection for pre-Socratic thought, this view of Heidegger is consistent with Habermas's conflation of Aristotelian and Heideggerian ontology in his *Philosophisch-politische Profile* (1971; *Philosophical-Political Profiles*). For there, too, Habermas offers a description of Heidegger as sentimentally yearning for origin, origin as a return to a privileged metaphysical site of Being: 'Thus Aristotle understood substance [Wesenheit] as a condition of being in the past [Ge-wesenheit], and Heidegger, as well, still understands the absent presencing of Being as the imminent return of something that was already past in the origin.'[36] Heidegger radically subverts the Aristotelian concept of a privileged and authoritative metaphysical origin – *Ur-sprung* as *Ur-sache*, origin as cause – by uncoupling *aitia* and *archē*.

Heidegger's belief in the lonely individuation of the *Seiendes* of human Dasein as Being-in-the-world is transformed by Habermas into a concept of transcendental subjectivity: 'The philosophy of origin's classical call for self-grounding and ultimate grounding isn't precisely rejected, but answered in the sense of a Fichtean act modified to a world design.'[37] Habermas judges the *Kehre* to be the result of Heidegger's unsuccessful effort to break out of the spell of the subjectivist philosophy that, Habermas believes, inevitably results from the philosophy of origin. This image of Heidegger's post–*Kehre* entanglement in a philosophy of origin contradicts an earlier pronouncement by Habermas in the *Philosophical-Political Profiles*, namely, that philosophy as the philosophy of origin became *impossible* for Heidegger after *Being and Time* because of Heidegger's confrontation during the composition of this work with the inevitably temporal nature of truth.[38] At any rate, the *Kehre* as Habermas interprets it in *The Philosophical Discourse of Modernity* represents Heidegger's attempt to turn *Ursprungsphilosophie* on its head by temporalizing the first principle of the philosophy of origin, which had lacked this finitude because the self-assertion of Heidegger's early subjectivity possessed a metaphysical authority that the *Kehre* forces it to cast off. Although in Habermas's view Heidegger's now temporalized philosophy of origin gives rise to a multiplicity of truths, these truths take on a sacral aura that allows them to appear at once provincial and total – a direct result of

Heidegger's endowing of the metahistorical and temporally fluid power of origin ('Ursprungsmacht') with the attribution of the event of truth.[39]

Habermas believes Heidegger's identification with national socialism is the path that led him to a temporalized philosophy of origin. Dasein as the ontological description of the historically constituted life of the individual is transformed through this path into the site of the collective destiny of the German people. After the fall of national socialism, Heidegger abdicates personal responsibility for his collaboration by asserting that an objective absence of truth had taken place. Fascism becomes a symptom for Heidegger, and the pathos of a letting-be ('Seinlassen') is the theoretical manifestation of Heidegger's abdication, although he remains under the spell of 'Subjektphilosophie.'[40]

I noted earlier that Adorno and Jaspers made a powerful case for linking Heidegger's philosophy of origin to his adherence in the 1930s to national socialist dogma. Although Habermas doesn't include the accusation of autochthonous totalitarianism in his critique of Heidegger's 'temporalized' philosophy of origin, he sees the same evil subjectivity at work there. Unsurprisingly, in view of Habermas's own philosophical priorities, his equation of Heidegger's philosophy of origin with a 'Subjektphilosophie' stems largely from what he sees as Heidegger's failure to adequately address the interpersonal element in human Dasein.[41] Habermas's association of Heidegger's notion of Dasein with a transcendental Fichtean subjectivity grounded in a philosophy of origin is, from my perspective, a reversal of Heidegger's real priorities; Heidegger actually draws on the principle of origin to show Dasein in its alterity, dissemination, and finitude. This temporal dimension of Heidegger's notion of origin is as evident *before* the 'turn' as it is *afterward*. There is indeed, as Habermas suggests, a certain Husserlian solipsism in Heidegger's view of intersubjectivity.[42] On balance, however, Habermas cannot entirely sustain his attempt to link Heidegger's principle of origin to an authoritarian philosophy rooted in a privileged metaphysical subject.[43]

It cannot be denied, of course, that Heidegger's philosophy of origin provided no obstacle to his embrace of Nazism in the Third

Reich's early years. Both Adorno and Habermas have shown, albeit in an overly one-sided manner, that Heidegger was quite capable of enacting *Ursprungsphilosophie* in its totalizing sense, and it requires no originary 'leap' to undertake a transition from totalizing philosophy to totalitarian practice. When origin is evoked as 'first causation' rather than as 'manifold origination,' to quote Schürmann again, then it is possible to embrace as 'destiny' the unique, autochthonously rooted dominion of a given *Volk*.[44] This evocation of primordial privilege was a core tendency of Nazism, and no one articulated it with greater pomposity than Heidegger. Schürmann, whose article on Heidegger's political thinking is cited approvingly by Habermas,[45] has shown, however, that Heidegger's opposition to teleology is tied to his advocacy of 'the destruction of a hypostatized First,' a dominant trend in his philosophy. This is the reason why Heidegger evokes origin more often as plurivalent than as unitary in his writing, why he sees it more often 'as the multifarious emergence of the phenomena around us' than as something to be conjured into the service of a hegemonic will to power.[46]

Habermas refers to Derrida's critique of Heidegger and to his general deconstruction of phonocentrism as an 'outbidding of the temporalized philosophy of origin.'[47] Although Derrida's irritated reaction to Habermas's reproach that he offers nothing new in his critique of Heidegger and that his deconstructive philosophy is essentially a Jewish mystical version of Heidegger's philosophy of origin is thoroughly justified, there is some merit in Habermas's use of this description as a subtitle for his essay on Derrida in *The Philosophical Discourse of Modernity*.[48] While recognizing the temporal dimension of Heidegger's principle of origin, Derrida still detects within it a strongly metaphysical telos. He takes note of Heidegger's distinction between originary and derivative time in *Being and Time* for example, and asks, 'Now, is not the opposition of the *originary* to the *derivative* still metaphysical? Is not the quest for an *archia* in general, no matter with what precautions one surrounds the concept, still the "essential" operation of metaphysics?'[49] Earlier, Derrida had described this distinction as one between 'originary and nonoriginary' time and as being inscribed by the Hegelianism Heidegger would overcome.[50] Derrida himself would overcome the 'metaphysics of presence' he discerns in Heidegger's treatment of time in Hegel through recourse to his own principle of *différance*, which allows us to 'think a writing without presence and without absence, without history, without cause, without *archia*, without *telos*.'[51] *Différance*, after all, subverts the quest for a privileged, empowering beginning – what Adorno would refer to as an absolute ground and what Derrida associates with the *archē*.[52] In this sense, Habermas's description of Derrida's project as an 'outbidding of the temporalized philosophy of origin' is accurate: Derrida would expose the dynamic temporality of Heidegger's notion of origin and the originary as inscribed by an atemporal metaphysics.[53] He would 'outbid' Heidegger's temporality by drawing on his own notion of *différance*, which subverts temporal and semantic closure and thus metaphysics by betraying their teleological trace in all Western discourse, whether that discourse is constituted by the empowering notion of the *archē* or by Heidegger's postulation of the ontic-ontological difference – the distinction between 'Being and beings.'[54]

The chief problem with Derrida's critique of Heidegger's notion of originary time is his tacit association of the Heideggerian *archē* with the post-Platonic rendering of this term. Heidegger and Derrida *both* view *archē* in its traditional sense as a normative and empowering first cause (*Ur-sache*). We must, however, answer Derrida's question about the necessity for equating the search for an *archia* with the 'essential' operation of metaphysics with a resounding 'no' because we can now see that Heidegger's uncoupling of *archē* and *aitia* allows *archē* to be inscribed by the antitranscendent, 'strategic and adventurous' operations of what Derrida came to call *différance*.[55] Pre-Socratic *archē*, after all, in its Heideggerian renaissance already suggests the nongrounded foregrounding of dissemination, alterity, and finitude evoked by Derrida's term. Derrida himself has shown that the Aristotelian *arkhē*, suggestive of 'beginning and commanding,' may be taken 'one step further toward a sort of original an-archy.' Given its political and academic consequences, this is a step Derrida would not like to take.[56] However, *archē* without *aitia* does not represent anarchy for Heidegger. His uncoupled *archē* lacks determinacy and thus resists any dialectical slippage into the radical overthrow of a determinate 'commanding.' With respect to Heidegger's reading of Hegel in *Being and Time*, it would be difficult to argue that creating an opposition between originary and derivative time and speaking of a 'fall' from originary, authentic time may be read as metaphysical.[57] One may argue, with Schürmann, however, that in spite of an apparently similar metaphysical resonance in the vocabularies of Hegel and Heidegger, 'Heideggerian phenomenology does not permit one to speak of a rationality underlying the reversals of history. For Heidegger, the essence of metaphysics is not itself metaphysical.'[58] Read in this way, the evocation of an *authentic* temporality in *originary* time can be seen as an attempt to evoke a historical space distinguished from *derivative* – that is, metaphysically constituted and subjectively manipulated – historical time.

Such a proposition is lent credence by Heidegger's *Der Satz vom Grund* (1957; *The Principle of Reason*). In an essay on the (usually neglected) aporias behind the 'principle of reason' by which the university, as an institution, likes to imagine itself governed, Derrida draws heavily on this late work. He notes that Heidegger calls the principle of reason into question by meditating on the long period of 'incubation' that separates its emergence and the scientific and technological practices to which it led from their common origin in Aristotle's metaphysical search for a *prima philosophia*. Derrida allies himself with Heidegger's praxis by calling the principle of reason into question.[59] However, Heidegger's evocation of an antimetaphysical temporality with which to undermine the unquestioned presuppositions of the principle of reason is even more subversive of this principle than Derrida's questioning of academic priorities. Heidegger objects to the subjective authoritarianism of the technological sciences, a dominance that has the principle of sufficient reason as its foundation (SG 201).[60] In a move parallel to his uncoupling of *aitia* and *archē*, Heidegger calls into question the conflation of Being and ratio (SG 175). Thought must risk a leap ('Sprung') that is a springing away from ('Absprung') the principle of reason. Instead of simply shedding it, however, thought appropriates it in a more originary ('ursprünglichere') way (SG 107).

Thought's leap must remain so originary, and thus radically temporal, that no metaphysical privileging from a principle of reason – Aristotelian, Hegelian, technological, or otherwise – can be sustained:

> 'Darin liegt: Das Denken muß den Sprung immer neu und ursprünglicher springen. Bei diesem immer anfänglicheren Springen des Sprunges gibt es keine Wiederholung und keine Wiederkehr. Es bedarf des Sprunges, bis das andenkende Vordenken in das Sein als Sein sich selber aus der Wahrheit des Seins zu einem anderen Sagen verwandelt hat.' (SG 159)

> [It follows that thought must leap the leap in an ever newer and more originary way. With this ever more incipient leap of the leap there is no repetition and no return. The leap is necessary until the remembering thinking ahead into Being as Being has transformed itself from the truth of Being to another telling.]

The originary leap, the *Ur-Sprung,* is volatile and escapes the quiescence and plenitude of a final truth. Like the praxis of deconstruction, the originary leap points to the fact of unlimited semiosis, to the circumstance that there must always be 'another telling.' Being invested with the dynamic of an originary leap always transcends itself and is irreducible to a single constitutive locus. It is only a projection of the leap itself. Heidegger's late articulation of Being thus has much in common with contemporary efforts informed by poststructuralist challenges to the concept of a static and isolated individual, to reconstellate this figure as a dynamic and multivalent construct. For example, John Smith, in his review essay on these efforts to recuperate the individual, draws both on Hegel's famous reconciliation of the subject/object dualism through the imagery of an annihilating bacchanalian dance and Derrida's deconstruction of this trope to arrive at a new proposal for conceptualizing individual *'transcendance'* (sic). Just as Heideggerian Being is defined through the originary leap itself and is invested with the choreography of a 'remembering thinking ahead,' Smith's individual is constituted through a choreographically informed motion, a series of coordinated but not foreordained steps. Moreover, neither Heidegger's originary leap nor Smith's 'dance' allow for reduction, regulative iteration, or predetermined signification in their formulations of, respectively, 'Being as Being' and the transcended individual. According to Smith, 'The individual's ontological status is closest to that of an actual performance: both are irreducible to a structure of representations (Labanotation notwithstanding); both can be repeated only in acts that point out their unrepeatability; both thus generate processes of interpretation without the telos of meaning.'[61]

Derrida's clearest attempt to distance himself from Heidegger's principle of origin comes at the outset of his early work *De la Grammatologie* (1967; *Of Grammatology*): 'The ontico-ontological difference and its ground (*Grund*) in the "transcendence of Dasein" are not absolutely originary. Differance by itself would be more "originary," but one would no longer be able to call it "origin" or "ground," those notions belonging essentially to the history of onto-theology, to the system functioning as the effacing of difference.'[62]

The thrust of this book has been to show that the notion of origin does *not* belong inevitably to this system. As was the case with Nietzsche, Benjamin, Adorno, and Rosenzweig, Heidegger's 'originary' thought serves to *heighten* our awareness of the difference, marginality, and dissemination that inscribe historically constituted Being-in-the-world. What Derrida seeks to evoke in the term *différance* is already elicited by Heideggerian *Ursprung,* namely, the radical alterity with which Dasein as elucidated in the 'ontico-ontological difference' confronts the subjective metaphysical construct of a unitary Being.

One of Derrida's more recent published engagements with Heidegger is found in his analysis of Heidegger's treatment of the concept 'spirit' (*Geist*): *De l'esprit: Heidegger et la question* (1987; *Of Spirit: Heidegger and the Question*). Derrida continues in this work to equate Heidegger's notion of origin and the originary with a refined view of temporal, historical antecedence, with a pointing toward what is earlier in time or even prior to it. Specifically, Derrida examines Heidegger's consistent attempt after *Being and Time* to invest the term *Geist* with an atemporal purity. In such works as *An Introduction to Metaphysics*, Heidegger characterizes the Germans

as the most metaphysical of peoples and alleges that they are en-
dowed with 'spiritual' powers that can bring them beyond and before history to Being's originary realm. Derrida is quite justified in
questioning the privilege Heidegger accords the words *Geist* and
geistlich in his later writing, insofar as Heidegger discovers in them
a more originary connotation than can be found in the Greek and
Latin *pneuma* and *spiritus*. For Derrida's Heidegger, *Geist* suggests
the destructive immolation of the flame, a flame closest to the complex resonance of the German form of 'spirit.' Although he never
does so directly, Derrida evokes the tremendous danger and du-
plicity of Heidegger's privileging; the white ash of the residue of
Geist as an exclusionary German 'trait,' a *Geist* that would ontologically efface and effect the 'brutal foreclose' of *pneuma, spiritus,*
and the Hebrew *ruah* cannot be divorced from the 'abyssal' power
of Nazi discourse.[63] For Derrida, it is no coincidence that *Geist* as a
leading term in Heidegger's vocabulary first leaves the shelter and
the restraint of quotation marks (the diacritical embrace that reins
in the authoritarian power of *Geist* in *Being and Time*) in his most
manifestly Nazi writing, the 'Rektoratsrede' ('Rectorial Address')
of 1933. Despite his subtlety, Derrida's message is clear: the destructive flame, the glow, and the white ash of Heideggerian *Geist*
are *spiritually* connected to the creation of the flame and the ashes
of history's ultimate exclusionary act, the Holocaust.

How does one evoke an *inclusionary* spirit, how does one create
through a dialogue with Heidegger's writing an alterity, a plurality,
a 'spirit,' that is 'entirely other' in the double sense of that term?
How can Heidegger's spirit 'still say something to us'?; how can a
'*we* which is perhaps not *given*' be brought into a discourse with Heidegger, with Heidegger's reading of Georg Trakl's poetry (where
Geist is brought into contiguity with *Flamme*)?[64] The answer is as-
tonishing, coming as it does from the individual most responsible
for bringing about the almost unquestioned contemporary equation of origin with univocality, with a metaphysical homogeneity.
What 'would lead back to the spirituality of a promise' is the inscription of Heidegger's reading of Trakl with 'an *other* birth and
an *other* essence, origin-heterogeneous (*hétérogène à l'origine*) to all
the testaments, all the promises, all the events, all the laws and

assignments which are our very memory.' Even more, it would be 'origin-heterogeneous because at the origin of the origin.'[65] If Derrida himself is capable of using the notion of origin to evoke heterogeneity and alterity, to reinvest Heidegger's reading of Trakl with a pluralism Heidegger seems to want to efface, if, indeed, there can be an affiliation for Derrida between what is heterogeneous and what is most originary, then perhaps a reassessment of origin is well under way.

Definitions and Implications
of Radical Origin

What kind of definition or definitions of radical origin emerge from the treatments and theories of *Ursprung* in the works of Nietzsche, Benjamin, Adorno, Rosenzweig, and Heidegger? What are the theoretical and philosophical implications of radical origin and the conclusions to be drawn from the constellation of ideas surrounding this issue in their work? A summary of their enactments of a philosophy of origin – their figuration of *Ursprung* as a rhetorically volatile signifier – allows, despite their differences, for the development of a coherent strand of thinking not so much antithetical to poststructuralism as anticipatory and corrective of it. Radical origin does not emerge as a counterposition to poststructuralist thought, but it does show that many of its leading proponents' one-sided attacks are misguided. In placing the principle of origin into an antithetical relationship with such sanctioned constructs as 'play' (Derrida), 'beginnings' (Said), 'genealogy,' (Foucault), and 'repetition' (Miller), binary oppositions are created. Because the deconstruction of binary oppositions is one of the primary means by which poststructuralists attempt to expose the fallacies of Western metaphysical thought and because current critical practices stress the radical indeterminacy of meaning in lexical signifiers, a genuinely poststructuralist reading of *Ursprung* should evoke its rich nuances, its polyvalent nature, and its resistance to the closure of one-sided definitions. I have attempted to show that such a reading of origin is not only possible but that *Ursprungsphilosophie* as a critical praxis of modern German thinking itself precisely constitutes a 'scene of origins' (Jameson) for poststructuralist thought.

Nietzsche was the first to appear on this scene. By inverting the terminological categories established by Foucault in his essay on Nietzsche and by adopting one of Foucault's common procedures and reading him 'against the grain' of his own discourse, I have

attempted to show that Nietzsche's originary genealogy is constituted by a dialectics of the interstice. This means that all epistemologies explored in his work, all ways of coming to know the world –
through art, religion, science, politics, and so forth – are formed by
the coming together of fundamentally conflicted discourses. Even
the divergent states of consciousness through which we perceive
the world can enact an originary interstice; the convergence of
dreaming and waking brings about the origin (*Ursprung*) of metaphysics. The intersection of the great oppositional ontologies in
antiquity, the Apollonian and the Dionysian, leads to the origin of
tragedy. These interstices do not, however, result from the simple
merging of binary oppositions to form a third category. Foucault's
conceptualization of the interstice is faithful to Nietzsche's genealogy in that it captures the radically overdetermined nature of the
categories that emerge in it. For example, the tragedy is inscribed
by *all* of the conflicted elements inherent in *both* the Apollonian
and Dionysian modalities. Tragedy, that is, cannot be defined as a
synthesis or reconciliation of these spheres.

Thus, Nietzsche's various origins are volatile and polyvalent,
and the originary interstice is a locus of multiple, indissoluble, and
dynamic tensions. This overdetermined character of the ideologies
and practices revealed by Nietzsche's exploration of their sites of
origin is the unique yet consistent trait that comes to the fore in
Nietzsche's *Ursprungsphilosophie*. His ability to evoke this character
in the ideologies and institutions he defines also constitutes his
particular contribution to a theory of radical origin. He shows that
the pursuit of origin can be tied to a genealogical praxis that allows
the objects of its exploration to emerge as richly heterogeneous
constructs. This is clearly a major desideratum of poststructuralist
critical thinking as well.

Walter Benjamin endows a theory of radical origin with an attribute rarely discussed in the analysis of discursive practices – a
rhythm. This rhythm is the result of the oscillation between destructive and redemptive ideals of praxis advocated and enacted
throughout Benjamin's writing. Benjamin does not state that the
rhythm of origin itself is inherently dualistic. Instead, the perceptual mode of those who would comprehend this rhythm must be

governed by a twofold methodology, informed by both destruction and redemption. The 'dual insight' attentive to the rhythm of origin desires to restore phenomena to their prelapsarian nominal integrity and yet retains an awareness of their fragmentary, open character. Like monads, phenomena under the sign of origin are imbued with a historical totality and yet are dynamically incomplete. Benjamin's insistence on the double character of origin-driven praxis is consistent throughout the course of his career although he focused initially on the origin of a literary genre, the German baroque *Trauerspiel.* He defines the rhythm of origin and the proper critical attitude toward it at the outset of his book on this subject, but the name of this attitude emerges as a specific praxis in the text: *allegoresis.*

As enacted in the *Trauerspiel* book, Benjaminian *allegoresis* subjects individual works to a sort of critical immolation, a microscopic analysis of disconnected details designed to reveal how the genre of the baroque *Trauerspiel,* as a specific literary phenomenon, is constituted by a concatenation of stylistic and tropological (figurative) extremities. Such a procedure has obvious attractions for poststructuralist critics, who rightly discern in such a destructive style of analysis an anticipation of contemporary deconstructive *allegoresis.* However, these critics not only elide or obfuscate the connection between origin and allegory in Benjamin's approach but, in so doing, suppress the second dimension of his originary praxis as well. Only in its dual aspect does Benjamin's methodology constitute a unique contribution to a theory of radical origin. Although there is an obvious metaphysical yearning in the redemptive dimension of Benjamin's aesthetics – an embrace of noumenal integrity at odds with most contemporary critical priorities – Benjamin's goal of imbuing the phenomena he examines with a historical totality (a telos consistently maintained throughout his career) is also an important component of his redemptive ideal. Benjamin regarded origin as a 'historical category,' and he emphasized this historical dimension much more intensely than the other figures examined in this book. For example, by treating the baroque *Trauerspiel* as an 'archetypal phenomenon of history' (which is how Benjamin retrospectively defined 'origin' itself), he invests this genre with a distinctive, discrete character that he finds missing in Nietzsche's less resolutely historical analysis of tragic forms.

The ideal of allowing phenomena to emerge in their historical totality, subsuming their pre- and posthistories, also forms the fundamental telos that operates in the two terms into which the concept of origin was transposed in Benjamin's later oeuvre: 'nowtime' and 'dialectical image.' A critical praxis closely attuned to the rhythm of origin attempts to establish these constructs in their synchronically holistic resonances, in the totality of their histories. Benjamin's book on the German baroque *Trauerspiel* offers a practical example of this procedure, alternating between culling and minutely examining a wealth of details from many individual works and analyzing the *Trauerspiel* as a genre not only throughout the course of its actual historical existence but in its prehistory (as anticipated by such forms as the classical tragedy) and posthistory (its resonance in such later manifestations as German expressionist drama) as well. This 'dual insight' evokes the rhythm of the *Trauerspiel's Ursprung*, and it is Benjamin's unique contribution to a theory of radical origin.

Far more than most poststructuralist thinkers – who are usually content to establish 'origin' as the negative term in a variety of binary oppositions – Adorno has shown us what an origin-based critical praxis should *not* be. In his unsparing assault on the philosophies of origin of figures such as Husserl, Heidegger, and Jaspers, Adorno exposes the authoritarian ideological trace latent in their trajectories when they attempt to establish transcendental first principles, subjective mastery of the natural world, and the primacy of the autochthonic. What Adorno regards as common to all such philosophies of origin is a backward or inwardly directed gaze; a dangerous nostalgia for nonalienated, intuitive forms of cognition anchored in subjective interiority or its opposite: a Heideggerian pseudomystical passive receptivity (*Gelassenheit*) toward the objects and forces of the external world. The overcoming of the objective world's alterity may also be sought through the attempt to go back into history to establish its starting point (*Beginn*), which Adorno believes was the objective of Hegel's philosophy of origin.

Thus, Adorno attempts, as previous analyses of his principle of origin have established, to ground *Ursprung* as a positive heuristic category in the alterity of history and to explore it from a resolutely contemporary perspective. This focus on the otherness of the external world and the determination to adhere to the present in all its ephemerality are the distinctive components of Adorno's elucidation of origin as a valid critical construct. In order to magnify the alterity of the nonsubjective, however, Adorno attempts to show that all discursive practices are constituted, *at their origin*, by the desire to overcome it. Modern art, modern science, and modern technology are present-day manifestations of the age-old effort to subvert and master natural domination. Nevertheless, Adorno is consistently interested much more in exploring the nuances of these manifestations *as* constructs of the present day than in analyzing their historical antecedents, except as these antecedents are relevant to, and can be seen inscribed in, contemporary phenomena. This is what is meant by Adorno's adherence to the present in his exploration of problems of origin and in his notion of origin as a positive critical principle. While origin is thus less of a historical category in Adorno's oeuvre than in Benjamin's, it is also free of the trace of nostalgia one discerns in Benjamin's yearning for the prelapsarian and in his desire to establish an 'urhistory of modernity.' This nostalgia, largely responsible for Adorno's dispute with Benjamin, should ideally be absent from a theory of radical origin. This was a lesson taught by Adorno more than anyone else.

All but one of the thinkers treated in this book are considered to have made an important impact on poststructuralist theories. Part of my intention, particularly in my chapters on Nietzsche and Benjamin, has been to show how those who use these figures as authoritative, indeed authorizing, voices in their own discourse suppress the name of one of the key principles that influenced their work, namely, 'origin.' The one major figure whose writing did not play a significant role in shaping current critical debate, and whose inclusion therefore provoked some consternation in one of the early readers of my manuscript, was Franz Rosenzweig. I included him because of the strong linkage in his work between a uniquely constellated principle of origin and a sphere of human life seen

as rigorously circumscribed by existential facticity, by the immanence (imposed by the certainty of death) no subjective idealistic
philosophy can transcend, and by God's unbridgeable distance
from the side of the creational equation occupied by man. The
strongest and most consistent charge made against the principle of
origin by the broad range of critical thinkers associated with poststructuralism is that it is an inevitably metaphysical category, a
term equated with the attainment of ideals projected to lie outside
the confinements of space, time, and language. Although Rosenzweig's magnum opus, *The Star of Redemption,* is a largely theological treatise, I have tried to show that his oeuvre, more than any
other, demonstrates that this charge is not always valid.

Even more powerfully than Adorno, Rosenzweig first anchors
his mundane conception of origin in a refutation of German idealism. The philosophy of origin developed by Rosenzweig after his
book on Hegel was largely inspired by his reading of Hermann
Cohen. Of fundamental interest to Rosenzweig in Cohen's 'logic of
origin' was the 'new concept' of the Nought. This category of determinate negation allows Cohen to anchor judgments concerning questions of origin in the real world, circumscribed by death,
ephemerality, and the confusion attendant upon the cognitive limitations faced by man, which no idealistic theorems can realisti-
cally hope to transcend. All judgments hoping to establish any
genuine ontological foundations for transcendent concepts held
dear by humanity, such as the soul, immortality, and infinity, must
first face the chaos and uncertainty posed by factical existence as
inscribed in the Nought. This is the 'judgment of origin.'

Cohen attempted to mitigate the fearsome negativity of such a
philosophy of origin by establishing a coherence among the units
of origin created in the transition from the Nought to the transcendent positivities associated with the Aught. Rosenzweig, however,
never attempts to avoid the looming nullities imposed by the transitory character of life. Although he, like Cohen, conceptualizes a
perfected metaphysical sphere associated with the Aught of God –
God in his internal fullness – he sees origins as essential, differentiated, and circumscribed by temporality. One can begin to think of
creation in its totality, according to Rosenzweig, only by first at-

tending to the ephemeral, the concrete, and the factical of mundane existence, and this pluralist, fractious character of real life is what inheres in origin. Despite his metaphysics, Rosenzweig's philosophy, more than any other, allows us to see that origin can be viewed as the very antithesis of transcendent metaphysical idealism, the character ascribed to it by such thinkers as Derrida, Foucault, and Said. In the oeuvre of Rosenzweig, the principle of origin is evoked as a category of immanent, multiple, factically grounded radical negation. Thus, as a specifically epistemological construct, origin in Rosenzweig has a signification, a particular semantic nuance, precisely opposite to what is intended by this term in the writing of almost all poststructuralists. I believe this circumstance justifies his inclusion in this book and suggests as well his important contribution to a theory of radical origin.

If, among the figures treated in this work, Rosenzweig as a philosopher of origin has drawn the least attention from contemporary theorists, a figure whose *Ursprungsphilosophie* bears some striking resemblances to Rosenzweig's has elicited the most attention. Like Rosenzweig, Heidegger's philosophical investigations never shrank from a resolute attention to the facticity of human Dasein. Indeed, their views are so closely allied in this fundamental domain that I decided to violate chronological sense by placing the chapters on these two thinkers next to each other. Nevertheless, Heidegger's thought differs from Rosenzweig's in that it lacks an avowedly metaphysical dimension. Indeed, Heidegger's project of writing an end to Western metaphysics constitutes the major source of his inspiration for leading deconstructionists such as Derrida and Miller. They attempt to further this project partly by exposing what they see as latent metaphysical tendencies in Heidegger's own writing, particularly where Heidegger adumbrates a philosophy of origin. For example, Derrida regards Heidegger's 'quest for an *archia*' as equivalent to a search for the transcendentally originary, for a metaphysics of presence rooted in the privileging of *Ursprung*. It is certainly true that Heidegger has constant recourse to the concept of *archē*, the rough Greek equivalent of 'origin.' However, deconstructionist critics tend to ignore Heidegger's grounding of *archē* as a philosophical paradigm in its pre-

Socratic roots prior to its conflation with the principle of *aitia* or 'cause.' This decoupling is perhaps Heidegger's most significant act for my purposes. This division allows *archē*, the 'origin' of Western conceptual 'origin' itself, to be seen as indeterminate, unfixed, multiple, and disseminated. Thus, origin cannot function as a stable ground for a metaphysics of presence. Reiner Schürmann has admirably demonstrated the remarkable multivalence signified by the term *Ursprung* as a seminal element in the Heideggerian vocabulary, and this multivalence is largely legitimated through Heidegger's originary decoupling.

Given the importance of the act of division in Heidegger's movement toward a radicalized notion of origin, it is somewhat ironic that the second important and unique facet of this movement lies in Heidegger's use of multiplication to create doubled or simultaneous origins. Like Nietzsche, Heidegger used the term *Herkunft* (meaning 'ancestry' or 'provenance') to indicate what traditional historiographies pursued by branches of science, such as anthropology, seek to establish. Like Foucault, Heidegger wanted to overcome the linearity inherent in the methodological procedures of the traditional historicist approaches to exploring the evolution of discursive practices. Early in his writings, he resorted frequently to the concept of *Gleichursprünglichkeit*, a term he apparently borrowed from Max Scheler and suggesting a simultaneity of origin, to evoke the possibility of a more dynamic historiography. He also drew on this principle as a way of establishing balance, of avoiding an overemphasis on or a possibly metaphysical favoring of any of the specific elements he drew upon in constellating his ontology. For example, he employs the term *gleichursprünglich* in *Being and Time* to show how human existence as 'Dasein,' as individuated Being-in-the-world, is rooted in a simultaneity of origin, insofar as Dasein is constituted equally and contemporaneously by human striving toward *perfectio* and human deliverance to a state of being thrown into the world, a state signified by Heidegger's famous term *Geworfenheit*. The simultaneity of origin informing Dasein is itself rooted in care. In order to expand upon Kant's dualistic view of cognition – his belief that cognition has its origin in both subjective reason and sensual modes of perception – Heidegger reverts to a related term, *Doppelursprung,* to suggest a double origin. Heidegger's use of such lexical formulas as 'double origin' and 'simultaneity of origin' stems from his desire to *avoid* any recourse to the establishment of unitary foundational sites in the constitution of his basic philosophical principles. When, as in his reading of Hölderlin, origin is tied to the inextricable entanglement of the conflicted elements inscribing Dasein, such as forgetting and remembrance or revelation and concealment, the turn to signifiers suggesting compounded and contemporaneous origins is rendered unnecessary. However, the concept of *Gleichursprünglichkeit* in particular serves to blunt the charge that Heidegger's philosophy of origin is tied solely to the conjuration of authoritarian first principles (Adorno) or to a metaphysical ground (Derrida). It also provides an intriguing dimension to a theory of radical origin.

A brief summary of the possible constitutive elements and approaches inhering in such a theory – at least of those elements suggested by the theories of origin of the five thinkers examined in this text – reveals a wealth of heuristic principles. An investigator attuned to the constellation of characteristics brought together in a theory of radical origin would be aware, as was Nietzsche, that the discourses one analyzes can arise from the coming together of fundamentally conflicted forces, resulting in overdetermined constructs whose origins are dynamic and volatile. In exploring these constructs, one might want to evoke the dialectical 'rhythm' of origin by examining them, as Benjamin did, in the totality of their histories (which encompasses both what preceded and what followed them) while at the same time dissecting and analyzing the phenomena that structure these constructs. Such an analysis would also draw on Adorno's awareness of the pitfalls of *Ursprungsphilosophie* and would avoid a recourse to subjectively intuited or primordial origins insofar as such a nostalgic pursuit can lead to authoritarian 'first principles' and a favoring of the autochthonous. Instead, the advocate of a theory of radical origin would examine questions of origin from a contemporary perspective and address contemporary issues (or at least issues of contemporary relevance) and would, like Adorno, be constantly aware of the alterity inherent in whatever objective constructs he or she is investigating.

A thinker whose crticial praxis is informed by a radical philosophy of origin could avoid looking for metaphysical solutions to existential dilemmas involving problems of origin by adhering to a principle of origin rooted in determinate negation, a negation based on the facticity of ephemeral, death-ridden life (an approach taken by Rosenzweig). This methodology would allow origins even in the theological domain to be probed without resorting to the metaphysics of idealism. Thinkers whose praxis is informed by the insights generated by a theory of radical origin could also use Heideggerian heuristic formulas such as 'simultaneity of origin' or 'double origin' to keep a balanced perspective when delineating the origin or origins of the constructs and practices he or she is investigating. A constant awareness of the pre-Socratic resonance of *archē* as it is reestablished by Heidegger – divorced, that is, from an unmediated link to authoritarian first causes – will also help sustain one's sense of radical origins as polyvalent and disseminated. The common thread in all of the philosophies of origin explored in this book – and the one imperative of all critical undertakings aware of the rich nuances in such lexical signifiers as *archē* and *Ursprung* – is, after all, a strict attention to the open, plural nature of all discourses. It is a plurality and openness inherent in – and capable of evocation through an exploration of – the origins of such discourses, as well as what is originary within them.

Most students of German literature are familiar with the parable of the rings in G. E. Lessing's play *Nathan der Weise* (1779; *Nathan the Wise*). Nathan, a Jewish merchant famed both for his wealth and erudition, is summoned to an audience with Sultan Saladin, a medieval sovereign in Jerusalem faced with a depleted treasury. Nathan is prepared to meet Saladin's material needs but is surprised to be confronted with a theological question: Saladin wants to know why this learned man has remained a Jew, why Judaism can claim to be the one true religion and thus superior to Christianity and Islam. After a moment's reflection, Nathan responds with his ring parable: in the distant past, a man who has inherited a ring with the secret power to make its possessor agreeable to God and man must decide which of his three sons shall inherit it. Because he loves his sons equally, he cannot bring himself to exclude two of them from his gift. He therefore has a talented artist produce two artificial rings, indistinguishable from the genuine article. Unable to distinguish the original, magic ring himself, he takes a last leave from each son, individually blesses them, and gives each one a ring, leading each of the sons to believe he alone is lord of the house. They turn to a judge to decide which of them possesses the authentic jewel. The judge tells them that because the original ring makes its bearer especially beloved in both the divine and earthly spheres and because each son seems to love himself above his brothers, the true ring must have been lost. He leaves them with the following advice: If each son believes he owns the magic ring, each one should strive to give evidence of this by leading a genuinely virtuous and agreeable life. The sons, in other words, should try to outdo one another in gentleness, accommodation, and devotion to God. If the rings should then express their powers after many generations, the sons' descendants should appear before the same court, where a wiser judge than himself will presumably be able to make a decision.

Lessing adapted the ring parable from a similar tale in Boccaccio's *Decameron* (1349–52). Boccaccio's story is constructed to highlight the Jew's cleverness in escaping his sultan's more straightforwardly extortionate scheme. Lessing reconfigured this episode in order to express in a parable what *Nathan the Wise* expresses as an allegory: no one religion can claim to be in possession of absolute truth, and Jews, Christians, and Moslems are truly brothers. If adherents of these three confessions nevertheless want to prove their own faith's special legitimacy, they should demonstrate it by living ethical, virtuous, and pious lives.

The search for the true, magical ring can be regarded as a search for foundational origin, the sort of search decried again and again by poststructuralists. Their repudiation of this search constitutes in large measure the foundational strategy that has generated the various movements grouped under the umbrella term 'poststructuralism.' This search is in turn associated with a whole range of deprecated philosophical constructs and social ills: logocentrism, authoritarianism, sexism, and philosophical first principles are the most striking. Lessing's parable suggests that the movement toward origin may be viewed in a different light. First, he shows that such a movement is inevitable, driven by human nature. People *will* search for the authentic, the original, and the foundational from religious and other motives no matter how much these efforts are decried and in spite of even legitimate attempts (today most evident in postmodern art) to call the boundaries separating fact from fiction and the authentic from the artificial into question.

How then can the endeavor to find origin and the use of origin as a heuristic principle be positive and constructive, respectful of pluralism and the alterity of the Other? By envisioning origin as marked by radical indeterminacy, by creating a task infinitely resistant to facile attempts to bridge the gap between origin and outcome, 'origin and goal,' Lessing again provides a hint toward an answer. He shows us in ethical terms what the philosophers examined in this book claim should govern *Ursprung* as a methodological principle; the probing of origin should not be treated as a simple historical look backward, as an attempt to find what is chronologically antecedent and therefore authentic. It must instead be grounded equally in facticity, and in the here-and-now of human morality. Such morality clearly encompasses a respect for difference. In Lessing's terms, this respect, equated with gentleness and tolerance, serves as a sign one is on the right path toward origin and as a commonsense corrective to poststructuralist celebrations of alterity and diversity in all forms, which have tended to treat these concepts as mere platitudes. Valuable as they are as genuine human ideals, concepts such as alterity and diversity need the link to genuine human proclivities suggested by Nathan's parable.

This link to human realities also has ramifications for a political dimension of a theory of radical origin. The commitments to 'pluralism' professed by many universities and other institutions may have achieved a few positive results, but they have mainly generated angry backlashes, cries of 'political correctness,' and a more deeply segregated society. Moreover, individual ethnic groups have tended to engage in searches for their own unique and discrete origins. Such searches teach us a great deal and balance the general Eurocentric focus traditionally regarded as possessing a universal validity for studies in the humanities. Exclusionary practices of any kind, however, tend to be quite divisive. In certain areas of the world they have led, and are leading once again, to genocide.

Human nature, however, will not allow us simply to abandon such searches – voyages of discovery for foundations, roots, and origin. My theory of radical origin has attempted to show the possibility of grounding pluralism, alterity, and openness (a better term perhaps than 'indeterminacy') *at* the origin, an origin that is inherently volatile and plurivalent and subject to constant reexamination. Such a theory may ideally allow the movement toward origins to generate harmony and fellowship rather than just divisions along national, religious, racial, ethnic, and epistemological lines. Future debates and future work will, it is hoped, further this project. When 'origin is the goal,' the goal is not always an end.

INTRODUCTION

1. Later published as *The Historical Perspective in German Genre Theory: Its Development from Gottsched to Hegel* (Stuttgart: Hans-Dieter Heinz, 1985).

2. George Steiner, introd. to *The Origin of German Tragic Drama*, by Walter Benjamin, trans. John Osborne (London: New Left Books, 1977), 16.

3. 'For Benjamin, as for every German thinker after Herder, the word *Ursprung* is resonant.' Steiner, *The Origin*, 15. Herder's arguments can be found in his *Abhandlung über den Ursprung der Sprache* (1772; *Essay on the Origin of Language*); see volume 2 of his *Werke*, ed. Wolfgang Pross (München: Carl Hanser, 1987), 251–399.

4. For a radically different view of Herder's treatment of the problem of the origin of language, which holds that Herder was able to 'bypass' this problem by denying such an origin actually existed, see Michael Morton, '*Verum est factum:* Critical Realism and the Discourse of Autonomy,' *German Quarterly* 64 (1991): 153–54.

5. Paul Ricoeur, 'Psychoanalysis and the Movement of Contemporary Culture,' trans. Willis Domingo, in *The Conflict of Interpretations: Essays in Hermeneutics*, ed. Don Ihde (Evanston IL: Northwestern UP, 1974), 121–59.

6. Jacques Derrida, 'Structure, Sign, and Play in the Discourse of the Human Sciences,' in *Writing and Difference*, trans. Alan Bass (London: Routledge & Kegan Paul, 1978), 292.

7. Derrida, *Of Spirit: Heidegger and the Question*, trans. Geoffrey Bennington and Rachel Bowlby (Chicago: U of Chicago P, 1989). See esp. 107–8, where Derrida adumbrates the possible latent meanings inscribing the term '*origin-heterogeneous (hétérogène à l'origine)*' without finding the heterogeneous and origin inherently antithetical as he had on previous occasions. An example of this earlier tendency can be found in the essays 'The Supplement of Origin' and 'Differance' in *Speech and Phenom-*

ena and Other Essays on Husserl's Theory of Signs, trans. David B. Allison (Evanston IL: Northwestern UP, 1973), 88–104, 129–60. In these essays, Derrida indicates that *differance* must *replace* origin in order to foreground the principle of alterity. Derrida's 'turn' will be discussed in chapter 5.

8. Roland Barthes, 'The Death of the Author' in *Image—Music—Text,* ed. and trans. Stephen Heath (New York: Hill & Wang, 1977), 142.

9. Barthes, *S/Z,* trans. Richard Miller (New York: Hill & Wang, 1974), 10.

10. Vincent B. Leitch, *Deconstructive Criticism: An Advanced Introduction* (New York: Columbia UP, 1983), 83.

11. See, for example, his critique of Harold Bloom in *Destructive Poetics: Heidegger and Modern American Poetry* (New York: Columbia UP, 1980), 11–13.

12. See, for example, his essay 'Hermeneutics and Memory: Destroying T. S. Eliot's *Four Quartets,*' *Genre* 11 (winter 1978): 523–73, esp. 535, 563.

13. Leitch, 50.

14. Miller, *The Linguistic Moment: From Wordsworth to Stevens* (Princeton: Princeton UP, 1985), 3–4.

15. Miller, 56–58, 60–61.

16. See, for example, Paul de Man, 'The Rhetoric of Temporality, Allegory and Symbol, Irony' in *Interpretation: Theory and Practice,* ed. Charles S. Singleton (Baltimore: Johns Hopkins UP, 1969), 191: 'Whereas the symbol postulates the possibility of an identity or identification, allegory designates primarily a distance in relation to its own origin, and, renouncing the nostalgia and the desire to coincide, it establishes its language in the void of this temporal difference.'

17. Julia Kristeva, *Desire in Language: A Semiotic Approach to Literature and Art,* ed. Leon S. Roudiez, trans. Thomas Gora, Alice Jardine, and Leon S. Roudiez (New York: Columbia UP, 1980), 275.

18. Luce Irigaray, *This Sex Which Is Not One,* trans. Catherine Porter and Carolyn Burke (Ithaca NY: Cornell UP, 1985), 25.

19. See Irigaray, esp. 65, 75, 82.

20. On New Historicism's tendency, inspired by Foucault, to downplay the importance of individuated human agency in history and literature, see Robert Holub, 'New Historicism and the New World Order: The Politics of Textuality and Power in German Studies' in *Monatshefte* 84 (1992): 171–82; and Peter Uwe Hohendahl, 'A Return to History? The New Historicism and Its Agenda,' *New German Critique* 55 (winter 1992): 87–104.

21. Stephen Greenblatt, *Shakespearean Negotiations: The Circulation of Social Energy in Renaissance England* (Berkeley: U of California P, 1988), 7.

22. Jeffrey T. Nealon, 'The Discipline of Deconstruction,' *PMLA* 107 (1992): 1275.

23. Jeffrey Williams, 'Saving Deconstruction,' *PMLA* 108 (1993): 1165.

24. For a summary of *clôtural* reading as an interpretative principle, see esp. Simon Critchley, *The Ethics of Deconstruction: Derrida and Levinas* (Oxford: Blackwell, 1992), 88–97.

25. This is the title of a bilingual collection of Rilke's French verse, which includes the 'Quatrains Valaisans,' entitled *The Astonishment of Origins: French Sequences by Rainer Maria Rilke*, trans. A. Poulin Jr. (Port Townsend WA: Graywolf Press, 1982).

1. ON FOUCAULT'S RECEPTION OF NIETZSCHE

References to Foucault's 'Nietzsche, Genealogy, History' are given parenthetically in the text with the abbreviation NGH. 'Nietzsche, Genealogy, History,' in *Language Countermemory, Practice: Selected Essays and Interviews,* ed. Donald F. Bouchard, trans. Donald F. Bouchard and Sherry Simon. Ithaca NY: Cornell UP, 1977.

1. Michel Foucault, *The Archaeology of Knowledge & The Discourse on Language,* trans. A. M. Sheridan Smith (New York: Pantheon, 1972), 13.

2. Foucault, *The Order of Things: An Archaeology of the Human Sciences* (New York: Pantheon, 1970), 305.

3. Foucault, *Order,* 334. Joseph N. Riddel (*The Inverted Bell: Mod-*

ernism and the Counterpoetics of William Carlos Williams [Baton Rouge: Louisiana State UP, 1974]) also cites Nietzsche (54–55) in discussing Williams's search for origin as an endless progression backward.

4. Stanley Corngold, *The Fate of the Self: German Writers and French Theory* (New York: Columbia UP, 1986), 105.

5. Friedrich Nietzsche, *Sämtliche Werke. Kritische Studienausgabe*, ed. Giorgio Colli and Mazzino Montinari (Berlin: Walter de Gruyter, 1980), 3, 471. Hereafter cited in the text by volume and page number.

6. De Man, *Allegories of Reading: Figural Language in Rousseau, Nietzsche, Rilke, and Proust* (New Haven CT: Yale UP, 1979), 81, de Man's emphasis. Foucault (NGH 161) asserts that Nietzsche uses the term 'monumental history' parodistically.

7. The other fragment singled out by Foucault from the *Genealogy* to demonstrate that '*Entstehung* or *Ursprung* serve equally well to denote the origin of duty or guilty conscience' (NGH 140) contains the above-cited discussion of the moral conceptual world's 'Entstehungsheerd' (5:300). Thus, as is the case with Foucault's assertion concerning the 'unstressed' use of *Ursprung* in *The Gay Science*'s critique of knowledge and logic, his own examples contradict his argument.

8. Edward W. Said, *Beginnings: Intention and Method* (New York: Basic, 1975), xiii.

9. Said, *Beginnings: Intention and Method*, 2d ed. (New York: Columbia UP, 1985), xii–xiii.

10. Said, *Beginnings*, 1st ed., 174, Said's emphasis.

11. See especially the chapter 'On Originality' in Said, *The World, the Text, and the Critic* (Cambridge: Harvard UP, 1983), 126–39.

12. Stephen Fredman, *Poet's Prose: The Crisis in American Verse* (Cambridge: Cambridge UP, 1983), 14, 150 n.6.

13. In this connection, it is worth taking note of consecutive post-humously published fragments stemming from 1870–71. In the first of them, Nietzsche proposes the following title for an 'aesthetic treatise': 'Ursprung und Ziel der Tragoedie' [Origin and goal of the tragedy]. The second fragment is a 'Tragic and Dramatic Dithyramb' and commences with the elliptical item-

ization of the antitheses delineated in *The Birth of Tragedy* as constituting the *Ursprung* of the Greek tragedy:

> Dionysian Apollonian.
> The Apollonian Genius and his preparation.
> The Dionysian Genius and his birth [Geburt]
> The double genius. (7:167)

Thinking of the Greek tragedy's origin as a pluralistic *Ursprung* rather than as a univocal birth perhaps helped to inspire this unmediated listing of aesthetic and philosophical polarities.

14. Cf. Werner Stegmaier, 'Darwin, Darwinismus, Nietzsche. Zum Problem der Evolution,' *Nietzsche-Studien* 16 (1987): 264–87. Stegmaier asserts (281) that Darwin actually rejects the doctrine of the instinctual self-preservation of the species and that Nietzsche's negative remarks concerning this doctrine are directed against the 'physiologists' rather than Darwin.

15. Martin Heidegger, *Nietzsche: Der Wille zur Macht als Kunst,* vol.43 of *Gesamtausgabe* (Frankfurt: Vittorio Klosterman, 1985), 70, Heidegger's emphasis.

16. Foucault, *Order*, 334.

17. Heidegger, 73.

18. R. J. Hollingdale, *Nietzsche: The Man and His Philosophy* (Baton Rouge: Louisiana State UP, 1965), 89.

19. Charles Darwin, *The Origin of Species by Means of Natural Selection, or the Preservation of Favored Races in the Struggle for Life,* 6th ed. (New York: Thomas Y. Crowell, 1901), 457.

20. Darwin, 474.

21. Stegmaier, 269–71.

22. Ernst Behler, 'Deconstruction versus Hermeneutics: Derrida and Gadamer on Text and Interpretation,' *Southern Humanities Review* 21 (1987): 216–17.

23. Fredric Jameson, 'Postmodernism, or the Cultural Logic of Late Capitalism,' *New Left Review* 146 (1984): 59.

24. See Foucault, 'Nietzsche, la genealogie, l'histoire,' *Hommage à Jean Hyppolite* (Paris: Presses Universitaires de France, 1971), 156 and Heidegger, 'Der Ursprung des Kunstwerkes,' in *Holzwege*, 2d ed. (Frankfurt: Vittorio Klostermann, 1952), 51.

25. Heidegger, 'Ursprung,' 64–65.

26. Heidegger, 'Ursprung,' 64.

27. Cf. Foucault (NGH 141), who cites this section in claiming the origin of religion is merely 'an invention (*Erfindung*), a sleight-of-hand, an artifice (*Kunststück*).'

28. Jeffrey Minson, *Genealogies of Morals: Nietzsche, Foucault, Donzelot and the Eccentricity of Ethics* (London: MacMillan, 1985), 7. See also 76–77.

29. Peter Heller, *Dialectics and Nihilism: Essays on Lessing, Nietzsche, Mann and Kafka* (Amherst: U of Massachusetts P, 1966), 71.

30. Minson, 77.

31. Walter Gebhard, *Nietzsches Totalismus: Philosophie der Natur zwischen Verklärung und Verhängnis* (Berlin: Walter de Gruyter, 1983), 86. For a discussion of Nietzsche's concept of 'active forgetfulness' as a way of coping with the burdens of historical and personal experience, see Minson, 64–66.

32. Hubert L. Dreyfus and Paul Rabinow, *Michel Foucault: Beyond Structuralism and Hermeneutics* (Chicago: U of Chicago P, 1982), xxi.

2. WALTER BENJAMIN

1. Walter Benjamin, *Gesammelte Schriften,* ed. Rolf Tiedemann and Hermann Schweppenhäuser (Frankfurt: Suhrkamp, 1972–), vol.1, 279–83. Hereafter cited in the text by volume and page number.

2. Ferenc Feher, 'Lukács and Benjamin: Parallels and Contrasts,' *New German Critique* 34 (1985): 125, Feher's emphasis. In mentioning Nietzsche's 'overwhelming authority,' Feher is referring, of course, to *The Birth of Tragedy.*

3. Richard Wolin, *Walter Benjamin: An Aesthetic of Redemption* (New York: Columbia UP, 1982), 43.

4. Cf. Leo Bersani, *The Culture of Redemption* (Cambridge: Harvard UP, 1990). In his section on Benjamin (48–63), Bersani argues that Benjamin's mystifying ahistoricism, embrace of an ideal prelapsarian language, and redemptive aesthetics are precisely what make him so attractive to contemporary critics, particularly deconstructionists. According to Bersani, the Ben-

jaminian telos of 'transcending' history through miraculous reading and Benjamin's notion that only criticism can redeem artistic beauty for knowledge correspond to deconstructive criticism's own hidden agenda.

5. Michael Jennings, 'Benjamin as a Reader of Hölderlin: The Origins of Benjamin's Theory of Literary Criticism,' *German Quarterly* 56 (1983): 551: 'Truth, which attains its full meaning only in the "final condition" described in detail in the preface to the *Trauerspielbuch,* is present in the world, albeit hidden in fragmentary form.'

6. David Couzens Hoy, *The Critical Circle: Literature, History, and Philosophical Hermeneutics* (Berkeley: U of California P, 1978), 5.

7. For an elaboration of this aspect of Benjamin's thought, see Lieselotte Wiesenthal, *Zur Wissenschaftstheorie Walter Benjamins* (Frankfurt: Athenäum, 1973), 35–47.

8. This oscillation between empiricism and metaphysics in Benjamin's phenomenology has been nicely summarized by Wolin, *Walter Benjamin,* 92–93.

9. This well-known accusation stems at least partially from Derrida's radical critique of points of beginning, which goes well beyond that of Gadamer: Gadamer's hermeneutic circle posits the existence of a discrete interpreting subject, while Derrida believes even the term 'I' as the signifier of a referential starting point is tinged by a false metaphysical certitude. For a more elaborate comparison, see Hoy, *Critical Circle,* 77–84.

10. My formulation of Benjamin's paradox is based on Michel Beaujour's discussion of the contradictions in Maurice Blanchot's views on literary taxonomies. Beaujour cites Blanchot's definition of Mallarmé's 'Book' as transgressing the classificatory power of the genre. According to Beaujour ('Genus Universum,' *Glyph* 7 [1980]: 16), 'the transgression of genre demanded by the Blanchotian Book does not do away with *norms.* On the contrary, the transgressive work will become a norm or a generic paradigm in its turn, thus establishing a new taxonomy of kinds' (Beaujour's emphasis).

11. Georg Simmel, *Goethe,* 4th ed. (Leipzig: Klinkhardt & Biermann, 1921), 56.

12. Rolf Tiedemann, *Studien zur Philosophie Walter Benjamins* (Frankfurt: Europäische Verlagsanstalt, 1965), 58.

13. René Wellek, 'The Early Literary Criticism of Walter Benjamin,' *Rice University Studies* 57 (1971): 132.

14. Peter Szondi, 'Hope in the Past: On Walter Benjamin,' trans. Harvey Mendelson, *Critical Inquiry* 4 (1978): 504.

15. See Sandor Radnoti, 'The Early Aesthetics of Walter Benjamin,' *International Journal of Sociology* 7 (1977): 93: 'Benjamin's theory of origin (*Ursprung*) contains the essence of the historical *method*. Origin is not identical with factual emergence; sometimes origin is not even expressed by the world of facts. The scholar has to select the facts, the inner structure of which is essential. Because his task is to recognize individuality as totality in the idea, in contrast to the individuality of the concept, he does not seek the average of facts, or conceptual generality, but he has to draft the circle of extremes of the facts that belong to the idea. Study of origin is the restoration of these facts, but it is by definition incomplete, unfinished' (Radnoti's emphasis).

16. Bernd Witte, *Walter Benjamin: Der Intellektuelle als Kritiker. Untersuchungen zu seinem Frühwerk* (Stuttgart: J. B. Metzler, 1976), 108.

17. Witte, *Walter Benjamin*, 109.

18. Michael Rumpf, *Spekulative Literaturtheorie: Zu Walter Benjamins Trauerspielbuch* (Königstein: Forum Academicum, 1980), 29.

19. See Terry Eagleton, *Walter Benjamin, or, Towards a Revolutionary Criticism* (London: New Left Books, 1981), 121: 'The historicist imprisoning of an artefact within its moment of genesis is to be rejected: the Benjamin of the *Trauerspiel* book instead grasps origin teleologically, as an unfolding dynamic structure within the work that is thoroughly caught up in the work's history, and of which that complete history is the only full account.' See also Heinz Schlaffer, 'Walter Benjamins Idee der Gattung' in *Walter Benjamin: Profane Erleuchtung und rettende Krtik*, ed. Norbert W. Bolz and Richard Faber, 2d ed. (Würzburg: Königshausen & Neumann, 1985), 48: '"Origin" indicates the historical structure of ideas of those aesthetic innovations that have

succeeded in creating an enduring formal scheme. Form is the telos for which the developing genre uses different factors from the sociopolitical realm and from literary history.'

20. Uwe Steiner, '"Zarte Empirie": Überlegungen zum Verhältnis von Urphänomen und Ursprung im Früh- und Spätwerk Walter Benjamins' in *Antike und Moderne: Zu Walter Benjamins 'Passagen*,' ed. Norbert W. Bolz and Richard Faber (Würzburg: Königshausen & Neumann, 1986), 30–31.

21. Stéphane Mosès, 'L'idée d'origine chez Walter Benjamin' in *Walter Benjamin et Paris*, ed. Heinz Wismann (Paris: Cerf, 1986), 815.

22. Wolin, *Walter Benjamin*, 98, Wolin's emphasis.

23. Nicholas Rescher, *Leibniz: An Introduction to His Philosophy* (Totowa NJ: Rowman & Littlefield, 1979), 68.

24. G. W. Leibniz, *Philosophical Papers and Letters*, ed. and trans. Leroy E. Loemker (Chicago: U of Chicago P, 1956), 2:1055.

25. Benjamin, *Briefe*, ed. Gershom Scholem and Theodor W. Adorno (1966; repr., Frankfurt: Suhrkamp, 1978), 1:323.

26. Benjamin, *Briefe*, 1:322.

27. Irving Wohlfarth, ('The Politics of Prose and the Art of Awakening: Walter Benjamin's Version of a German Romantic Motif,' *Glyph* 7 [1980]) has also taken note of this shift: 'For the later Benjamin, "continuum" becomes a primarily negative category – already *The Origin of German Baroque Drama* replaces the unitary *Reflexionsmedium* with a discontinuous plurality of ideas – and the romantic faith in a sustaining center persists only in muted form' (137). This 'discontinuous plurality' – what I referred to as an 'infinite heterogeneity' – is a corollary of Benjamin's notion of origin.

28. Jürgen Habermas, 'Bewußtmachende oder rettende Kritik – die Aktualität Walter Benjamins' in *Zur Aktualität Walter Benjamins*, ed. Siegfried Unseld (Frankfurt: Suhrkamp, 1972), 182–83.

29. See Wolin, 71.

30. Wolin, 64.

31. Jesse Gellrich, 'Deconstructing Allegory' *Genre* 18 (fall 1985): 197.

32. Gellrich, 203–6.

33. De Man, 'Rhetoric of Temporality,' 176. See also 173.

34. De Man, 'Rhetoric of Temporality,' 191.

35. Miller, 'The Two Allegories' in *Allegory, Myth, and Symbol*, Harvard English Studies, ed. Morton W. Bloomfield, no. 9 (Cambridge: Harvard UP, 1981), 362–65.

36. Miller, 'The Two Allegories,' 363.

37. Miller, 'Narrative and History,' ELH 41 (1974): 459. Hereafter cited in the text.

38. Michael Löwy, *Redemption and Utopia: Jewish Libertarian Thought in Central Europe*, trans. Hope Heaney (London: Athlone, 1992), 95–126.

39. Löwy, 123.

40. On Benjamin's negative attitude toward natural history, see Jennings, *Dialectical Images: Walter Benjamin's Theory of Literary Criticism* (Ithaca NY: Cornell UP, 1987), 64.

41. Habermas, 187–88.

42. Wolin, 281 n.24.

43. This line represents an interesting inversion of the definition of the *authentic* as the seal of *origin* in the prologue to the *Trauerspiel* book: 'Das Echte – jenes Ursprungssiegel in den Phänomenen – ist Gegenstand einer Entdeckung, einer Entdeckung, die in einzigartiger Weise sich mit dem Wiedererkennen verbindet.' (1:227) [The authentic – that seal of origin in the phenomena – is the object of a discovery, a discovery that is bound in a singular way to the act of re-cognition]. Obviously, origin and authenticity are, for Benjamin, inextricably intertwined. However, this connection is later somewhat mitigated. See note 51.

44. See Hannah Arendt, 'Walter Benjamin,' *Merkur* 22 (1968): 305–15. Arendt elucidates the destructive/redemptive element in Benjamin's own citational praxis. She also detects in Benjamin's obsession with collections, collecting, and collectors the same equation of the 'seal of authenticity on the phenomena' with 'origin' formulated by Benjamin in his treatment of Kraus's notion of origin (2:360). For Arendt, Benjamin's collection impulse is also characterized by the productive demolition of tradition and context. See esp. 309.

45. Habermas, 213.

46. See Wohlfarth, ' "Immer radikal, niemals konsequent . . . ". Zur theologisch-politischen Standortsbestimmung Walter Benjamins' in *Antique und Moderne*, 116–37.

47. See Uwe Steiner (38), who believes this fragment reconstitutes the object of history as a phenomenon of origin ('Ursprungsphänomen').

48. In employing this leaf simile, Benjamin probably had in mind the famous hypothesis made by Goethe during the course of his Italian Journey: 'All is leaf, and this simplicity makes possible the greatest diversity.' In Johann Wolfgang von Goethe, *Naturwissenschaftliche Schriften*, vol.7 (Weimar: Hermann Böhlau, 1892), 282.

49. Habermas, 220.

50. Thomas Dörr, *Kritik und Übersetzung: Die Praxis der Reproduktion im Frühwerk Walter Benjamins* (Giessen: Focus, 1988), 34–38.

51. Derrida, 'Ein Porträt Benjamins,' trans. B. Lindner, in *'Links hatte noch alles sich zu enträtseln . . . ' Walter Benjamin im Kontext*, ed. Burkhardt Lindner (Frankfurt: Syndikat, 1978), 172. Derrida is fundamentally correct. Benjamin seems to equate the authenticity – here equated with the 'aura' – of an object with its origin in the 'Kunstwerk' essay: 'Die Echtheit einer Sache ist der Inbegriff alles von Ursprung her an ihr Tradierbaren, von ihrer materiellen Dauer bis zu ihrer geschichtlichen Zeugenschaft' (1:477) [The authenticity of a thing is the essence of all that it is capable of transmitting from its point of origin, ranging from its material duration to its character as a historical witness]. In a passage partially cited by Derrida, Benjamin indicates that when the criterion of authenticity in the production of an artwork fails, the function of art becomes politicized (1:482). In the 'Kunstwerk' essay, Benjamin views this politicization as a desideratum. However, because 'the work of art has always been fundamentally reproducible' (1:474), its reproducibility is also inscribed in its origin. In this second version of the 'Kunstwerk' essay, on the other hand, Benjamin makes it clear that authenticity is *not* reproducible (1:476 n.3). This implies the separation of origin and authenticity.

52. Dörr, 43–46 and 163. Dörr believes that 'das Denken einer Ur-sprungslosigkeit, eines Ursprungs als Wiederholung, die kein Wiederholtes birgt, sondern es erst erzeugt' [the thinking of an originlessness, of an origin as repetition, which does not shelter that which is repeated, but first generates it] is the central theme of Derrida's philosophy (46). Dörr equates Benjamin's 'Ur-Sprung' with 'reproduction,' which is a 'duality at the beginning' (163).

53. See also Mosès, who suggests that Benjamin's view of origin in the first version of the *Trauerspiel* book anticipates his investment of the unfolding of historical time with ruptures in the historico-philosophical theses (824–25).

54. Points of contact, as well as differences, in the philosophies of Rosenzweig and Benjamin have been elucidated by Mosès, 'Walter Benjamin and Franz Rosenzweig,' trans. Deborah Johnson, *Philosophical Forum* 15 (fall–winter 1983–84): 188–205. Mosès does not compare their respective concepts of origin. For a brief contrast between their language theories, see Martin Jay, *Permanent Exiles: Essays on the Intellectual Migration from Germany to America* (New York: Columbia UP, 1985), 211–13.

3. PROBING THEODOR ADORNO'S ANTIMONIES

1. Theodor W. Adorno, *Gesammelte Schriften,* ed. Rolf Tiedemann (Frankfurt: Suhrkamp, 1970–), 8:104. Hereafter cited in the text by volume and page number.

2. For comprehensive introductions to Adorno's philosophy, see Gillian Rose, *The Melancholy Science: An Introduction to the Thought of Theodor W. Adorno* (New York: Columbia UP, 1978); and Jay, *Adorno* (Cambridge: Harvard UP, 1984).

3. Buck-Morss, *The Origin of Negative Dialectics: Theodor W. Adorno, Walter Benjamin, and the Frankfurt Institute* (New York: Free Press, 1977), 47, Buck-Morss's emphasis.

4. See especially 6, 111–14.

5. See Buck-Morss, 47.

6. Jay, *Adorno,* 32.

7. Adorno, *Philosophische Terminologie,* ed. Rudolf zur Lippe (Frankfurt: Suhrkamp, 1973), 1:150–51.

8. Hermann Mörchen, *Adorno und Heidegger: Untersuchung einer philosophischen Kommunikationsverweigerung* (Stuttgart: Klett-Cotta, 1981), 364.

9. Adorno, *Philosophische Terminologie*, 1:151–53. Both this lecture and the subsequent one (delivered on 12 July 1962) contain Adorno's harshest attack on the philosophy of origin as (even in its most innocent guise) the attempt, informed by a traditional rigidity, to dominate nature and control social relationships and to establish the epistemological primacy of the temporally prior. See *Philosophische Terminologie*, 1:148–73.

10. Rose, 71.

11. Gerhard Kaiser, *Benjamin. Adorno. Zwei Studien* (Frankfurt: Athenäum, 1974), 48 n.82.

12. In *Aesthetic Theory*, Adorno again borrows Kraus's motto. However, here he uses it to *expose* subjective domination. In this case, the subject is man as artistic creator, and the object is natural beauty (7:104).

13. While Adorno developed his principle of nonidentity largely in opposition to what he saw as identitarian tendencies in the philosophies of Hegel and Marx, Fredric Jameson has convincingly argued that Adorno drew heavily on the Marxist distinction between 'exchange value' and 'use value' in structuring his own identity/nonidentity binarism. See *Late Marxism: Adorno, or the Persistence of the Dialectic* (London: Verso, 1990), esp. 15–24.

14. Rose, 42. Adorno's objections to the *Urgeschichte* project are detailed in a letter to Benjamin dated 2 August 1935. See Adorno, *Über Walter Benjamin*, ed. Rolf Tiedemann (Frankfurt: Suhrkamp, 1970), 111–25.

15. Buck-Morss, 60.

16. Jameson, *Late Marxism*, 100.

17. Jameson, *Late Marxism*, 149. Jürgen Habermas *does* show an awareness of this resonance when he notes how the myth of origin staged in the *Dialectic of Enlightenment* captures the conflicted reaction of Homeric man to moments when this mastery seems to be achieved: 'The myth of origin adheres to the *double meaning* of "leaping away" ["des Entspringens"]: a shudder at the uprooting and a sigh of relief at the escape.' In *Der phi-*

losophische Diskurs der Moderne, 3d ed. (Frankfurt: Suhrkamp, 1986), 132, Habermas's emphasis.

18. Miriam Hansen, 'Mass Culture as Hieroglyphic Writing: Adorno, Derrida, Kracauer,' *New German Critique* 56 (spring–summer 1992): 52–53.

19. See Richard E. Palmer, *Hermeneutics: Interpretation Theory in Schleiermacher, Dilthey, Heidegger and Gadamer* (Evanston IL: Northwestern UP, 1969).

20. Jameson, *Late Marxism*, 217.

21. I am referring specifically to Kant's famous essay 'Beantwortung der Frage: Was ist Aufklärung?' (1784; 'What is Enlightenment?'). See Immanuel Kant, *Sämmtliche Werke*, ed. J. H. von Kirchmann, vol.5 (Berlin: L. Heimann, 1870), 109–19.

22. Herman Rapaport, *Heidegger & Derrida: Reflections on Time and Language* (Lincoln: U of Nebraska P, 1989), 136. Another recent study concludes that Heidegger sought 'authentic' meanings but that features of language such as paronomasia counteract traditional etymological attempts to ascribe such univocal, historically determined significations to words. See Derek Attridge, 'Language as History/History as Language: Saussure and the Romance of Etymology' in *Post-Structuralism and the Question of History*, ed. Attridge et al. (Cambridge: Cambridge UP, 1987), 183–211.

23. For a brief outline of the evolution of this break, see Hans Saner's forward to Karl Jaspers, *Notizen zu Martin Heidegger*, ed. Hans Saner (München: R. Piper, 1978), 7–21.

24. See *Notizen*, 61 n.33 and 158 n.140.

25. Jaspers, *Vom Ursprung und Ziel der Geschichte* (München: R. Piper, 1949), 17–18.

26. See Jay, *Adorno*, 63.

27. See Jay, *Adorno*, 64: 'For Adorno, any philosophy which lamented the lost origins of humanity's wholeness with the world or identified utopia with its future realization was not merely misguided, but potentially pernicious as well.'

28. Jay, *Marxism and Totality: The Adventures of a Concept from Lukács to Habermas* (Berkeley: U of California P, 1984), 419.

29. Jay, *Marxism and Totality*, 259. Jay does, however, indicate that

Althusser and Adorno shared a general aversion to 'idealistic meta-subjects,' 'myths of original unity,' 'philosophical first principles,' and 'absolute historicism,' while they both sustained a belief that authentic art's relationship to knowledge is characterized by difference (413–15).

30. My interpretation of Adorno's jazz essay owes much to that of Buck-Morss, although I would not concur with her view that Adorno's discussion of the figure of the 'eccentric' in the essay provides an illustration of his use of the term *Ursprung* as a critical tool; he does not use it in connection with this 'prototype of the jazz subject' (17:97). See Buck-Morss, 100, 105, 259 n.34, and 261–62 n.67.

31. For a more detailed comparison of Benjamin's and Adorno's use of this principle, see Jameson, *Late Marxism*, 49–58.

32. As Rainer Nägele has already noted in 'The Scene of the Other: Theodor W. Adorno's Negative Dialectic in the Context of Poststructuralism,' *boundary 2* 11 (1982–83): 59–60.

33. Elsewhere, Adorno emphasizes that artworks are not to be confused with, and should be freed from, their genesis ('Genese') (7:153, 267, 400, 513). For a discussion of Nietzsche's influence on Adorno's aesthetics, see Norbert W. Bolz, 'Nietzsches Spur in der Ästhetischen Theorie' in *Materialien zur ästhetischen Theorie Th. W. Adornos Konstruktion der Moderne*, ed. Burkhardt Lindner and W. Martin Lüdke (Frankfurt: Suhrkamp, 1979), 369–96.

34. Jameson indicates that Adorno saw the refutation of broad artistic categories (genres and styles) as symptomatic of a particular trend in the history of aesthetics. This tendency, a major theme in Adorno's own aesthetics, can be cast in broader terms as 'the repudiation of the universal' and can be defined as 'nominalism.' Adorno identifies Croce's work as its first manifestation. Such a repudiation is also a general tendency of poststructuralism but Adorno localizes it as a specific episode in aesthetic history. Because of its 'anti-historical anxieties,' poststructuralism turns what Adorno regards as a historically generated impulse into its own temporally unconstricted universal. See *Late Marxism*, 157–58.

35. Adorno's disenchantment of art's magical origin should not be

interpreted as suggesting that he advocated the disenchantment of art itself. Adorno was quite concerned about the disenchantment of art by the mass media; this is one of the reasons for his dispute with Benjamin's celebration of the destruction of the aura of the artwork. In the draft introduction to *Aesthetic Theory,* Adorno even equates the attempt to banish mystery ('das Geheime') from art with a false concern with art's origin (7:531). Of course, Adorno did not propose that modern art should be reinvested with magic either. For a brief but comprehensive summary of Adorno's views concerning the disenchantment of art, see Karol Sauerland, *Einführung in die Ästhetik Adornos* (Berlin: Walter de Gruyter, 1979), 45–53.

36. Heidegger, 'Der Ursprung des Kunstwerkes,' 7.
37. Buck-Morss, 259 n.34.
38. Jameson, *Late Marxism,* 15.
39. An example of such a view can be found in Nägele's analysis of Adorno's critique of Heidegger in the *Negative Dialectics*: 'Adorno's proximity to Derrida and his conflictual affinity to Heidegger show most clearly in his critique of "origin"' ('Scene of the Other,' 67).
40. Buck-Morss, 60.

4. FRANZ ROSENZWEIG

References to Rosenzweig's works are given parenthetically in the text.

HS *Hegel und der Staat,* 2 vols. (1920) repr. Aalen: Scientia Verlag, 1962.

BT *Briefe und Tagebücher,* ed. Rachel Rosenzweig and Edith Rosenzweig-Scheinmann, with the assistance of Bernhard Casper. Vol. 1 of *Der Mensch und sein Werk. Gesammelte Schriften:* The Hague: Martinus Nijhoff, 1979.

SE *Der Stern der Erlösung,* 4th ed. Vol. 2 of *Der Mensch und sein Werk: Gesammelte Schriften.* The Hague: Martinus Nijhoff, 1976.

z   *Zweistromland: Kleinere Schriften zu Glauben und Denken,* ed. Reinhold and Annemarie Mayer. Vol 3 of *Der Mensch und sein Werk: Gesammelte Schriften.* Dordrecht: Martinus Nijhoff, 1984.

1. Said, *Beginnings,* 1st ed., xiii.
2. Alan Udoff made this remark in the course of an informal lecture presented at the University of Washington in 1987.
3. Buck-Morss, 5. It should be noted, however, that Evelyn Adunka, in her 1988 University of Vienna 'Diplomarbeit,' entitled 'Das messianische Denken Adornos: Eine Studie zur jüdischen Philosophie und Identität in diesem Jahrhundert,' cites an unpublished letter from Adorno to Dr. Achim von Borries, dated 8 March 1955, in which Adorno accuses Rosenzweig of conformism, of a failure to engage in the sort of radical thinking Adorno discerns in the works of Benjamin and the early Ernst Bloch. See Adunka, 62, 155 n.158.
4. Buck-Morss, 60.
5. Alexander Altmann, 'Franz Rosenzweig on History' in *The Philosophy of Franz Rosenzweig,* ed. Paul Mendes-Flohr (Hanover NH: UP of New England, 1988), 135.
6. See Jameson, *Late Marxism,* 22.
7. Buck-Morss, 5.
8. Nathan Rotenstreich, 'Rosenzweig's Notion of Metaethics' in *Philosophy of Franz Rosenzweig,* 72.
9. For an interesting, although speculative, account of this experience and its significance for Rosenzweig's subsequent writings, see Nahum N. Glatzer, *Franz Rosenzweig: His Life and Thought* (New York: Schocken, 1953), xvi–xxii.
10. Otto Pöggeler, 'Between Enlightenment and Romanticism: Rosenzweig and Hegel' in *Philosophy of Franz Rosenzweig,* 108.
11. Else-Rahel Freund, *Franz Rosenzweig's Philosophy of Existence: An Analysis of "The Star of Redemption,"* ed. Paul R. Mendes-Flohr, trans. Stephen L. Weinstein and Robert Israel (The Hague: Martinus Nijhoff, 1979), 87.
12. Paul Mendes-Flohr, 'Introduction: Franz Rosenzweig and the German Philosophical Tradition' in *Philosophy of Franz Rosenzweig,* 1–2.
13. It is interesting to note that one of the foremost Rosenzweig scholars, Stéphane Mosès, has called Rosenzweig's spiritual cri-

sis in 1913, and his decision to remain Jewish, a dialectical movement because the rich universality Rosenzweig discovers in Judaism itself derives from assimilation. See Mosès, 'Hegel pris au mot: La critique de l'histoire chez Franz Rosenzweig,' *Revue de métaphysique et de morale* 90 (1985): 329.

14. On the history of this term as a linguistic marker of middle-class Germany's attempt to forge a distinct social, and then national, identity, see Norbert Elias, *The Civilizing Process: The History of Manners,* trans. Edmund Jephcott (New York: Urizen, 1978), 3–34.

15. Buck-Morss, 5.

16. On the attempt by German philosophers since the eighteenth century to regard the state as the ideal collective manifestation of *Kultur* and as a necessary abstraction and institutionalization of the spiritual community, see Joseph Chytry, *The Aesthetic State: A Quest in Modern German Thought* (Berkeley: U of California P, 1989).

17. Eliezer Berkovits, *Major Themes in Modern Philosophies of Judaism* (New York: Ktav, 1974), 5.

18. Berkovits, 6.

19. Hermann Cohen, *Logik der reinen Erkenntnis,* 2d ed. (Berlin: Bruno Cassirer, 1914), 13, Cohen's emphasis.

20. Cohen, 15–31.

21. Cohen, 35–36.

22. Cohen, 31–35.

23. Walter Kinkel, 'Das Urteil des Ursprungs' *Kantstudien* 17 (1912): 278–79.

24. Cohen, 37. See also 31–38.

25. I borrow the terms 'the Nought,' 'the Aught,' 'the Nay,' and 'the Yea' from William W. Hallo's translation of *Der Stern der Erlösung.* The original terms are, respectively, 'das Nichts,' 'das Etwas,' 'das Nein,' and 'das Ja.' See Rosenzweig, *The Star of Redemption,* trans. William W. Hallow (Notre Dame: Notre Dame P, 1985), 24.

26. Cohen, 84.

27. Cohen, 79–80.

28. Cohen, 88–89.

29. Cohen, 91.

30. Cohen, 596–97.

31. Rotenstreich, 69, Rotenstreich's emphasis.

32. At the same time, as Rotenstreich suggests, Rosenzweig ultimately came to disagree with what he felt was Cohen's conflation of the metaethical and metaphysical spheres from a false concept of origin: 'Rosenzweig's polemic with Cohen, which he never made explicit, was directed against Cohen's attempt to place the individual within the purview of morality, namely, via religion, the "Religion of Reason," specifically calling Judaism a source (*Ursprung*) of the latter' (83).

33. Cohen, 79.

34. For a discussion of the intricacies of Rosenzweig's Cohenian analytic equations, see Norbert M. Samuelson, 'The Concept of "Nichts" in Rosenzweig's "Star of Redemption" in *Der Philosoph Franz Rosenzweig (1886–1929), Internationaler Kongreß – Kassel 1986*, vol.2, ed. Wolfdietrich Schmied-Kowarzik (Freiburg, München: Karl Alber, 1988), 643–56. In addition to offering a concise summary of Rosenzweig's logical and metalogical theorems as they relate to the concept of the Nought in the first part of *The Star of Redemption*, Samuelson points to some interesting parallels in the ontologies of Rosenzweig and Aristotle.

35. See Mosès, *Système et Révélation: La philosophie de Franz Rosenzweig* (Paris: Éditions du Seuil, 1982), 128.

36. Cohen, 79–80.

37. In the geometric configuration of Rosenzweig's triangular star, result is below and origin is above (SE 286).

38. See SE 91–99.

39. Freund, 95.

40. On Rosenzweig's language theory, see Susan A. Handelman, *Fragments of Redemption: Jewish Thought and Literary Theory in Benjamin, Scholem, and Levinas* (Bloomington: Indiana UP, 1991), 217–23.

41. See note 2.

42. Michael Theunissen, *The Other: Studies in the Social Ontology of Husserl, Heidegger, Sartre, and Buber*, trans. Christopher Macann (Cambridge: MIT Press, 1984), 312, 260.

43. See Löwy, 59.

5. MARTIN HEIDEGGER

References to Heidegger's works are given parenthetically in the text.

GA   *Gesamtausgabe.* Frankfurt: V. Klostermann. Vol.2: *Sein und Zeit,* 1977. Vol.4: *Erläuterungen zu Hölderlins Dichtung,* 1981. Vol.5: *Holzwege,* 1977. Vol.9: *Wegmarken,* 1976. Vol.25: *Phänomenologische Interpretation von Kants Kritik der reinen Vernunft,* 1977. Vol.26: *Metaphysische Anfangsgründe der Logik im Ausgang von Leibniz,* 1978. Vol.32: *Hegels Phänomenologie des Geistes,* 1980. Vol.40: *Einführung in die Metaphysik,* 1983. Vol.52: *Hölderlins Hymne "Andenken,"* 1982. Vol.55: *Heraklit,* 1979.

ID   *Identität und Differenz.* Pfullingen: G. Neske, 1957.

KM   *Kant und das Problem der Metaphysik,* 2d ed. Frankfurt: V. Klostermann, 1951.

N   *Nietzsche II,* 2d ed. Pfullingen: G. Neske, 1961.

SG   *Der Satz vom Grund.* Pfullingen: G. Neske, 1957.

VA   *Vorträge und Aufsätze,* 2d ed. Pfullingen: G. Neske, 1959.

ZSD *Zur Sache des Denkens.* Tübingen: M. Niemeyer, 1969.

1. Karl Löwith, 'M. Heidegger and F. Rosenzweig: A Postscript to *Being and Time*' in *Nature, History, and Existentialism,* ed. Arnold Levison (Evanston IL: Northwestern UP, 1966), 52.

2. Löwith, 52.

3. Löwith, 57–58, 76.

4. This is especially true with respect to Adorno's reception of Heidegger. On this point, see Mörchen, 364–70. The most eloquent case made by an English-language writer for the view that Heidegger's obsession with origins was fundamentally backward looking and nostalgic is put forward by Allan Megill, *Prophets of Extremity: Nietzsche, Heidegger, Foucault, Derrida* (Berkeley: U of California P, 1985), 103–80. However, like Adorno, Megill ignores the multivalence inherent in Heidegger's use of the term *Ursprung* and its derivations.

5. Udoff, 'Rosenzweig's Heidegger Reception and the re-Origination of Jewish Thinking' in *Der Philosoph Franz Rosenzweig,* vol.2, 923–24.

6. Udoff, 'Rosenzweig's Heidegger Reception,' 950.

7. Udoff, 'Rosenzweig's Heidegger Reception,' 949.

8. The use of the comparative *ursprünglicher* ('more originary') would be a logical absurdity if origin (*Ursprung*) itself always represented for Heidegger some absolute first ground or *prima philosophia*, as critics such as Adorno have charged. Perhaps to underscore the very lack of fixity he attaches to the term, Heidegger employs it more often in adjectival than in nominal forms. For a different perspective on Heidegger's use of comparative and superlative forms of *ursprünglich* ('originary') see Erasmus Schöfer, *Die Sprache Heideggers* (Pfullingen: G. Neske, 1962), 223–24.

9. Jaspers, *Notizen,* 61 n.33.

10. Ricoeur, 'The Task of Hermeneutics,' trans. David Pellauer, in *Heidegger and Modern Philosophy,* ed. Michael Murray (New Haven CT: Yale UP, 1978), 146. Heidegger himself cites Dilthey as *the* exemplary life philosopher later in the essay on Jaspers (GS 9:13–14).

11. Rapaport, 8–9.

12. Heidegger's anchoring of the ego in concrete historicity has not spared him from charges by figures such as Herbert Marcuse and Jürgen Habermas that his constant invocation of Being dehistoricizes his philosophy. Heideggerian historicity, in their view, attempts to elide what is truly concrete in history – its social, economic, and political dimensions – in favor of a suprahistorical foundationalism. See the discussion in Rapaport, 259–64.

13. Elisabeth Young-Bruehl, *Freedom and Karl Jaspers's Philosophy* (New Haven CT: Yale UP, 1981), 44.

14. Young-Bruehl, 162.

15. Mörchen, 370 and 370 n.313.

16. Max Scheler, *Die Wissensformen und die Gesellschaft,* 2d ed., ed. Maria Scheler (Bern: Francke, 1960), 107.

17. Scheler, 124, Scheler's emphasis.

18. In his *Metaphysische Anfangsgründe der Logik im Ausgang von Leibniz* (1928; *The Metaphysical Foundations of Logic*), Heidegger qualifies his rejection of the principle of an isolated philoso-

phizing subjectivity. He speaks here of the metaphysical isolation of the individual and contrasts this with the false notion of an existentially isolated individual who thereby becomes the philosophizing center of the world. This is the view of the subject that he rejects in Kantian philosophy. In contrast, he notes that 'Die metaphysische Neutralität des innerlichst isolierten Menschen als Dasein ist . . . das eigentlich Konkrete des Ursprunges, das Noch-nicht der faktischen Zerstreutheit' (GS 26:172–73) [The metaphysical neutrality as Dasein of the most inwardly isolated human being is . . . that which is origin's authentic concreteness, the not-yet of factical dissemination]. The facticity of Dasein – its concrete origin – is the metaphysical neutrality that grounds Dasein's temporal dissemination. Thus, concrete origin is the very opposite of a fixed, atemporal, and subjectively authoritarian first ground, as Adorno and other critics of Heidegger would have it. Instead, concrete origin is the ground of factical alterity, temporality – dissemination.

19. Werner Marx, *Heidegger and the Tradition*, trans. Theodore Kisiel and Murray Greene [Evanston IL: Northwestern UP, 1971), 98. In the original German, '"original" time' is '"ursprüngliche" Zeit.' See Marx, *Heidegger und die Tradition: Eine problemgeschichtliche Einführung in die Grundbestimmungen des Seins* (Stuttgart: W. Kohlhammer, 1961), 106.

20. Kant, *Gesammelte Schriften*, vol.3 (Berlin: Georg Reimer, 1904), 77–78.

21. The complex relationship between foundation, freedom, and transcendence in *The Essence of Reasons* is most usefully articulated in Rapaport's brief discussion of this treatise. Rapaport notes that transcendence is developed in *The Essence of Reasons* as a 'stepping beyond' foundations and principles grounded in traditional boundaries between identity and difference. Dasein's rootedness in a discrete subject is called into question through temporality. Transcendence as an event is more originary than principles (such as 'sufficient reason' and the subject/ object distinction) based on the identity/difference dichotomy. Transcendence is Dasein's most powerful confrontation with its temporality and enacts a 'stepping beyond' delimiting grounds.

As Rapaport notes, 'Heidegger will conclude that the essence of reason is manifested in the always already of the *Überstieg,* through which Dasein discloses itself as the freedom through which reasons or grounds are posited' (95). In *The Essence of Reasons,* the temporal event of transcendence 'steps beyond' all grounds and foundations rooted in identity and difference, and this allows foundation at its origin to emerge as *nothing but* freedom.

22. Löwith, *Heidegger: Denker in dürftiger Zeit,* 2d ed. (Göttingen: Vandenhoeck & Ruprecht, 1960), 18–19.

23. Andrzej Warminski, *Readings in Interpretation: Hölderlin, Hegel, Heidegger* (Minneapolis: U of Minnesota P, 1987), 45–71.

24. In discussing Heidegger's reading of Hölderlin's hymn 'Germanien,' for example, Warminski simply equates 'beginning' with a leading into/transformation into origin (65, 67).

25. In spite of Heidegger's antilinear grounding of the origin of the work of art between the unconcealedness of Earth and the concealedness of World, I nevertheless maintain that his equation of *Herkunft* ('ancestry') and *Ursprung* ('origin') at the outset of 'Der Ursprung des Kunstwerkes' (GS 5:1–2) legitimizes the critique of Heidegger's search for art's essence (*Wesen*) found in the chapter on Adorno.

26. Reiner Schürmann, 'Political Thinking in Heidegger,' *Social Research* 45 (spring 1978): 212–13, Schürmann's emphasis.

27. Otto Pöggeler, *Der Denkweg Martin Heideggers* (Pfullingen: G. Neske, 1963), 227.

28. Mörchen, 372.

29. On this point, see esp. *Sein und Zeit* – GS 2:97–102.

30. Heidegger asserts that the *Sein/Seiende* dichotomy is itself the *Ursprung* of the fissure between ordinary and essential thinking (GA 55:150). Schürmann sees in this passage from the *Heraklit* lectures (1943–44) a reflection of Heidegger's view that pre-Socratic thought is essential because it 'does not pursue ultimate entities' and instead evokes the 'correspondence' of phenomena inscribed by *phusis* as 'the locus of the origin.' See Schürmann's book *Heidegger on Being and Acting: From Principles to Anarchy,* trans. Christine-Marie Gros in collaboration

with the author (Bloomington: Indiana UP, 1987), 125. The attempt to overcome the pursuit of ultimate entities and to make a *phusis*-grounded correspondence the locus of origin has as its implicit telos the reestablishment of the phenomenal world in its historical, plurivocal, and nonhierarchic balance.

31. Mörchen, 372, Mörchen's emphasis.

32. Louis Althusser and Étienne Balibar, *Reading Capital*, trans. Ben Brewster (New York: Pantheon, 1970), 182–93.

33. On the element of contradiction in structural causality and for a brief analysis of this concept's weaknesses, see Ted Benton, *The Rise and Fall of Structural Marxism: Althusser and His Influence* (New York: St. Martin's, 1984), 64–65. See also Mörchen, 372.

34. Jameson, *Late Marxism*, 59–60. For a discussion of synchronicity in the concept of structural causality, see Jay's essay on Althusser in *Marxism and Totality*, 385–422, esp. 408.

35. Habermas, *Moderne*, 158, 161, 162.

36. Habermas, *Philosophisch-politische Profile*, 2d ed. (Frankfurt: Suhrkamp, 1973), 148.

37. Habermas, *Moderne*, 179.

38. Habermas, *Profile*, 80.

39. Habermas, *Moderne*, 180–83.

40. Habermas, *Moderne*, 184–90.

41. See esp. Habermas, *Moderne*, 178–79.

42. Habermas, *Moderne*, 178.

43. See also John D. Caputo, *Radical Hermeneutics: Repetition, Deconstruction and the Hermeneutic Project* (Bloomington: Indiana UP, 1987), 236–40. Caputo demonstrates Heidegger's strong *critique* of a 'metaphysics of subjectivity,' which Heidegger would replace with an 'originary ethos.'

44. Schürmann, 'Political Thinking in Heidegger,' 213.

45. Habermas, *Moderne*, 189 n.40.

46. Schürmann, 'Political Thinking in Heidegger,' 220, 213. For a balanced overview of Heidegger's political writings during the national socialist period – when he seems to exhibit a tendentious nationalism but still subtly suggests that only a *will to knowledge* is capable of understanding Dasein in its comprehensiveness – see Philippe Lacoue-Labarthe, 'Transcendence

Ends in Politics,' *Typography: Mimesis, Philosophy, Politics*, ed. Christopher Fynsk (Cambridge: Harvard UP, 1989), 267–300.

47. See Habermas, *Moderne*, 191–218.

48. See Derrida, *Positionen*, ed. Peter Engelmann, trans. Dorothea Schmidt (Graz, Wien: H. Böhlaus Nachfolger, 1986), 27–30.

49. Derrida, *Margins of Philosophy*, trans. Alan Bass (Chicago: U of Chicago P, 1982), 63, Derrida's emphasis. I have deviated from Bass's translation in rendering 'originaire' as 'originary' rather than 'primordial.' English translators and interpreters of Heidegger have the unfortunate tendency of translating *ursprüng-lich* with 'primordial.' As the very notion of 'primordiality' suggests some numinous point in time before time, some prehistoric but transcendental locus, the employment of this term denotes a tacit agreement with Adorno's interpretation of Heidegger's *Ursprungsphilosophie* as the search for a *prima philosophia* and an autochthonous ground. This chapter has attempted to demonstrate that this view is overly simplistic. As Derrida uses the term 'originaire' rather than 'primordial,' I believe the term 'originary' is more accurate here as well. The French original of the passage in question is in *Marges de la philosophie* (Paris: Minuit, 1972), 73–74.

50. Derrida, *Margins*, 35 n.11.

51. Derrida, *Margins*, 65–67.

52. Derrida, *Margins*, 6.

53. Derrida's *Speech and Phenomena and Other Essays on Husserl's Theory of Signs* offers similar but more abbreviated critiques of Heidegger's 'metaphysics of presence' (74 n.4) and 'temporalization' (83).

54. Derrida, *Margins*, 23.

55. Derrida, *Margins*, 7.

56. Derrida, 'The Principle of Reason: The University in the Eyes of its Pupils,' trans. Catherine Porter and Edward P. Morris, *diacritics* 13 (1983): 18–19.

57. Derrida, *Margins*, 63.

58. Schürmann, *Heidegger on Being and Acting*, 316 n.9. Schürmann's book itself offers an admirable elucidation of the multivalence inherent in Heidegger's notion of *Ursprung*. See esp. 88–151.

59. Derrida, 'Principle,' 8–9.

60. Habermas argues that Heidegger's attack on reason is so all-encompassing that it fails to differentiate between the instrumental reason putatively guiding modern technology and the universal, intersubjective ideals posited in the Enlightenment concept of *Vernunft*. This distortion of reason even leads Heidegger to characterize the (admittedly deficient) exercise of everyday human communication as vulgar and oblivious to Being. See *Moderne*, 160, 167. Habermas's critique is well founded, although it should be noted that Heidegger's attack against modern technology is largely based on its alleged refusal to allow Being *sufficient* oblivion and forgottenness. Relentless contemporary scientific research imbues earth and its human inhabitants with a deep-seated exhaustion. See SG 201–2.

61. John H. Smith, 'The *Transcendance* of the Individual,' *diacritics* 19, no. 2 (1989): 92–93.

62. Derrida, *Of Grammatology,* trans. Gayatri Chakravorty Spivak (Baltimore: Johns Hopkins UP, 1976), 23.

63. Derrida, *Of Spirit,* 100, 109.

64. Derrida, *Of Spirit,* 113.

65. Derrida, *Of Spirit,* 107–8. All italics are Derrida's.

INDEX

Index

211